Garfield keeps his chins up

BY JIM DAVIS

Ballantine Books • New York

2011 Ballantine Books Trade Paperback Edition

Published in the United States by Ballantine Books, an imprint of The Random House Publishing Group,
a division of Random House, Inc., New York.

Ballantine and colophon are registered trademarks of Random House, Inc.

Originally published in slightly different form in the United States by Ballantine Books, an imprint of
The Random House Publishing Group, a division of Random House, Inc., in 1992.

ISBN 978-0-345-52559-8

Printed in the United States of America

www.ballantinebooks.com

9 8 7 6 5 4 3 2 1

First Colorized Edition

YOU KNOW YOU'RE GETTING FAT WHEN...

SOMEONE TRIES TO CLIMB YOUR NORTH SLOPE

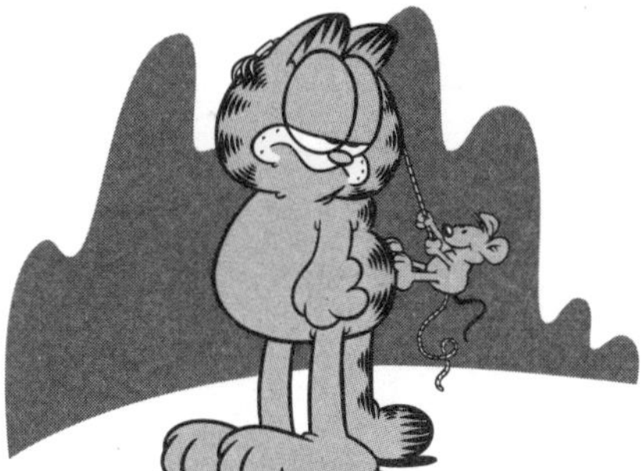

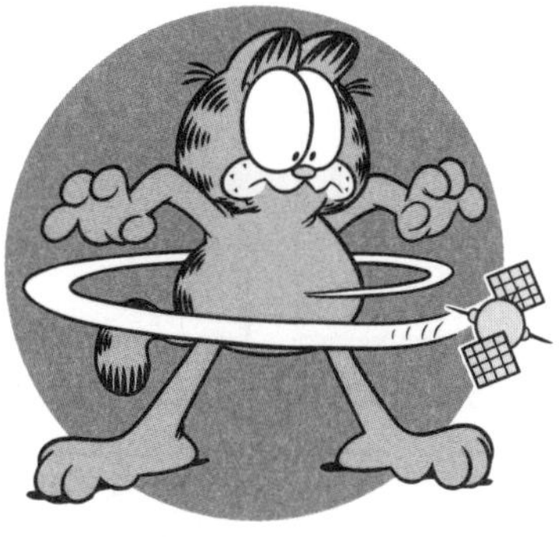

NASA ORBITS A SATELLITE AROUND YOU

YOU HAVE THIS TREMENDOUS URGE TO GRAZE

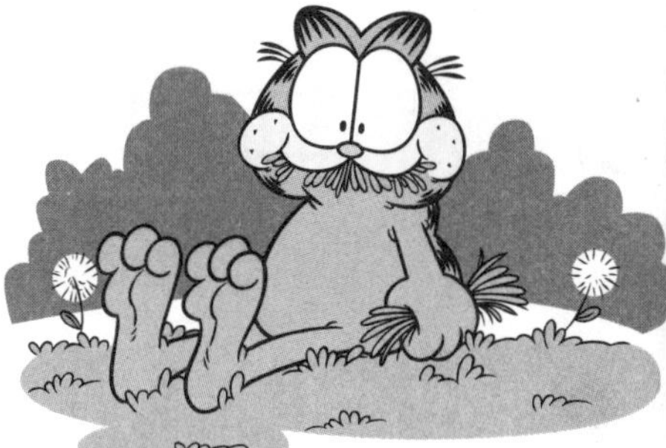

YOUR PICTURE IS POSTED IN ALL-YOU-CAN-EAT RESTAURANTS

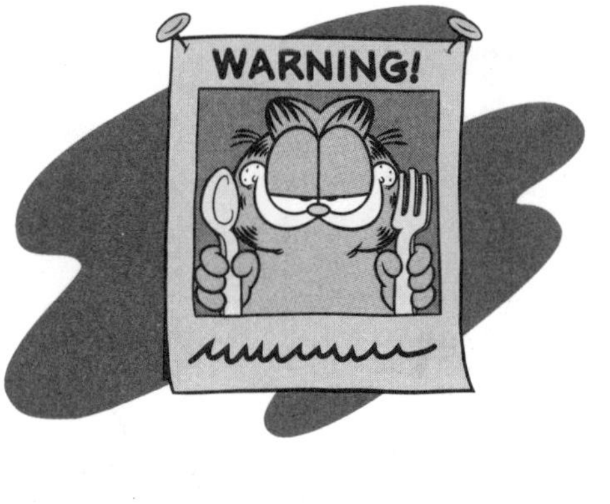
WARNING!

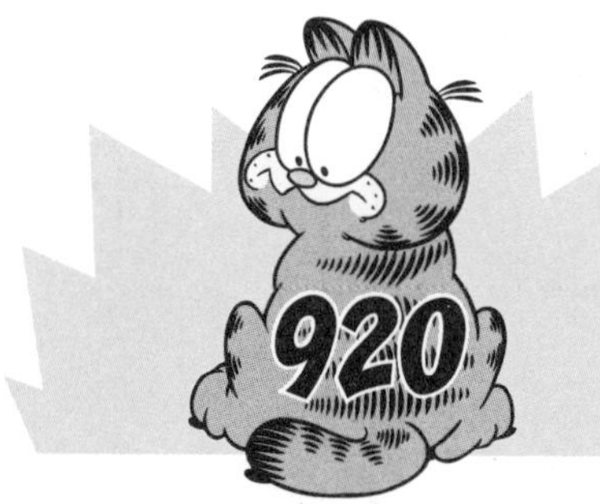
920

THE PHONE COMPANY GIVES YOU YOUR OWN AREA CODE

EVERY TIME YOU GO TO THE BEACH, THE TIDE COMES IN

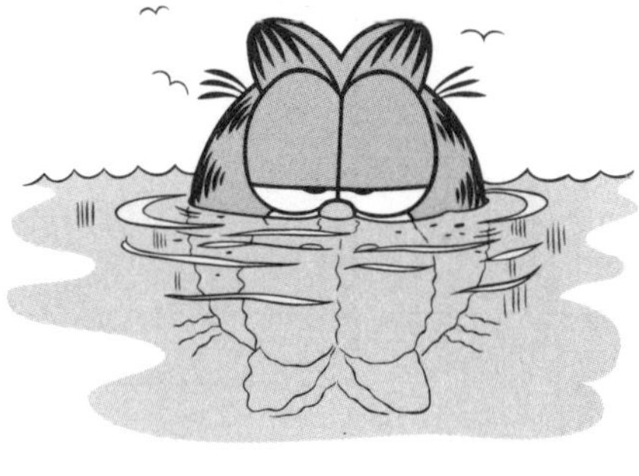

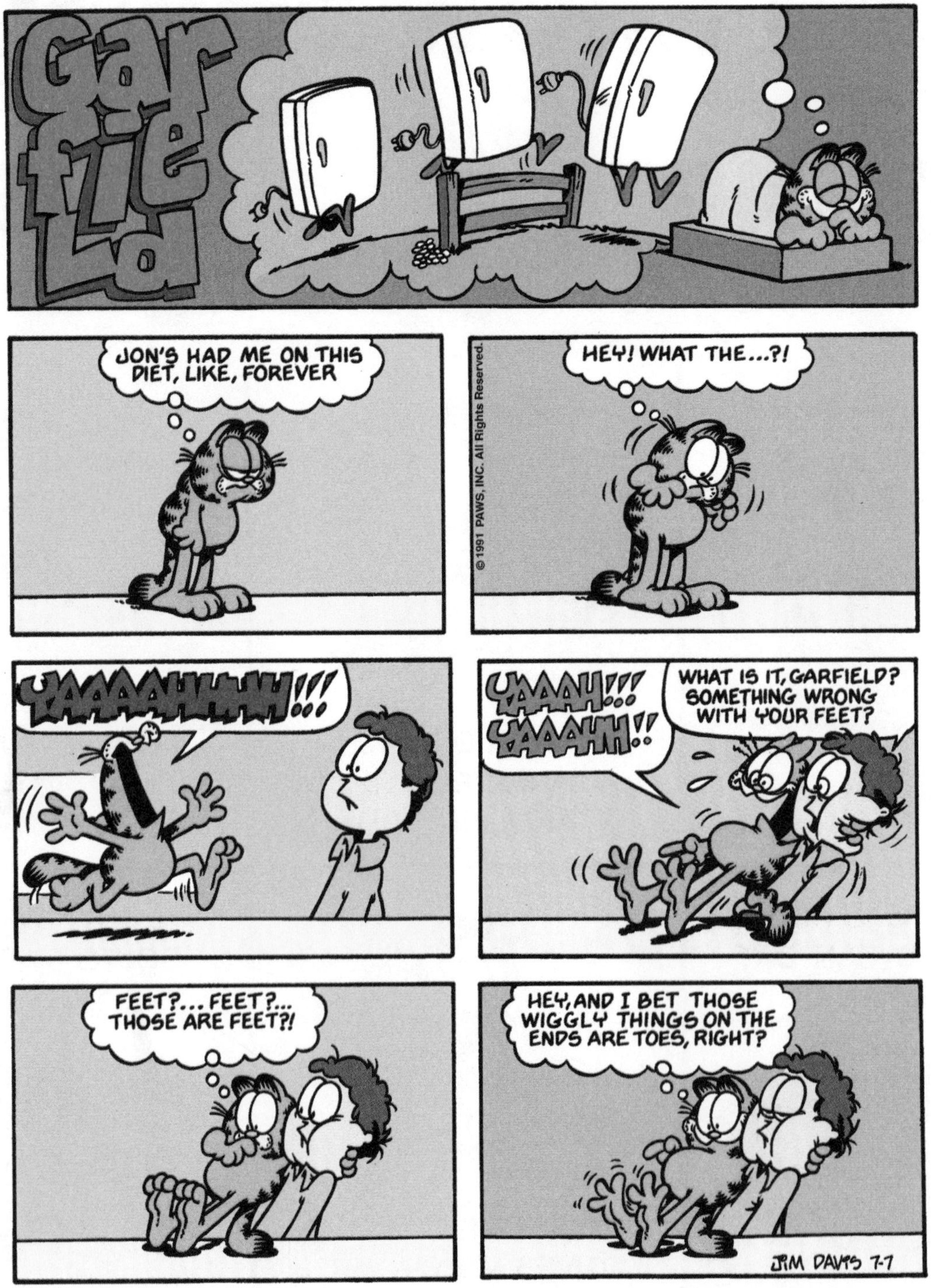
Garfield
JON'S HAD ME ON THIS DIET, LIKE, FOREVER
© 1991 PAWS, INC. All Rights Reserved.
HEY! WHAT THE...?!
YAAAAHHHH!!!
YAAAH!!! YAAAHH!!
WHAT IS IT, GARFIELD? SOMETHING WRONG WITH YOUR FEET?
FEET?... FEET?... THOSE ARE FEET?!
HEY, AND I BET THOSE WIGGLY THINGS ON THE ENDS ARE TOES, RIGHT?
JIM DAVIS 7-7

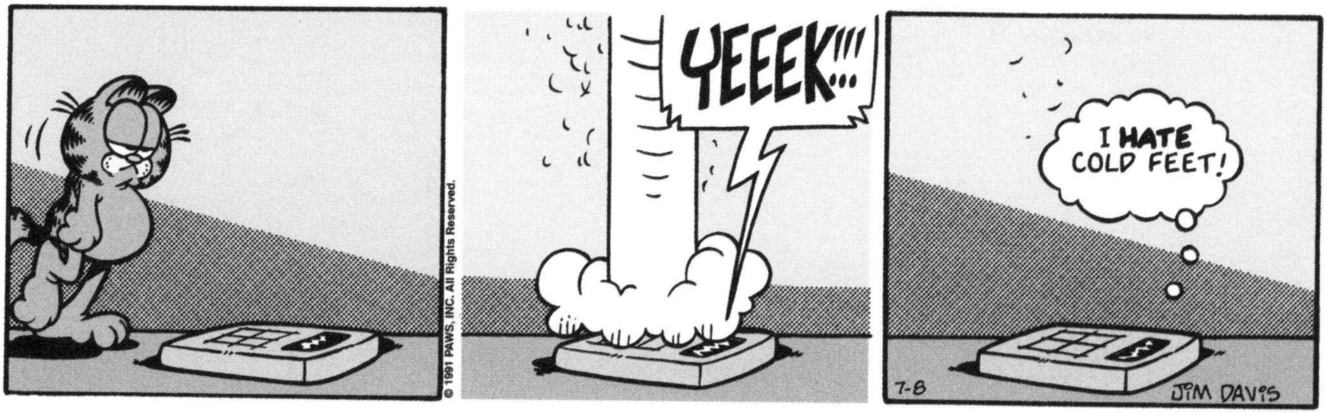
© 1991 PAWS, INC. All Rights Reserved.
YEEEK!!!...
I HATE COLD FEET!
7-8
JIM DAVIS

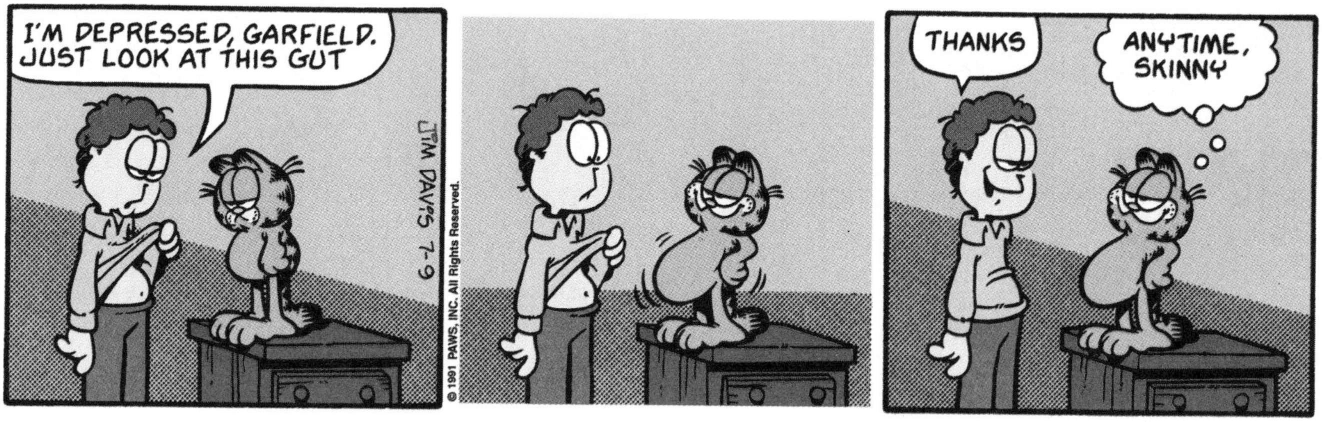
I'M DEPRESSED, GARFIELD. JUST LOOK AT THIS GUT
JIM DAVIS 7-9
© 1991 PAWS, INC. All Rights Reserved.
THANKS
ANYTIME, SKINNY

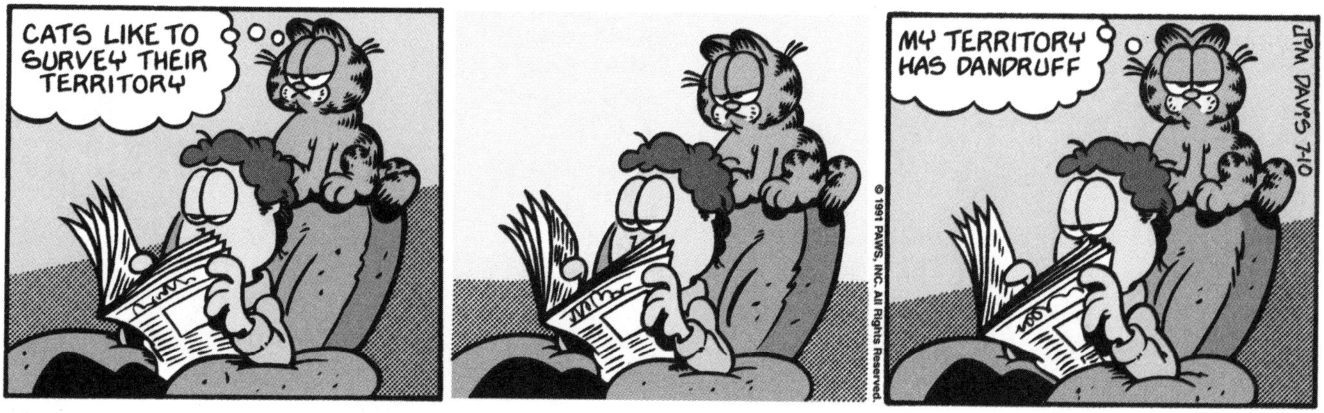
CATS LIKE TO SURVEY THEIR TERRITORY
© 1991 PAWS, INC. All Rights Reserved.
MY TERRITORY HAS DANDRUFF
JIM DAVIS 7-10

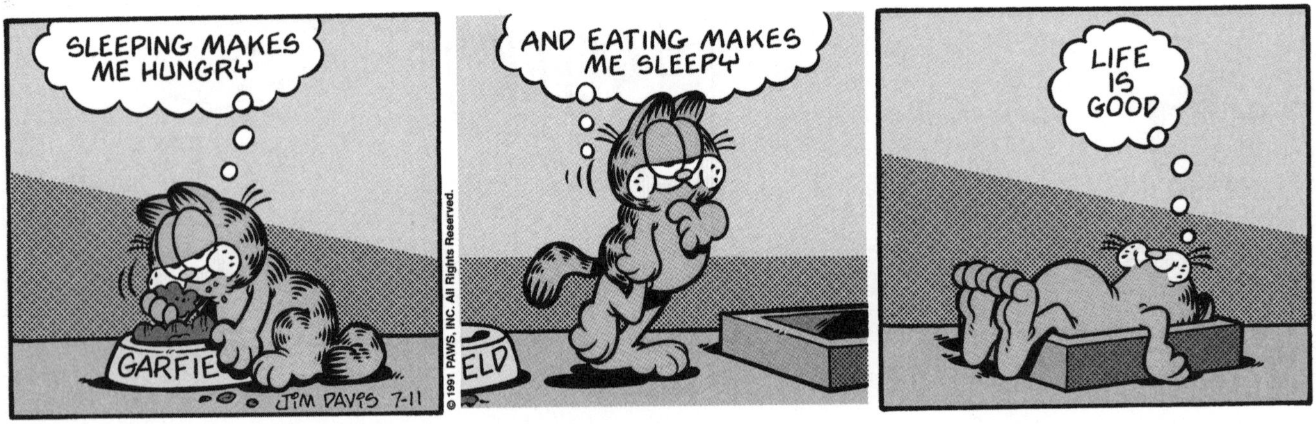
SLEEPING MAKES ME HUNGRY
GARFIE
AND EATING MAKES ME SLEEPY
ELD
LIFE IS GOOD
JIM DAVIS 7-11

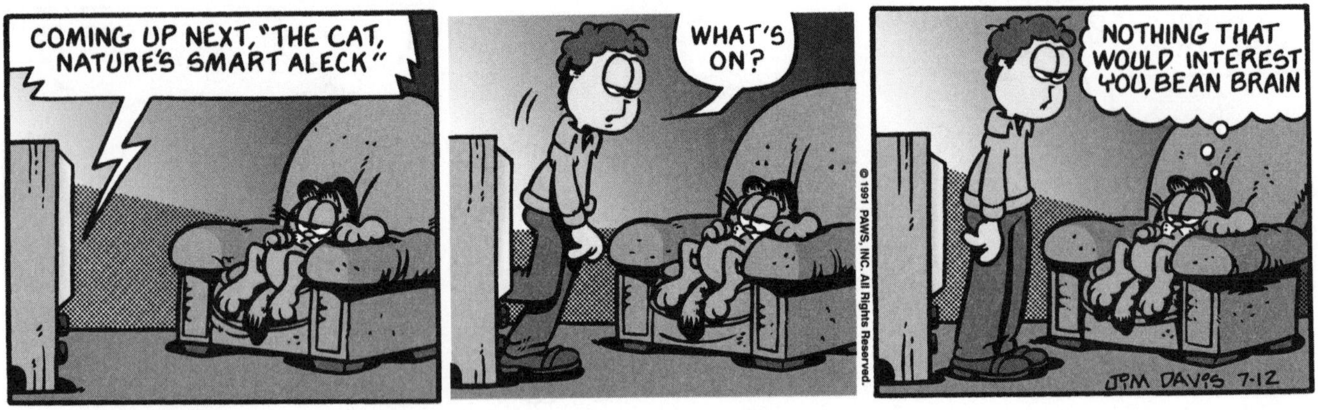
COMING UP NEXT, "THE CAT, NATURE'S SMART ALECK"
WHAT'S ON?
NOTHING THAT WOULD INTEREST YOU, BEAN BRAIN
JIM DAVIS 7-12

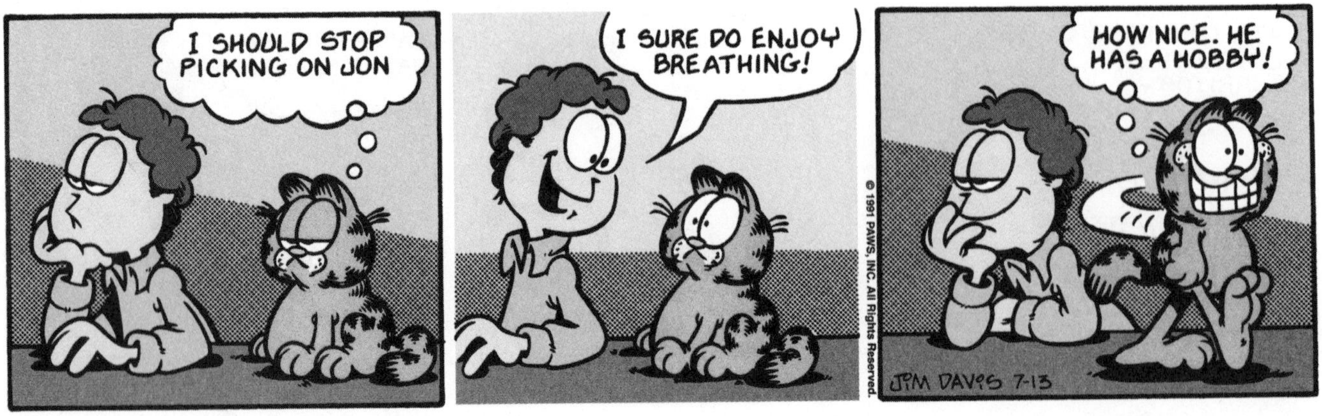
I SHOULD STOP PICKING ON JON
I SURE DO ENJOY BREATHING!
HOW NICE. HE HAS A HOBBY!
JIM DAVIS 7-13

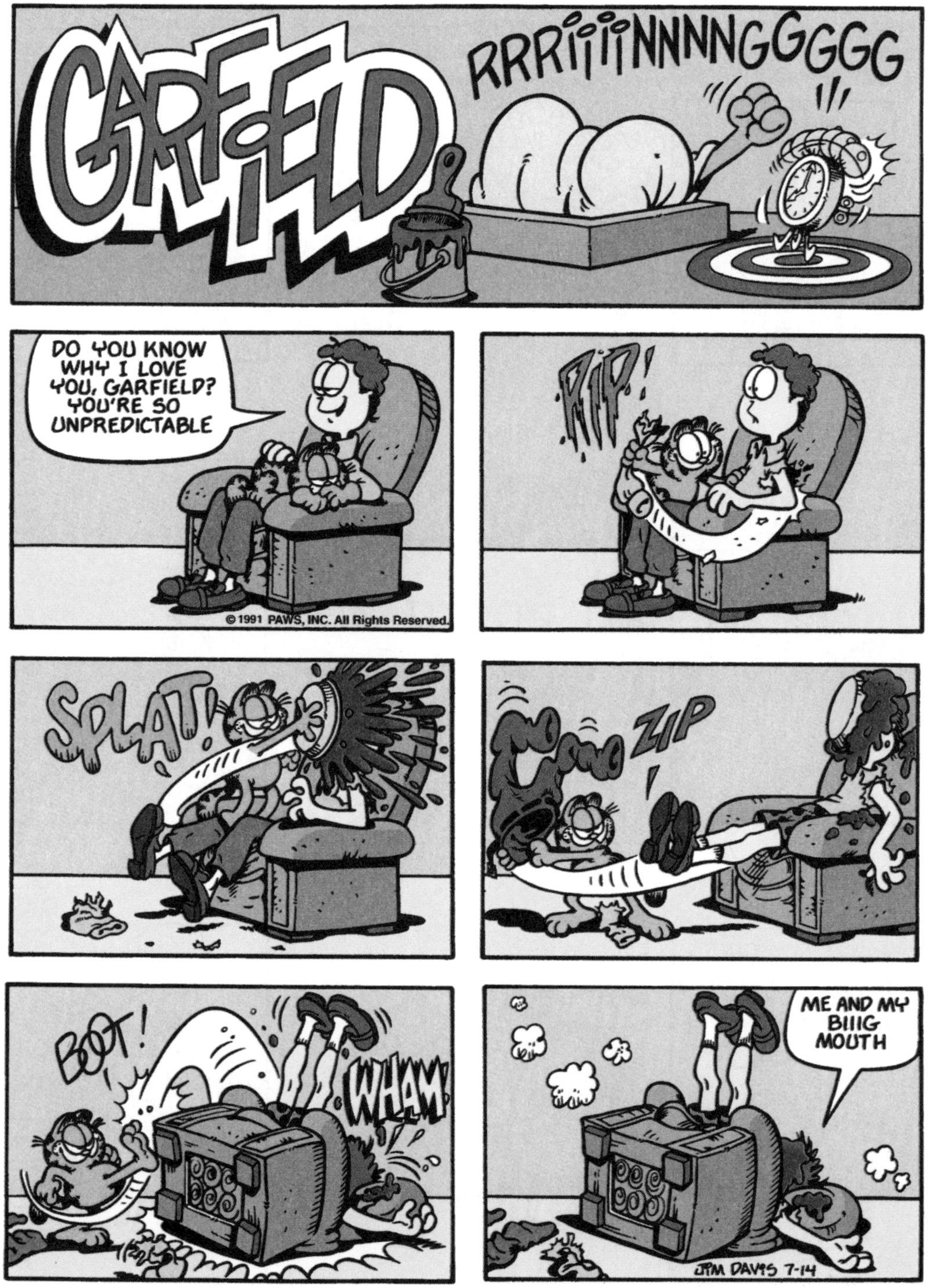
GARFIELD
RRRIIIINNNNGGGGG
DO YOU KNOW WHY I LOVE YOU, GARFIELD? YOU'RE SO UNPREDICTABLE
© 1991 PAWS, INC. All Rights Reserved.
RIP!
SPLAT!
ZIP
BOOT!
WHAM!
ME AND MY BIIIG MOUTH
JIM DAVIS 7-14

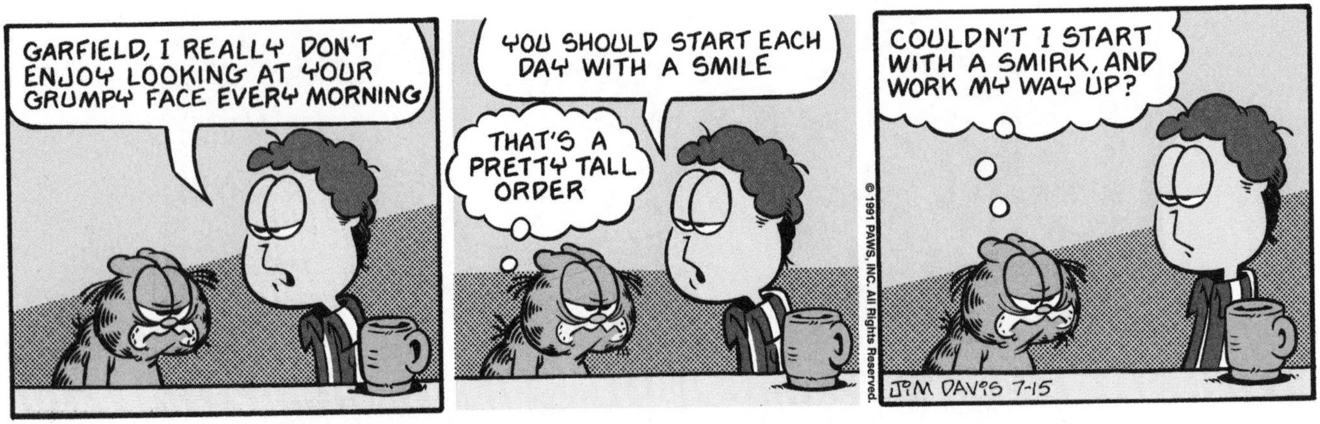
GARFIELD, I REALLY DON'T ENJOY LOOKING AT YOUR GRUMPY FACE EVERY MORNING
YOU SHOULD START EACH DAY WITH A SMILE
THAT'S A PRETTY TALL ORDER
COULDN'T I START WITH A SMIRK, AND WORK MY WAY UP?
© 1991 PAWS, INC. All Rights Reserved.
JIM DAVIS 7-15

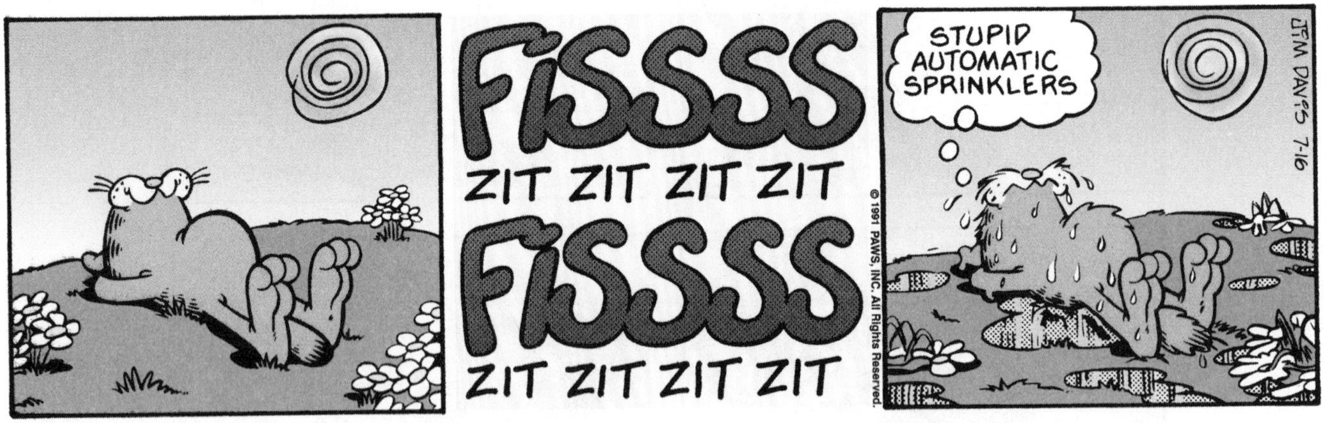
FISSSS
ZIT ZIT ZIT ZIT
FISSSS
ZIT ZIT ZIT ZIT
STUPID AUTOMATIC SPRINKLERS
© 1991 PAWS, INC. All Rights Reserved.
JIM DAVIS 7-16

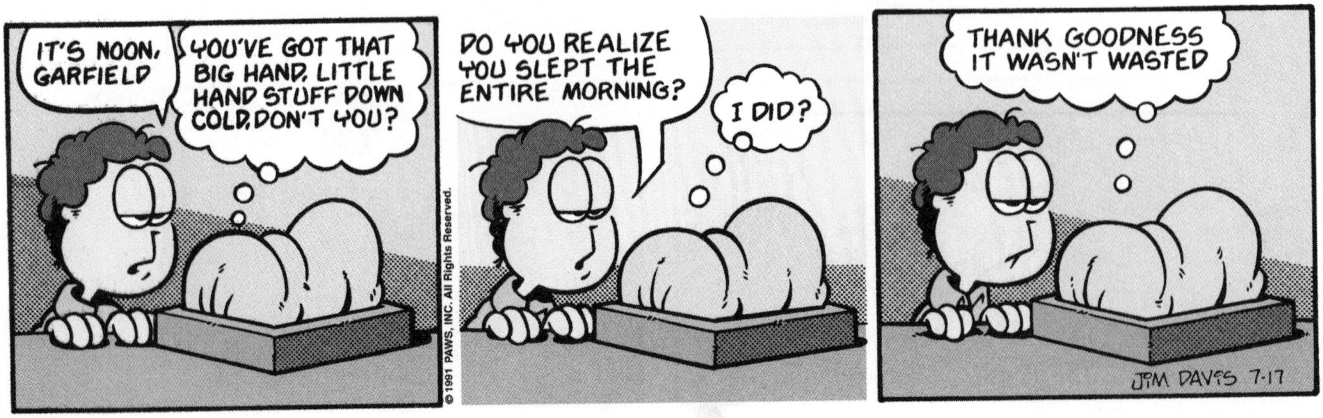
IT'S NOON, GARFIELD
YOU'VE GOT THAT BIG HAND, LITTLE HAND STUFF DOWN COLD, DON'T YOU?
DO YOU REALIZE YOU SLEPT THE ENTIRE MORNING?
I DID?
THANK GOODNESS IT WASN'T WASTED
© 1991 PAWS, INC. All Rights Reserved.
JIM DAVIS 7-17

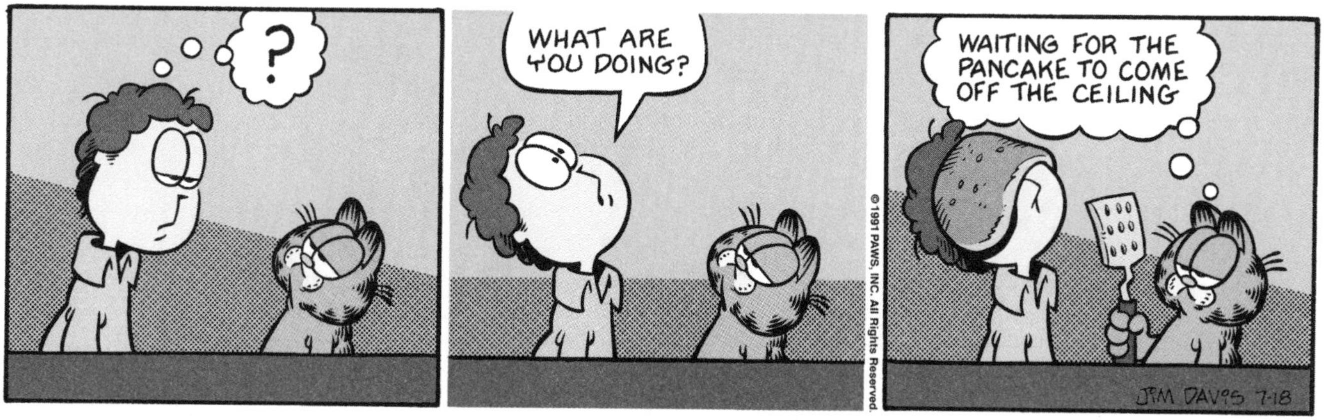
?
WHAT ARE YOU DOING?
WAITING FOR THE PANCAKE TO COME OFF THE CEILING
© 1991 PAWS, INC. All Rights Reserved.
JIM DAVIS 7-18

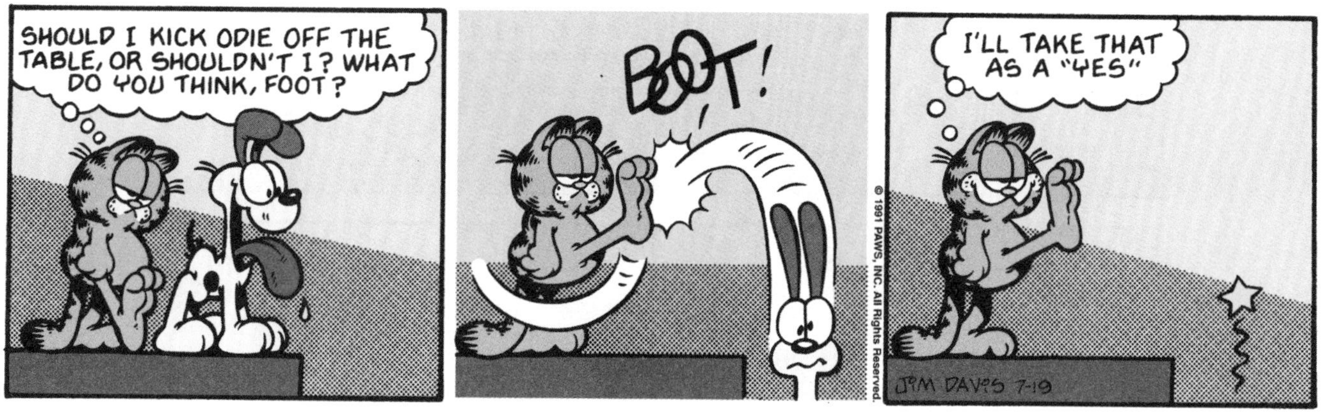
SHOULD I KICK ODIE OFF THE TABLE, OR SHOULDN'T I? WHAT DO YOU THINK, FOOT?
BOOT!
I'LL TAKE THAT AS A "YES"
© 1991 PAWS, INC. All Rights Reserved.
JIM DAVIS 7-19

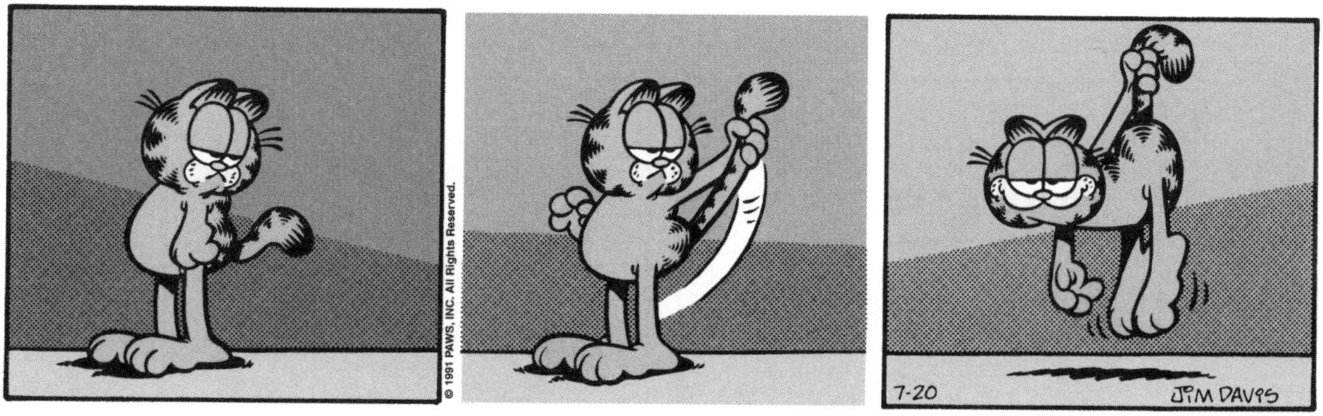
© 1991 PAWS, INC. All Rights Reserved.
7-20
JIM DAVIS

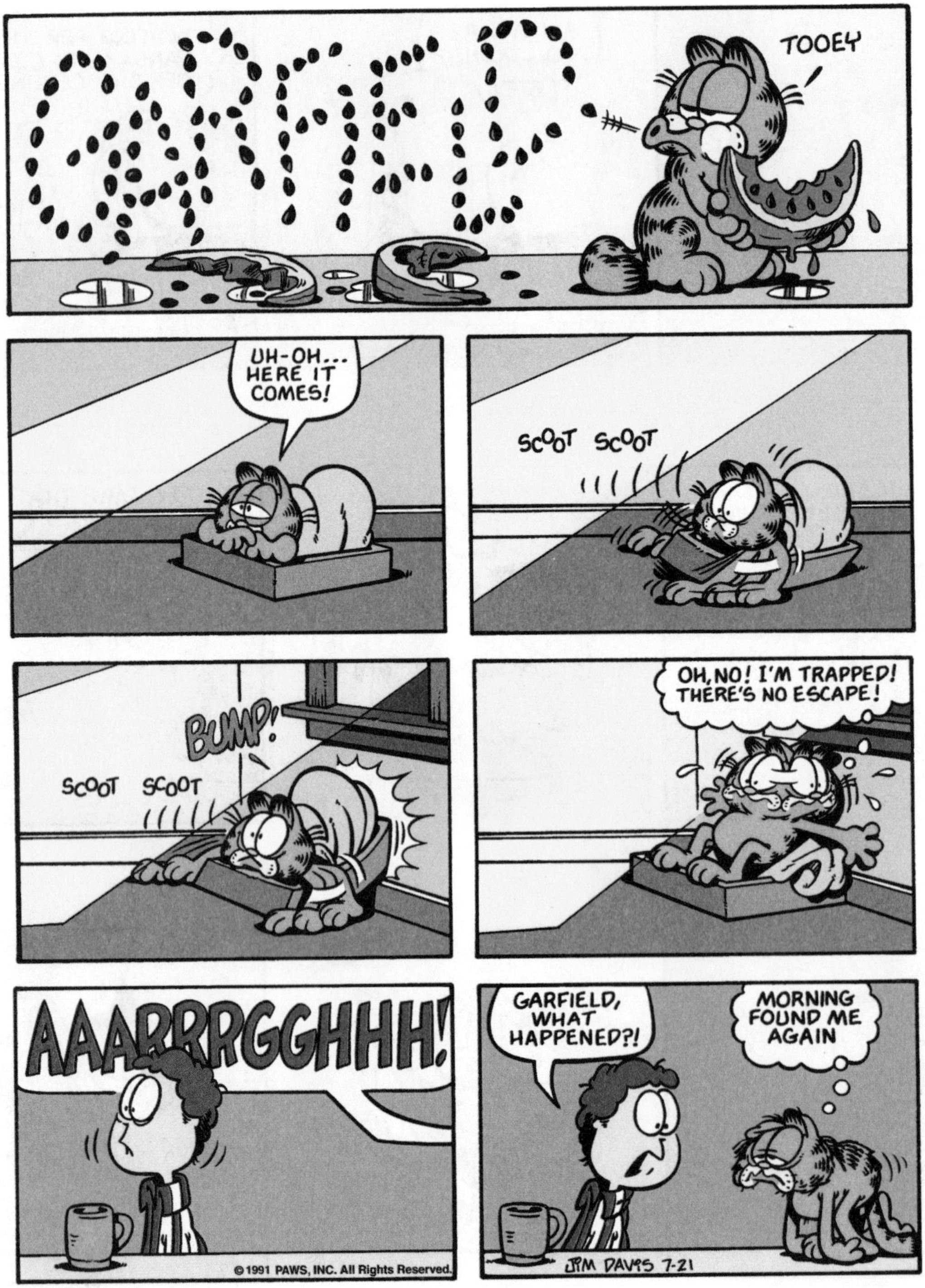
GARFIELD
TOOEY
UH-OH... HERE IT COMES!
SCOOT SCOOT
SCOOT SCOOT
BUMP!
OH, NO! I'M TRAPPED! THERE'S NO ESCAPE!
AAARRRGGHHH!
GARFIELD, WHAT HAPPENED?!
MORNING FOUND ME AGAIN
JIM DAVIS 7-21

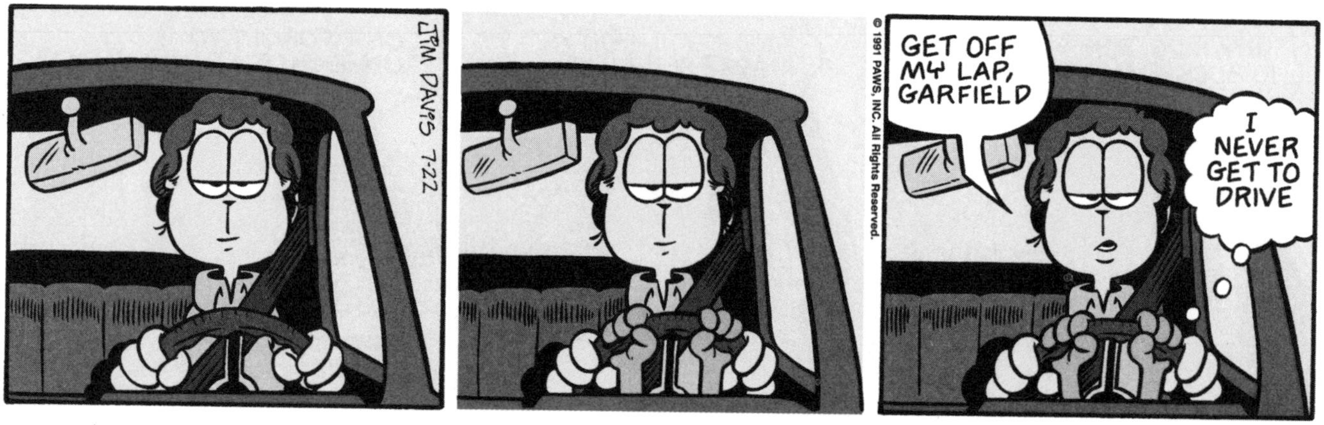
JIM DAVIS 7-22
© 1991 PAWS, INC. All Rights Reserved.
GET OFF MY LAP, GARFIELD
I NEVER GET TO DRIVE

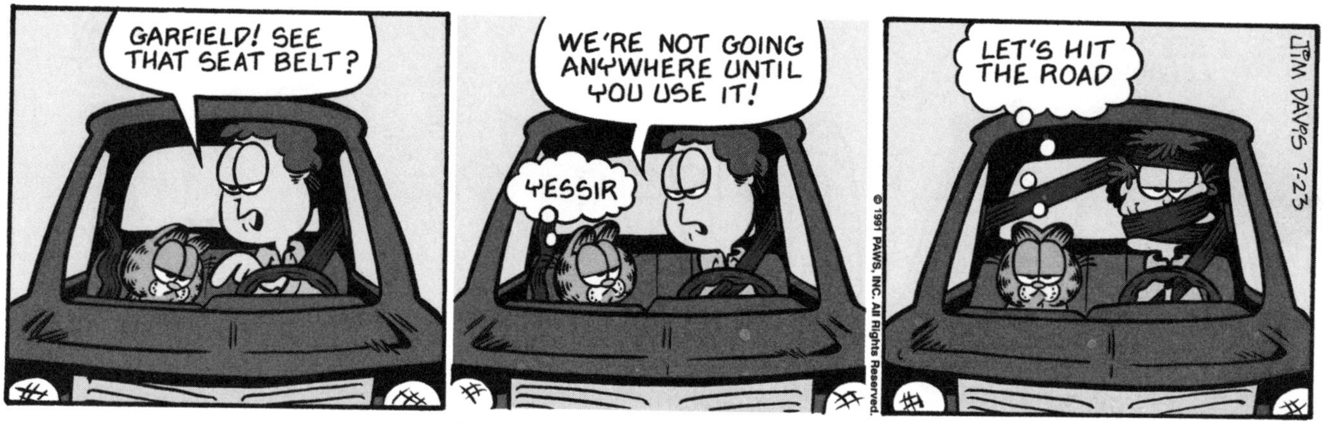
GARFIELD! SEE THAT SEAT BELT?
WE'RE NOT GOING ANYWHERE UNTIL YOU USE IT!
YESSIR
© 1991 PAWS, INC. All Rights Reserved.
LET'S HIT THE ROAD
JIM DAVIS 7-23

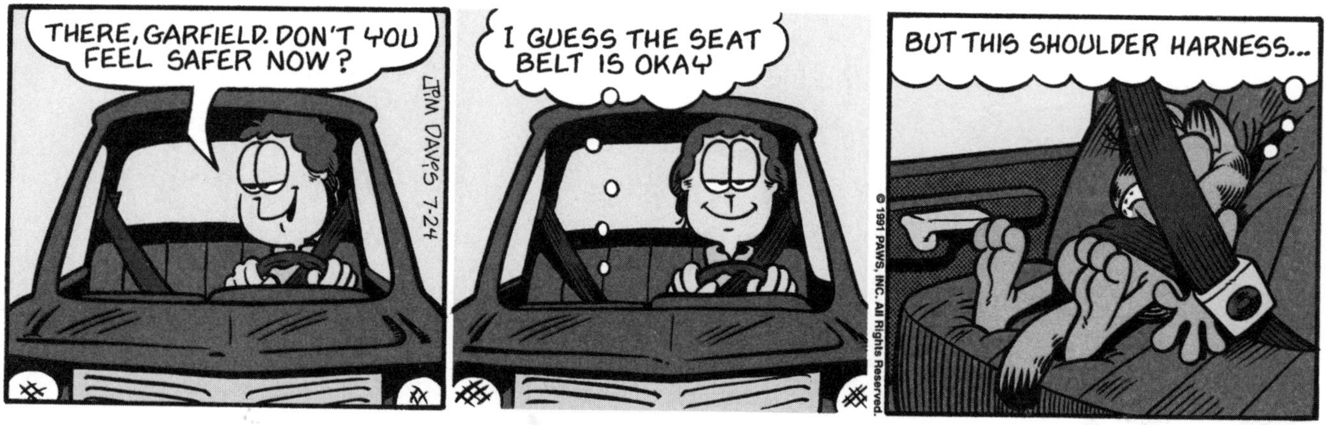
THERE, GARFIELD. DON'T YOU FEEL SAFER NOW?
JIM DAVIS 7-24
I GUESS THE SEAT BELT IS OKAY
© 1991 PAWS, INC. All Rights Reserved.
BUT THIS SHOULDER HARNESS...

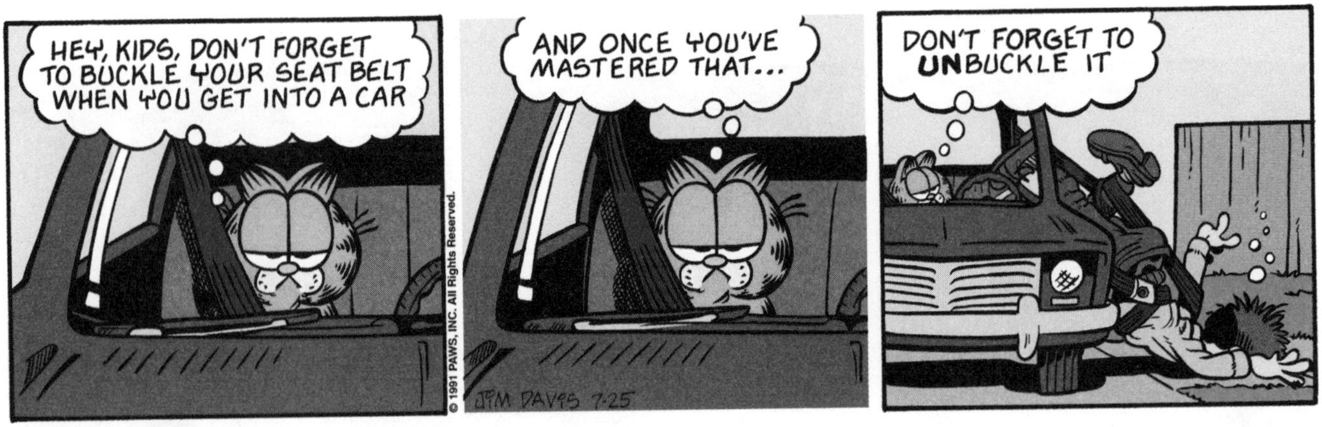
HEY, KIDS, DON'T FORGET TO BUCKLE YOUR SEAT BELT WHEN YOU GET INTO A CAR
© 1991 PAWS, INC. All Rights Reserved.
AND ONCE YOU'VE MASTERED THAT...
JIM DAVIS 7-25
DON'T FORGET TO **UN**BUCKLE IT

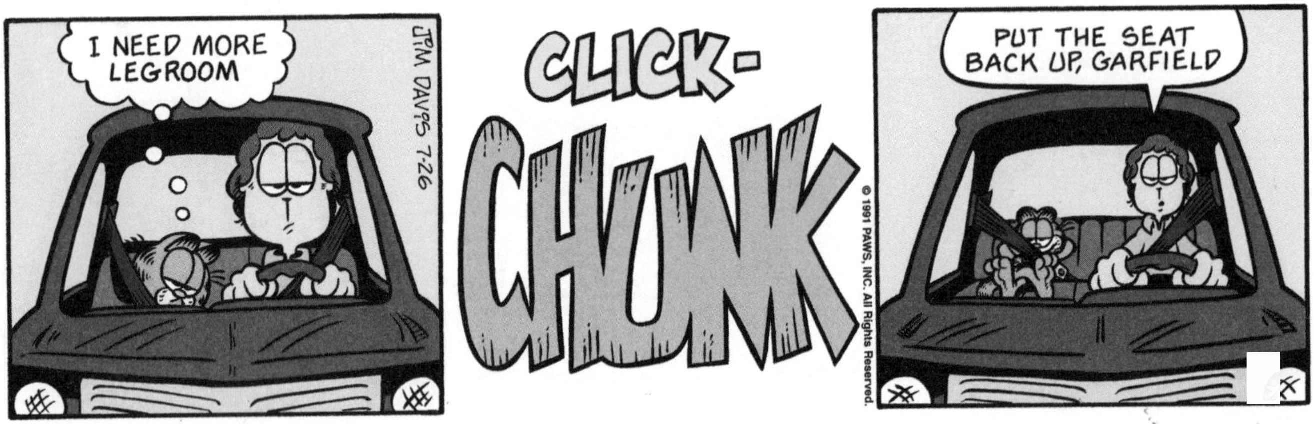
I NEED MORE LEGROOM
JIM DAVIS 7-26
CLICK-
CHUNK
© 1991 PAWS, INC. All Rights Reserved.
PUT THE SEAT BACK UP, GARFIELD

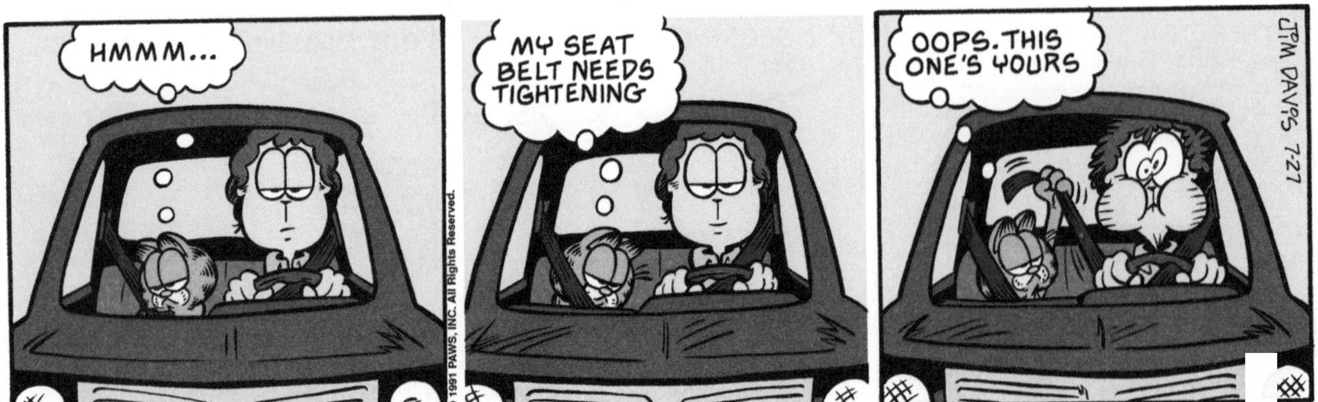
HMMM...
© 1991 PAWS, INC. All Rights Reserved.
MY SEAT BELT NEEDS TIGHTENING
OOPS. THIS ONE'S YOURS
JIM DAVIS 7-27

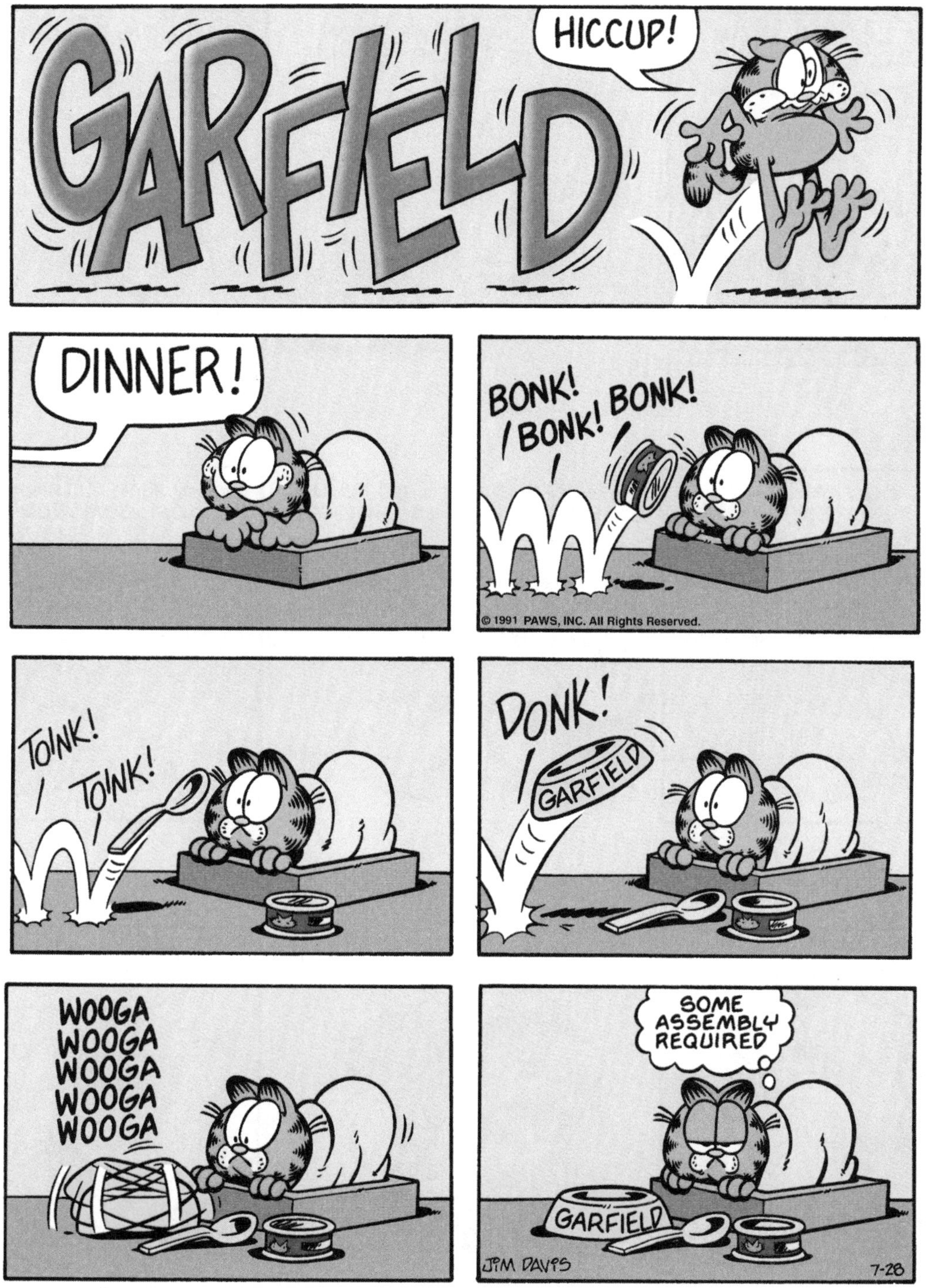
GARFIELD
HICCUP!
DINNER!
BONK! BONK! BONK!
© 1991 PAWS, INC. All Rights Reserved.
TOINK! TOINK!
DONK!
GARFIELD
WOOGA WOOGA WOOGA WOOGA WOOGA
SOME ASSEMBLY REQUIRED
GARFIELD
JIM DAVIS
7-28

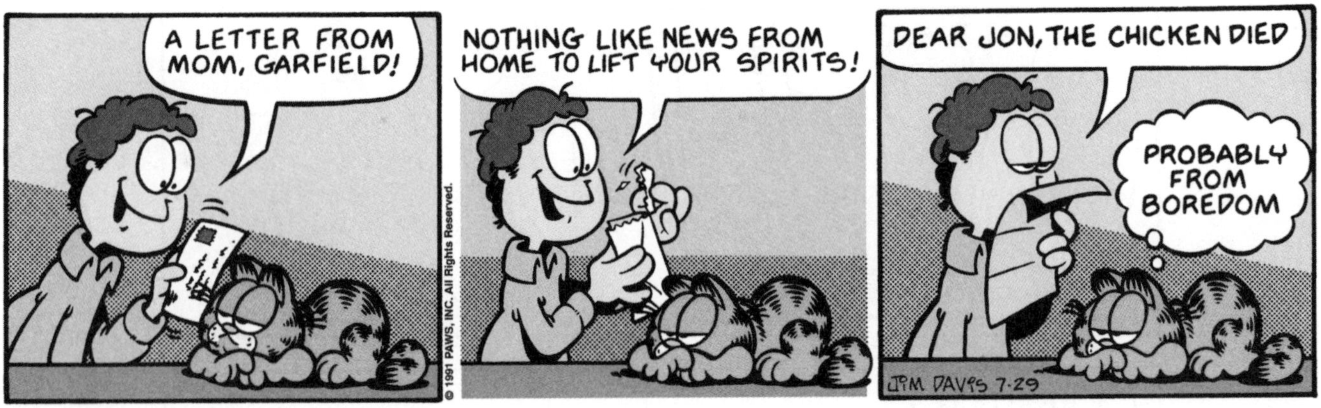
A LETTER FROM MOM, GARFIELD!
NOTHING LIKE NEWS FROM HOME TO LIFT YOUR SPIRITS!
DEAR JON, THE CHICKEN DIED
PROBABLY FROM BOREDOM
© 1991 PAWS, INC. All Rights Reserved.
JIM DAVIS 7-29

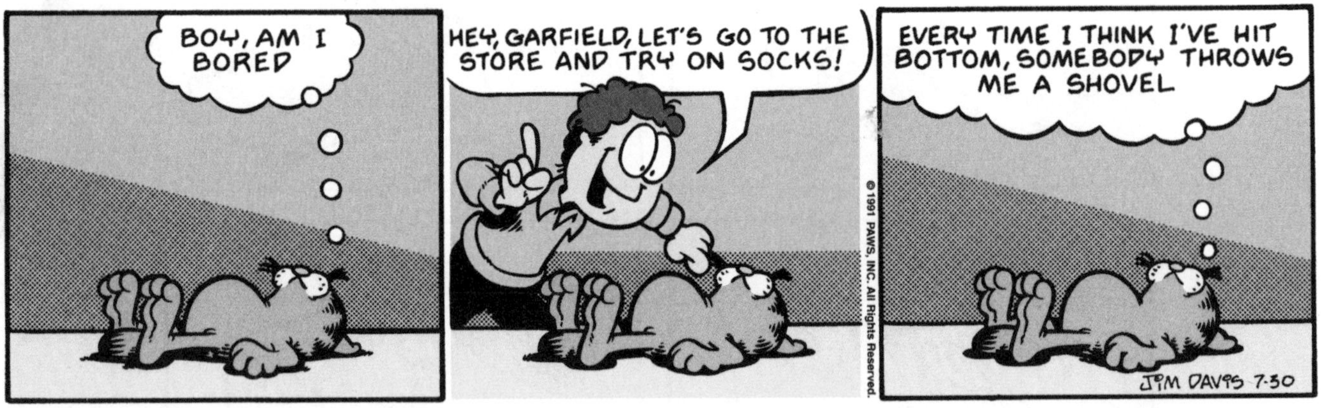
BOY, AM I BORED
HEY, GARFIELD, LET'S GO TO THE STORE AND TRY ON SOCKS!
EVERY TIME I THINK I'VE HIT BOTTOM, SOMEBODY THROWS ME A SHOVEL
© 1991 PAWS, INC. All Rights Reserved.
JIM DAVIS 7-30

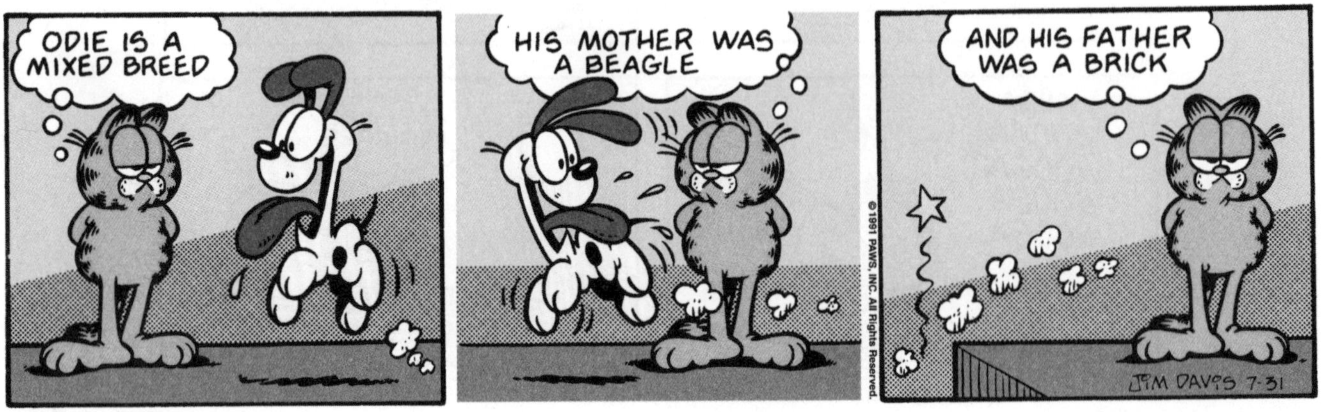
ODIE IS A MIXED BREED
HIS MOTHER WAS A BEAGLE
AND HIS FATHER WAS A BRICK
© 1991 PAWS, INC. All Rights Reserved.
JIM DAVIS 7-31

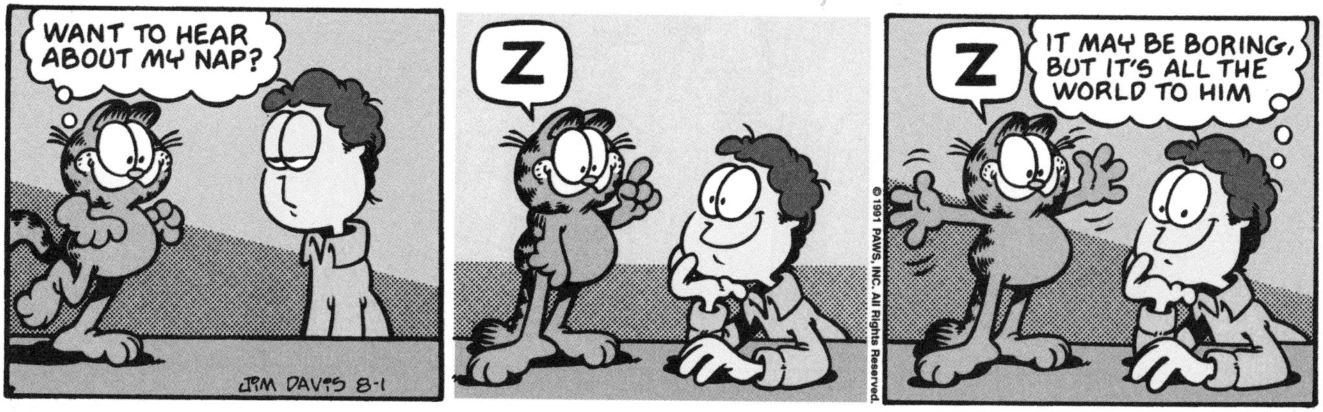
WANT TO HEAR ABOUT MY NAP?
JIM DAVIS 8-1
Z
© 1991 PAWS, INC. All Rights Reserved.
Z
IT MAY BE BORING, BUT IT'S ALL THE WORLD TO HIM

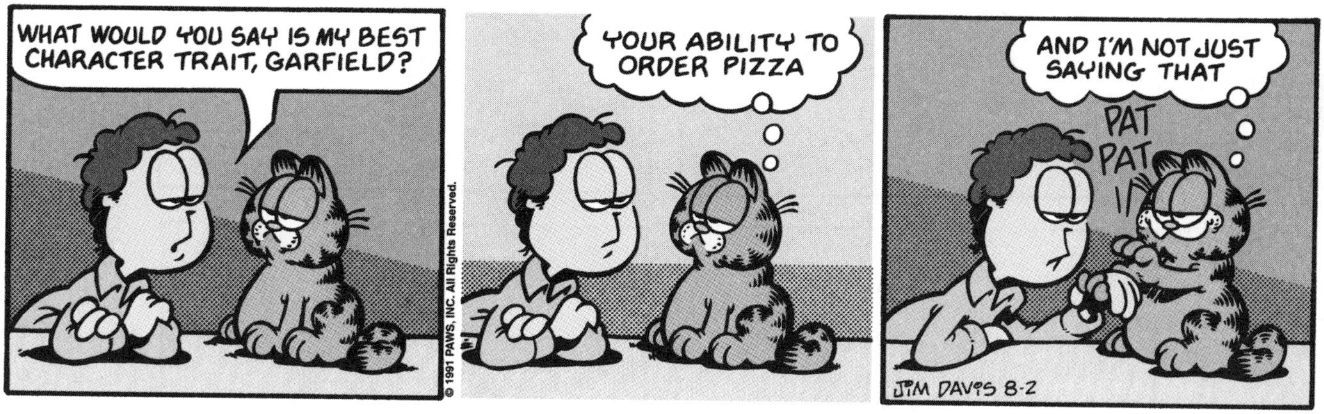
WHAT WOULD YOU SAY IS MY BEST CHARACTER TRAIT, GARFIELD?
© 1991 PAWS, INC. All Rights Reserved.
YOUR ABILITY TO ORDER PIZZA
AND I'M NOT JUST SAYING THAT
PAT PAT
JIM DAVIS 8-2

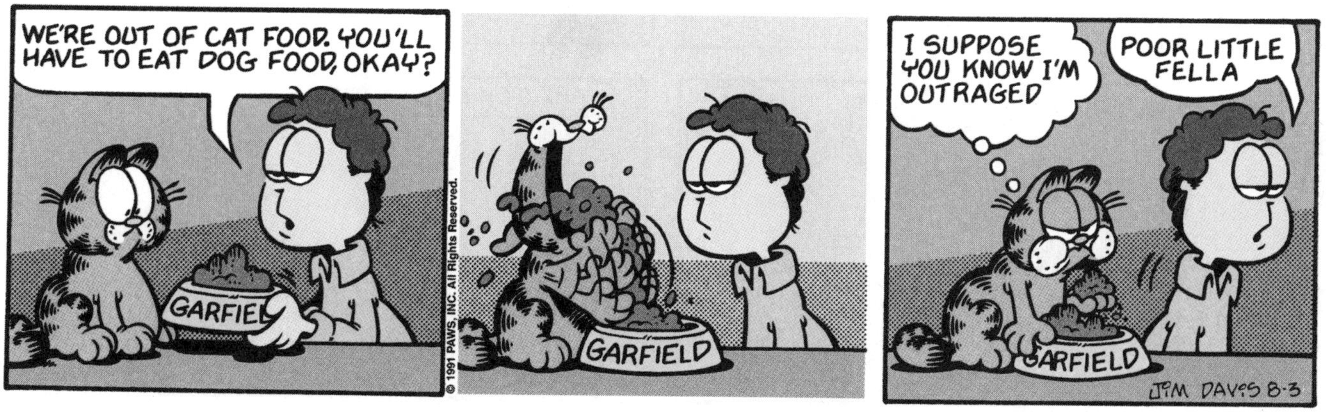
WE'RE OUT OF CAT FOOD. YOU'LL HAVE TO EAT DOG FOOD, OKAY?
GARFIEL
© 1991 PAWS, INC. All Rights Reserved.
GARFIELD
I SUPPOSE YOU KNOW I'M OUTRAGED
POOR LITTLE FELLA
GARFIELD
JIM DAVIS 8-3

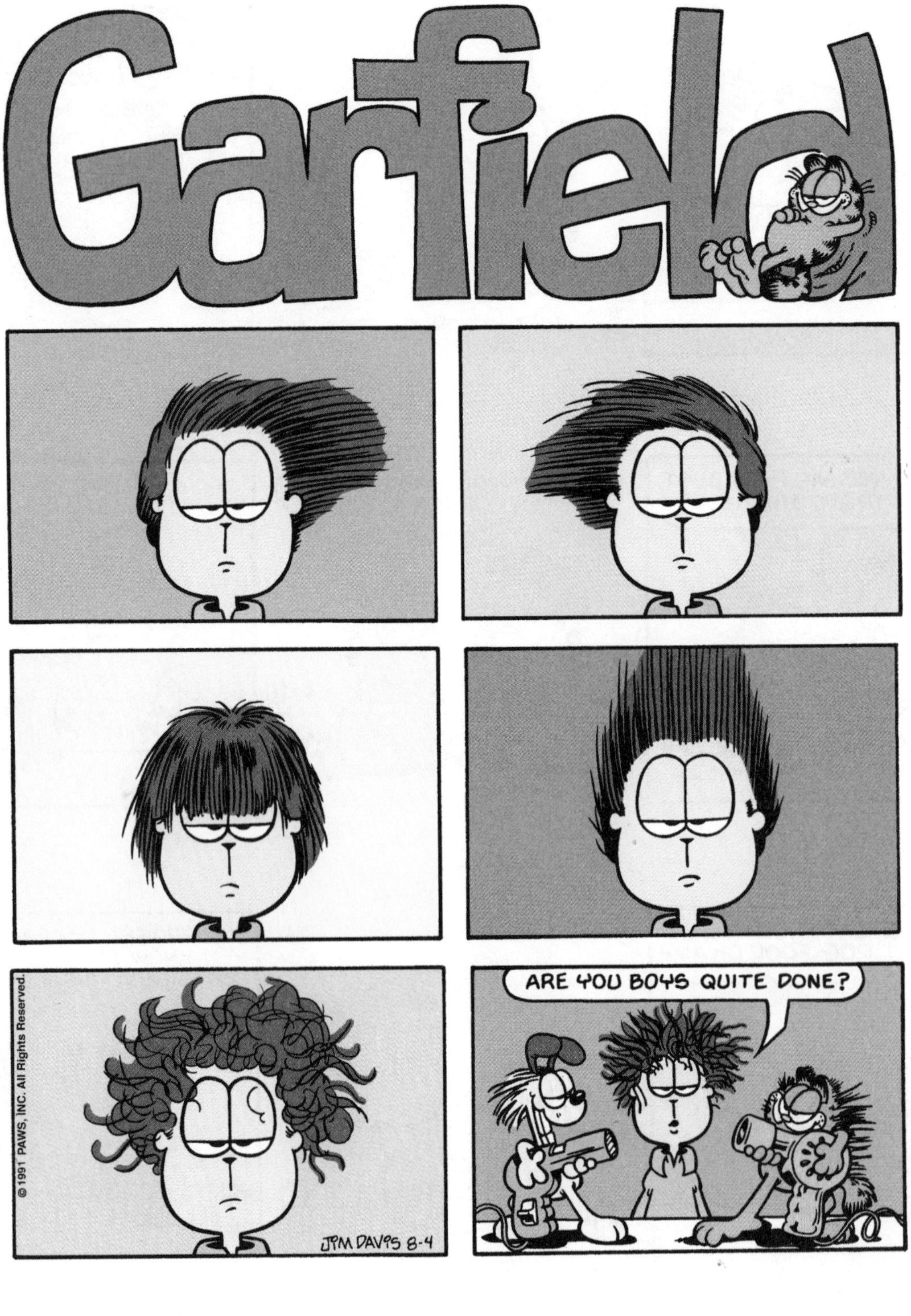
Garfield
©1991 PAWS, INC. All Rights Reserved.
JIM DAVIS 8-4
ARE YOU BOYS QUITE DONE?

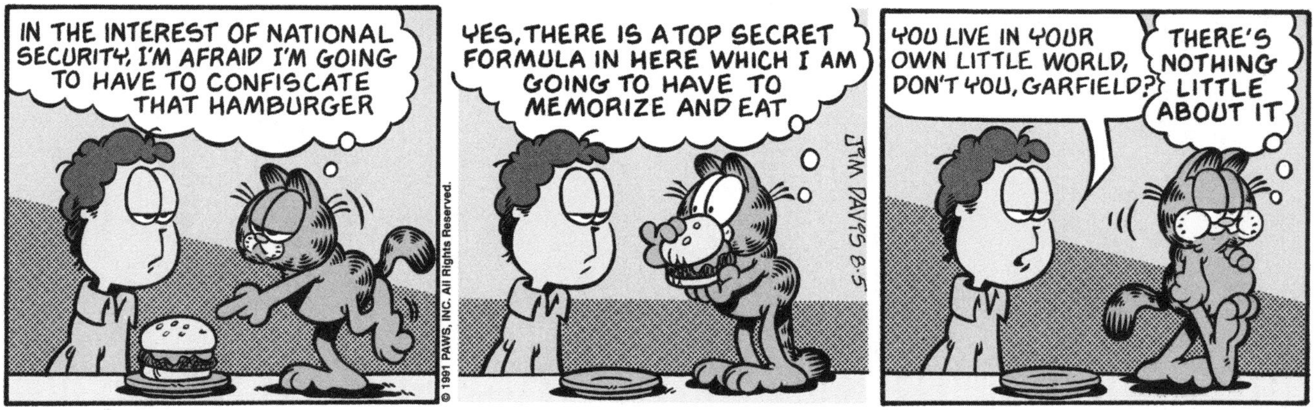
IN THE INTEREST OF NATIONAL SECURITY, I'M AFRAID I'M GOING TO HAVE TO CONFISCATE THAT HAMBURGER
© 1991 PAWS, INC. All Rights Reserved.
YES, THERE IS A TOP SECRET FORMULA IN HERE WHICH I AM GOING TO HAVE TO MEMORIZE AND EAT
JIM DAVIS 8-5
YOU LIVE IN YOUR OWN LITTLE WORLD, DON'T YOU, GARFIELD?
THERE'S NOTHING LITTLE ABOUT IT

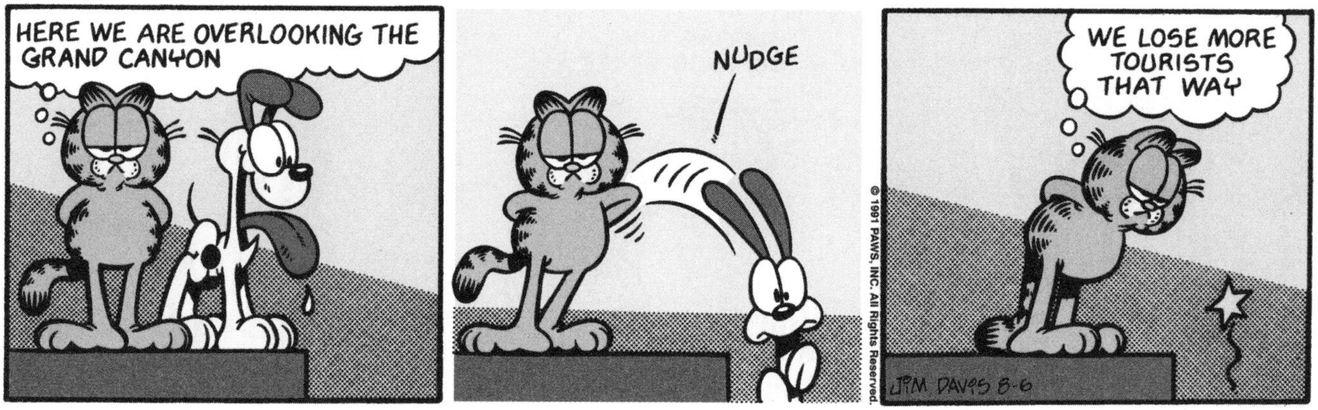
HERE WE ARE OVERLOOKING THE GRAND CANYON
NUDGE
© 1991 PAWS, INC. All Rights Reserved.
WE LOSE MORE TOURISTS THAT WAY
JIM DAVIS 8-6

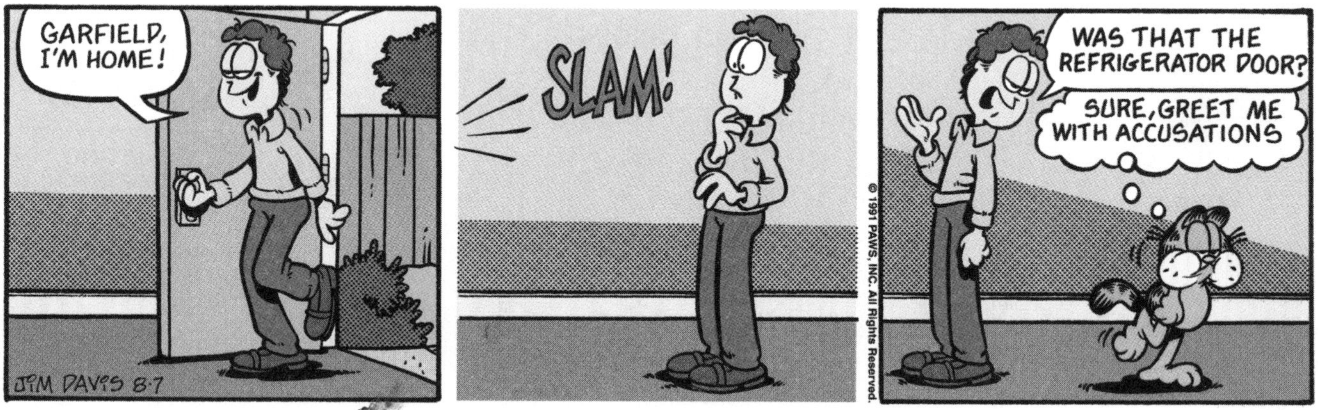
GARFIELD, I'M HOME!
JIM DAVIS 8-7
SLAM!
© 1991 PAWS, INC. All Rights Reserved.
WAS THAT THE REFRIGERATOR DOOR?
SURE, GREET ME WITH ACCUSATIONS

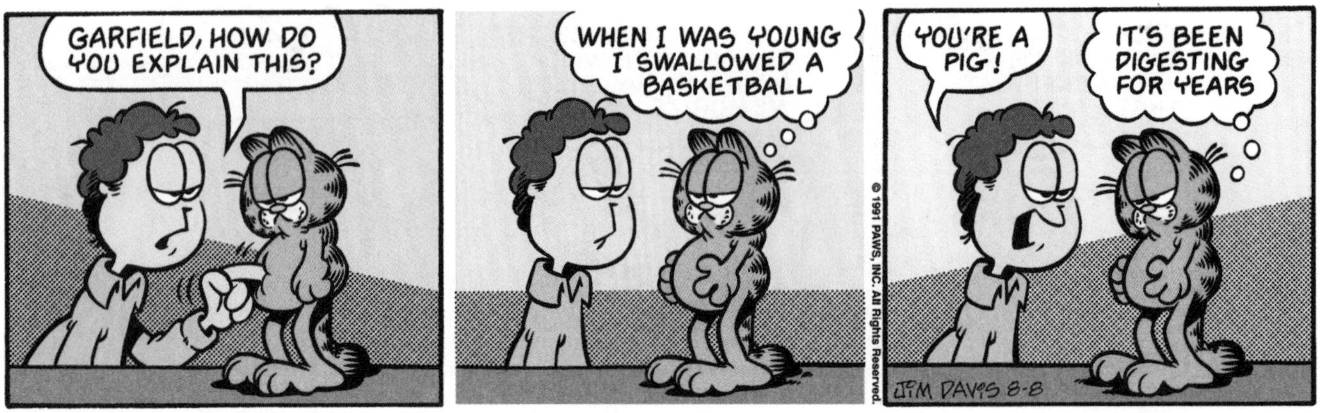
GARFIELD, HOW DO YOU EXPLAIN THIS?
WHEN I WAS YOUNG I SWALLOWED A BASKETBALL
YOU'RE A PIG!
IT'S BEEN DIGESTING FOR YEARS
© 1991 PAWS, INC. All Rights Reserved.
JIM DAVIS 8-8

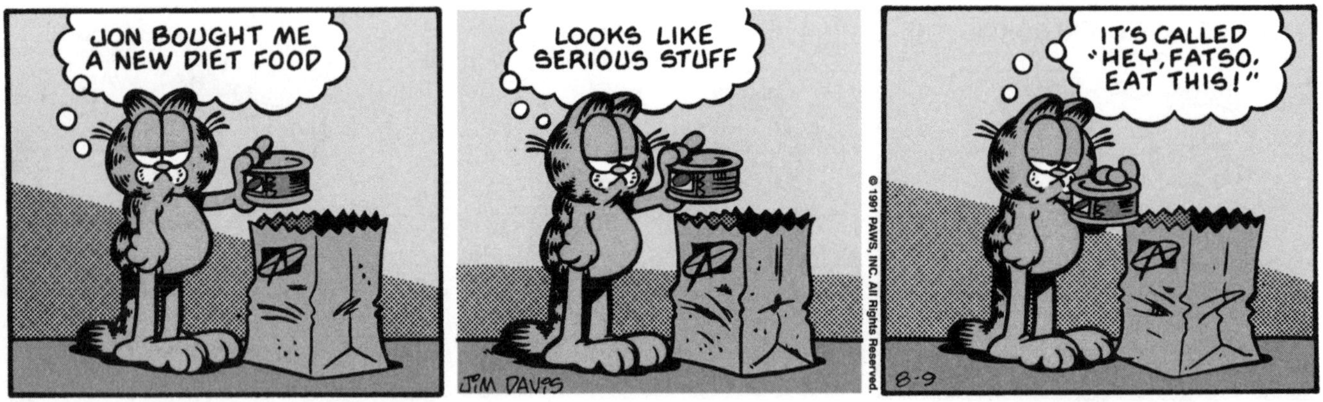
JON BOUGHT ME A NEW DIET FOOD
LOOKS LIKE SERIOUS STUFF
IT'S CALLED "HEY, FATSO, EAT THIS!"
JIM DAVIS
© 1991 PAWS, INC. All Rights Reserved.
8-9

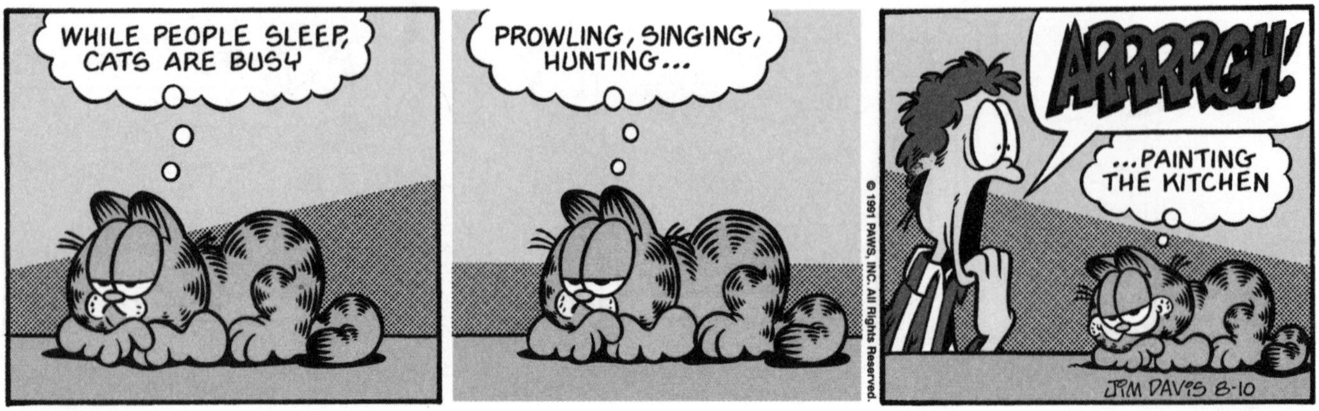
WHILE PEOPLE SLEEP, CATS ARE BUSY
PROWLING, SINGING, HUNTING...
ARRRRGH!
...PAINTING THE KITCHEN
© 1991 PAWS, INC. All Rights Reserved.
JIM DAVIS 8-10

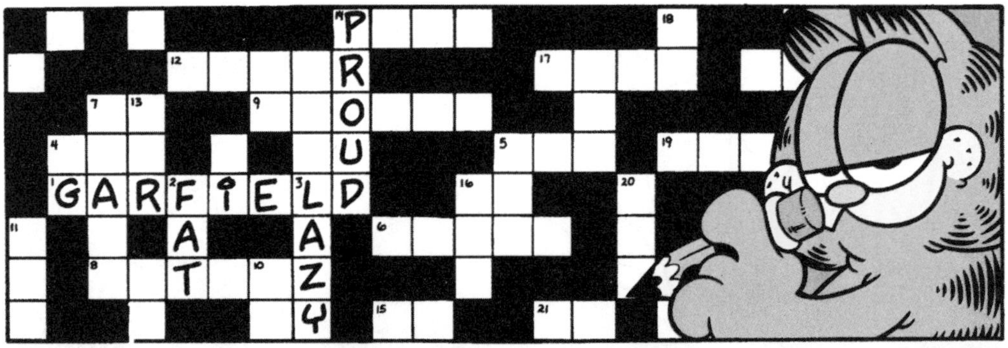
GARFIELD
PROUD
FAT
LAZY

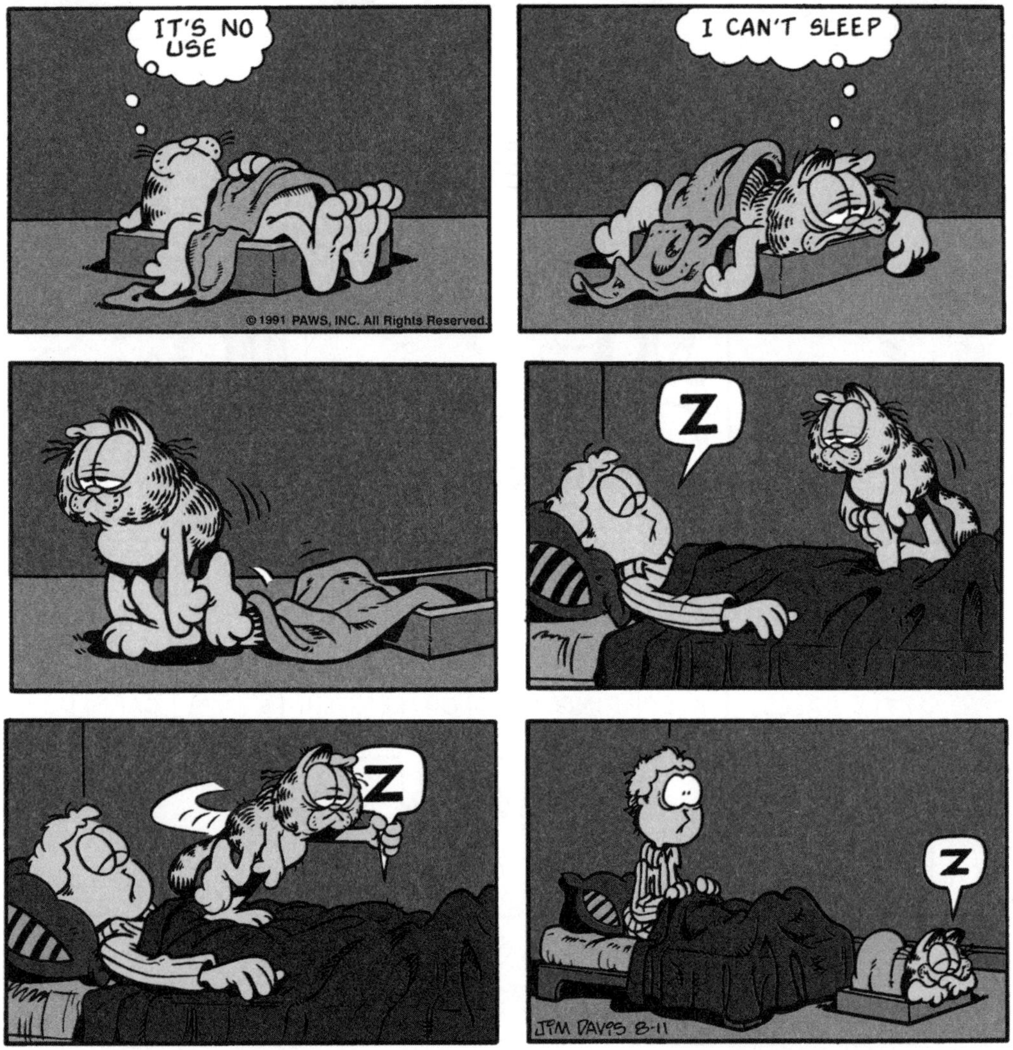
IT'S NO USE
I CAN'T SLEEP
© 1991 PAWS, INC. All Rights Reserved.
Z
Z
Z
JIM DAVIS 8-11

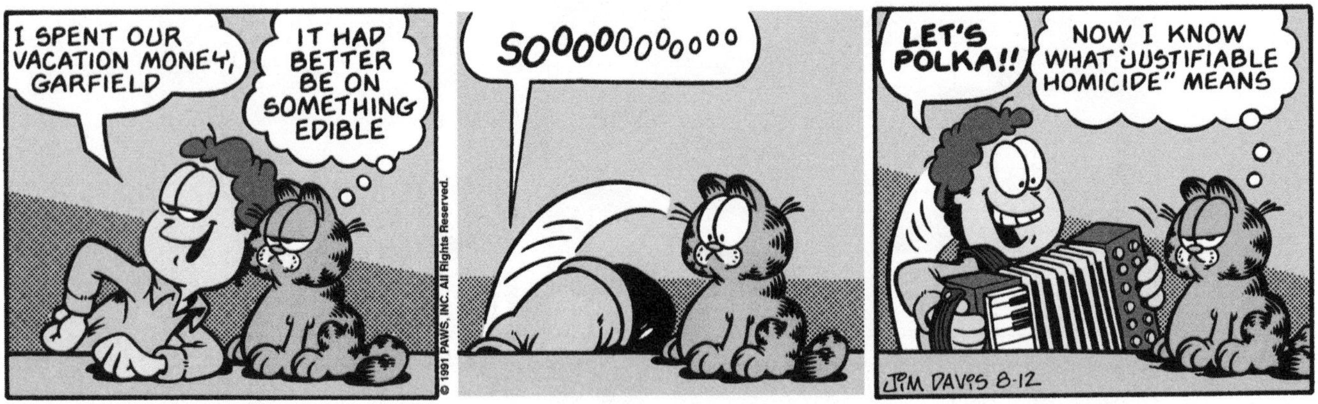
I SPENT OUR VACATION MONEY, GARFIELD
IT HAD BETTER BE ON SOMETHING EDIBLE
© 1991 PAWS, INC. All Rights Reserved.
SOOOOOOOOOOO
LET'S POLKA!!
NOW I KNOW WHAT "JUSTIFIABLE HOMICIDE" MEANS
JIM DAVIS 8-12

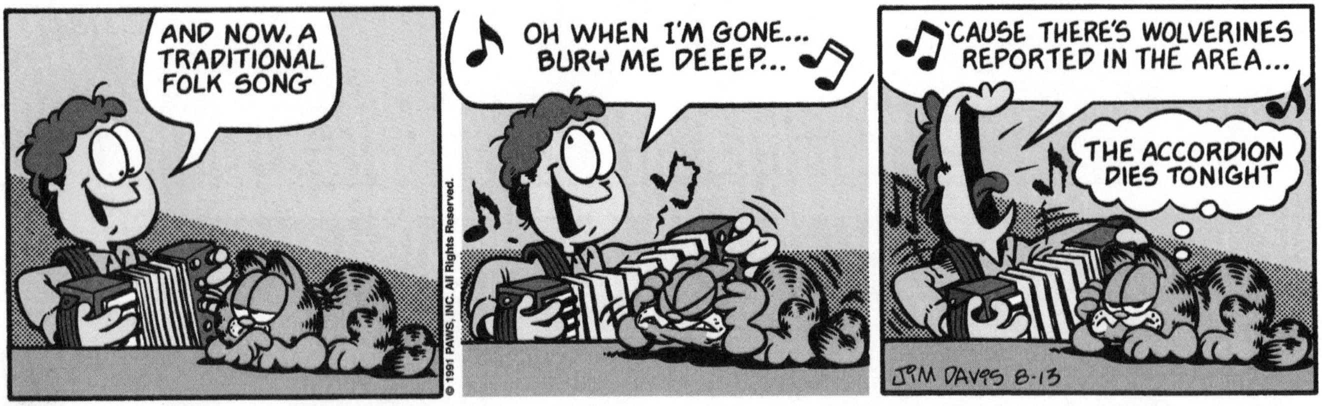
AND NOW, A TRADITIONAL FOLK SONG
© 1991 PAWS, INC. All Rights Reserved.
OH WHEN I'M GONE... BURY ME DEEEP...
'CAUSE THERE'S WOLVERINES REPORTED IN THE AREA...
THE ACCORDION DIES TONIGHT
JIM DAVIS 8-13

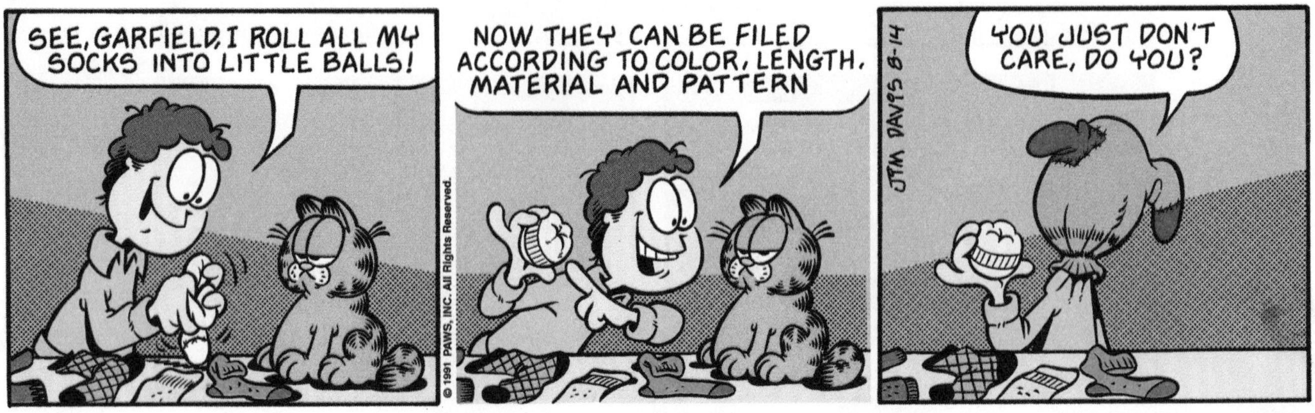
SEE, GARFIELD, I ROLL ALL MY SOCKS INTO LITTLE BALLS!
© 1991 PAWS, INC. All Rights Reserved.
NOW THEY CAN BE FILED ACCORDING TO COLOR, LENGTH, MATERIAL AND PATTERN
JIM DAVIS 8-14
YOU JUST DON'T CARE, DO YOU?

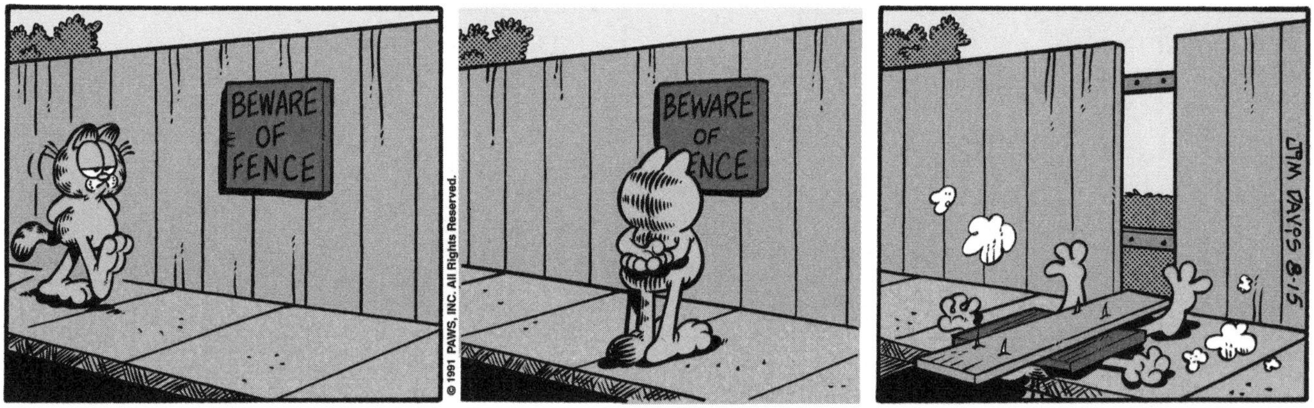
BEWARE OF FENCE
© 1991 PAWS, INC. All Rights Reserved.
BEWARE OF FENCE
JIM DAVIS 8-15

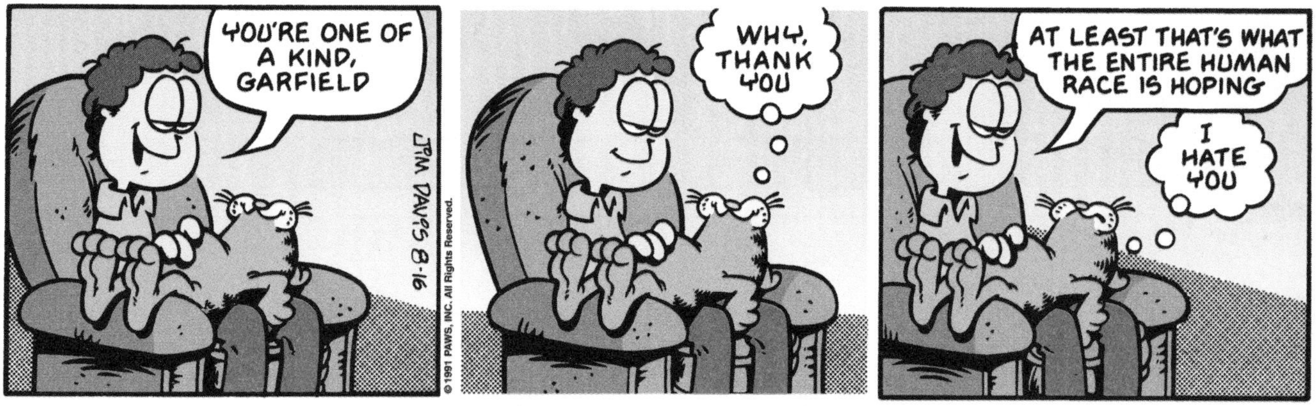
YOU'RE ONE OF A KIND, GARFIELD
JIM DAVIS 8-16
© 1991 PAWS, INC. All Rights Reserved.
WHY, THANK YOU
AT LEAST THAT'S WHAT THE ENTIRE HUMAN RACE IS HOPING
I HATE YOU

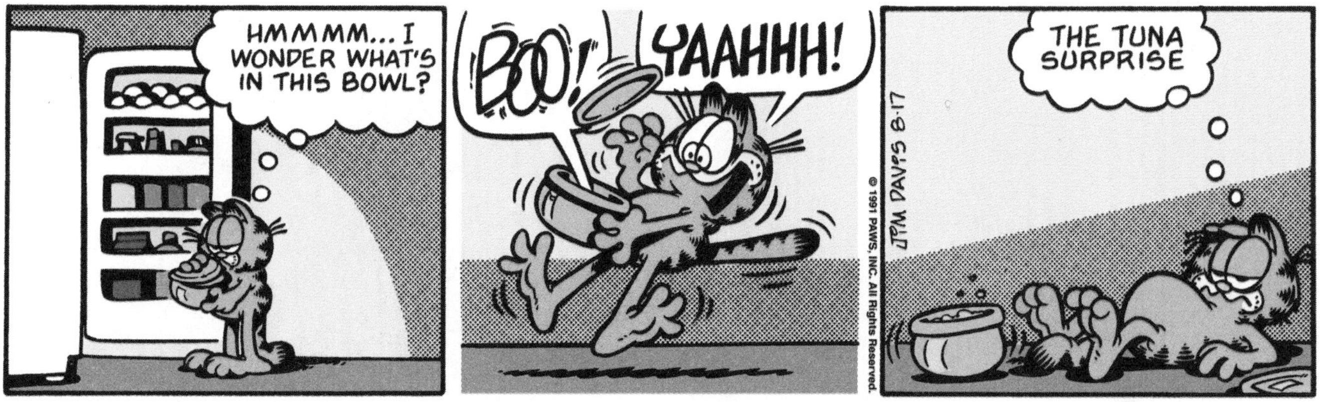
HMMMM... I WONDER WHAT'S IN THIS BOWL?
BOO!
YAAHHH!
JIM DAVIS 8-17
© 1991 PAWS, INC. All Rights Reserved.
THE TUNA SURPRISE

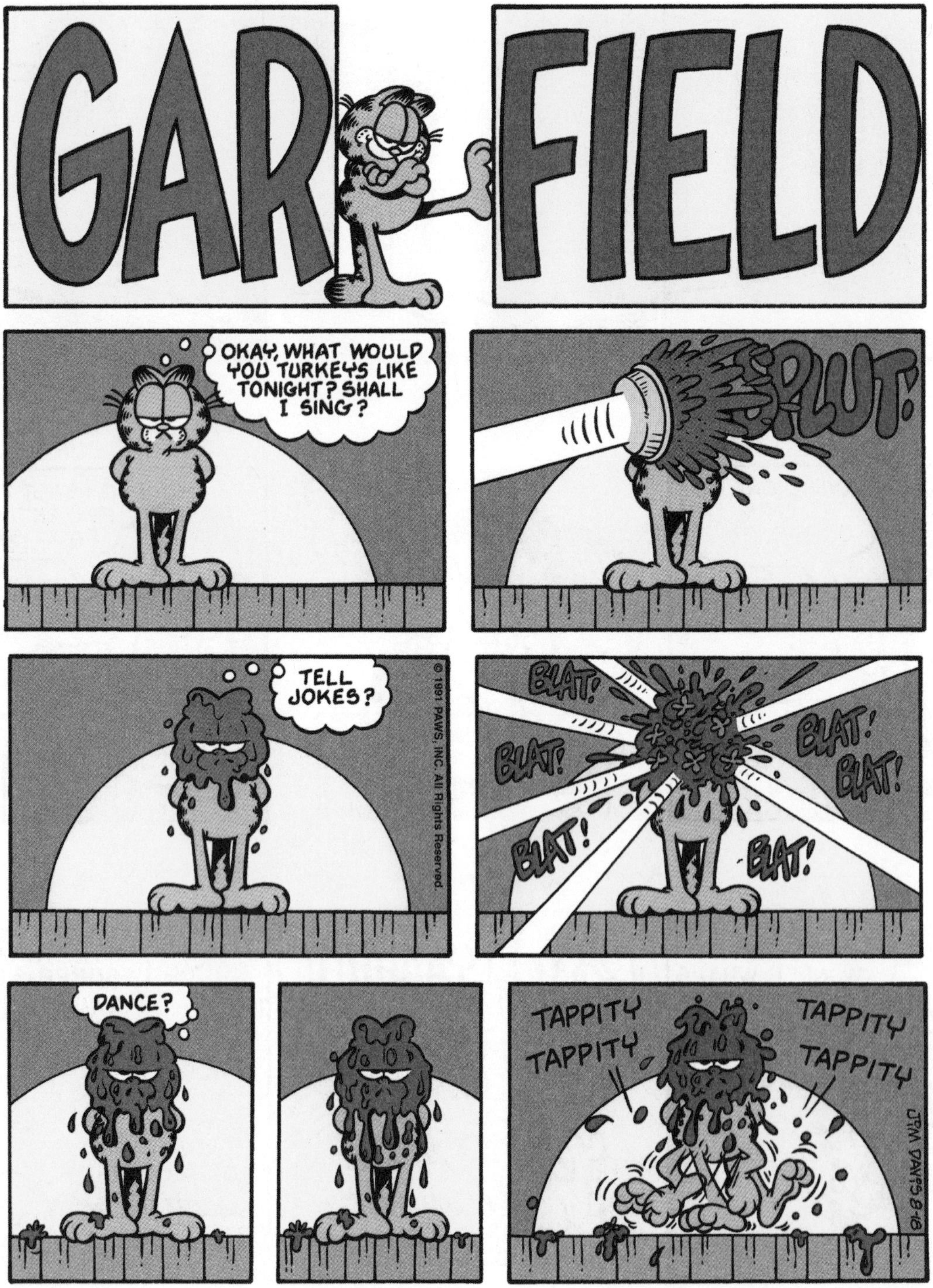
GARFIELD
OKAY, WHAT WOULD YOU TURKEYS LIKE TONIGHT? SHALL I SING?
SPLUT!
TELL JOKES?
© 1991 PAWS, INC. All Rights Reserved.
BLAT!
BLAT!
BLAT!
BLAT!
BLAT!
BLAT!
DANCE?
TAPPITY
TAPPITY
TAPPITY
TAPPITY
JIM DAVIS 8-18

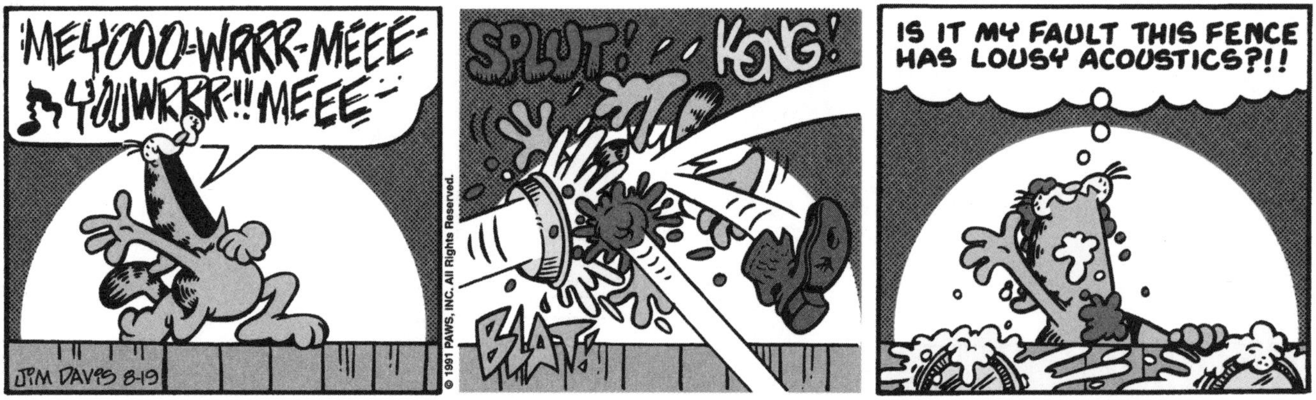
MEYOOO-WRRR-MEEE-
YOUWRRR!! MEEE-
SPLUT! KONG! BLAT!
IS IT MY FAULT THIS FENCE HAS LOUSY ACOUSTICS?!!
JIM DAVIS 8-19
© 1991 PAWS, INC. All Rights Reserved.

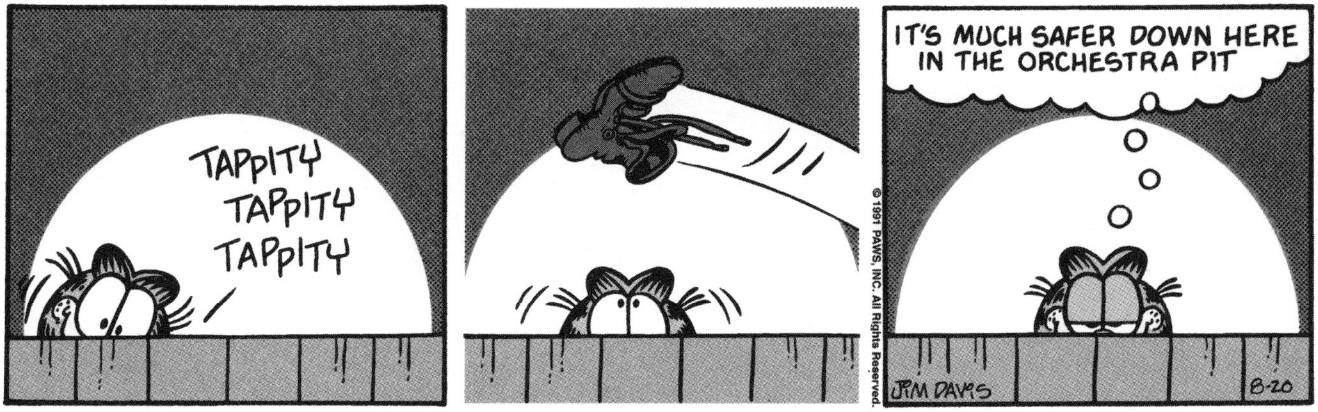
TAPPITY
TAPPITY
TAPPITY
IT'S MUCH SAFER DOWN HERE IN THE ORCHESTRA PIT
JIM DAVIS 8-20
© 1991 PAWS, INC. All Rights Reserved.

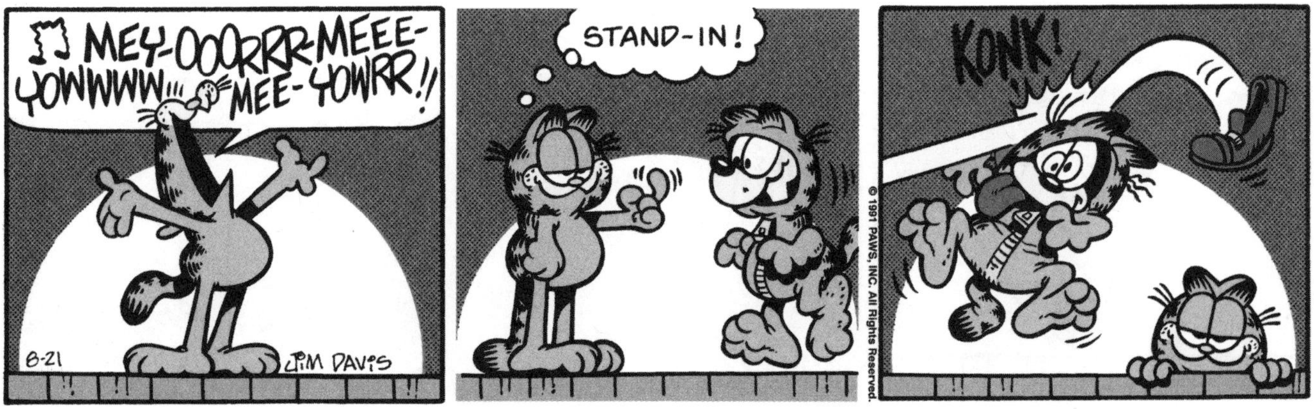
MEY-OOORRR-MEEE-
YOWWWW MEE-YOWRR!!
8-21 JIM DAVIS
STAND-IN!
KONK!
© 1991 PAWS, INC. All Rights Reserved.

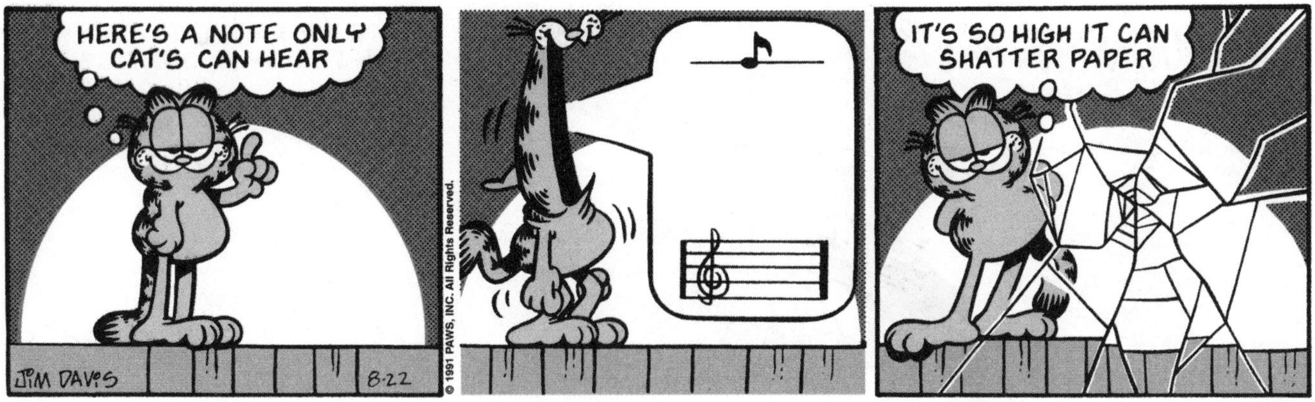
HERE'S A NOTE ONLY CAT'S CAN HEAR
JIM DAVIS
8-22
© 1991 PAWS, INC. All Rights Reserved.
IT'S SO HIGH IT CAN SHATTER PAPER

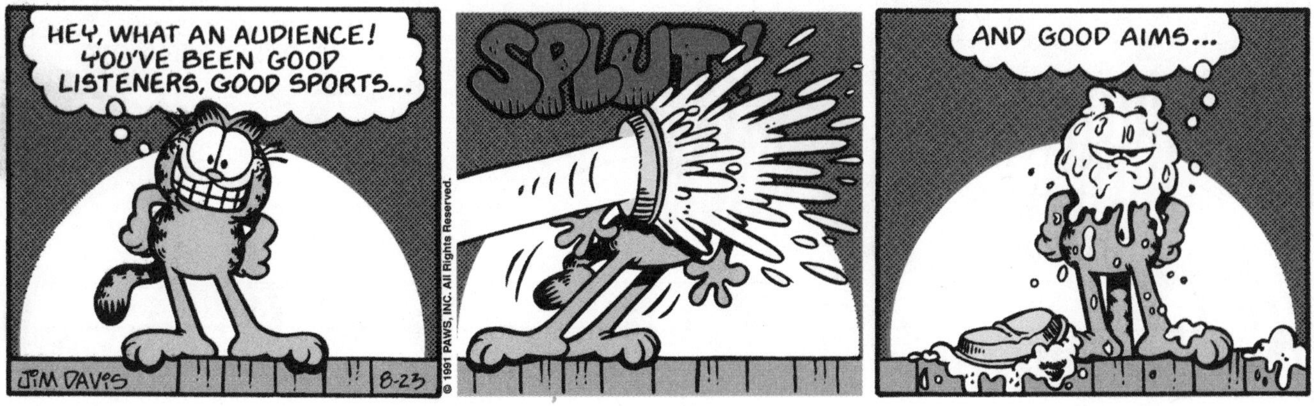
HEY, WHAT AN AUDIENCE! YOU'VE BEEN GOOD LISTENERS, GOOD SPORTS...
JIM DAVIS
8-23
SPLUT!
© 1991 PAWS, INC. All Rights Reserved.
AND GOOD AIMS...

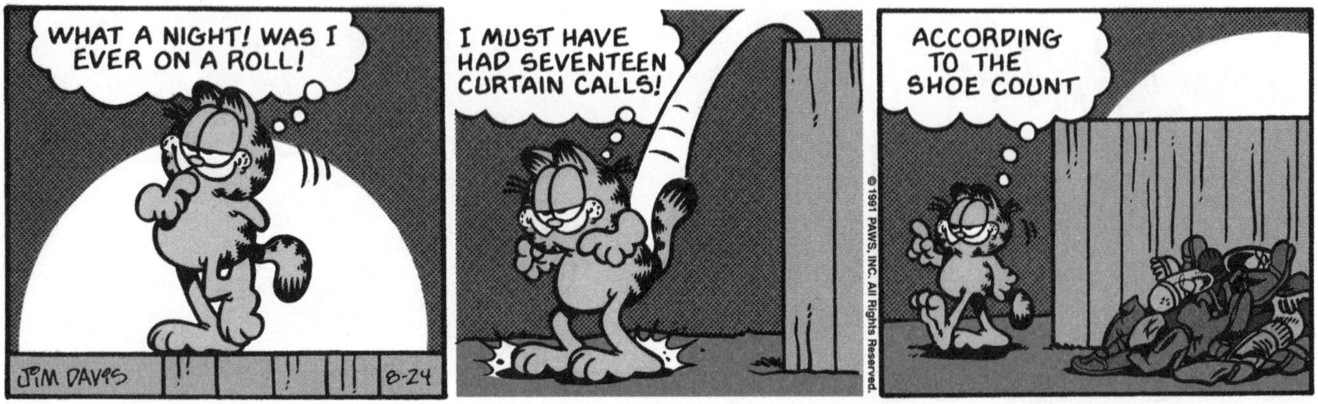
WHAT A NIGHT! WAS I EVER ON A ROLL!
JIM DAVIS
8-24
I MUST HAVE HAD SEVENTEEN CURTAIN CALLS!
© 1991 PAWS, INC. All Rights Reserved.
ACCORDING TO THE SHOE COUNT

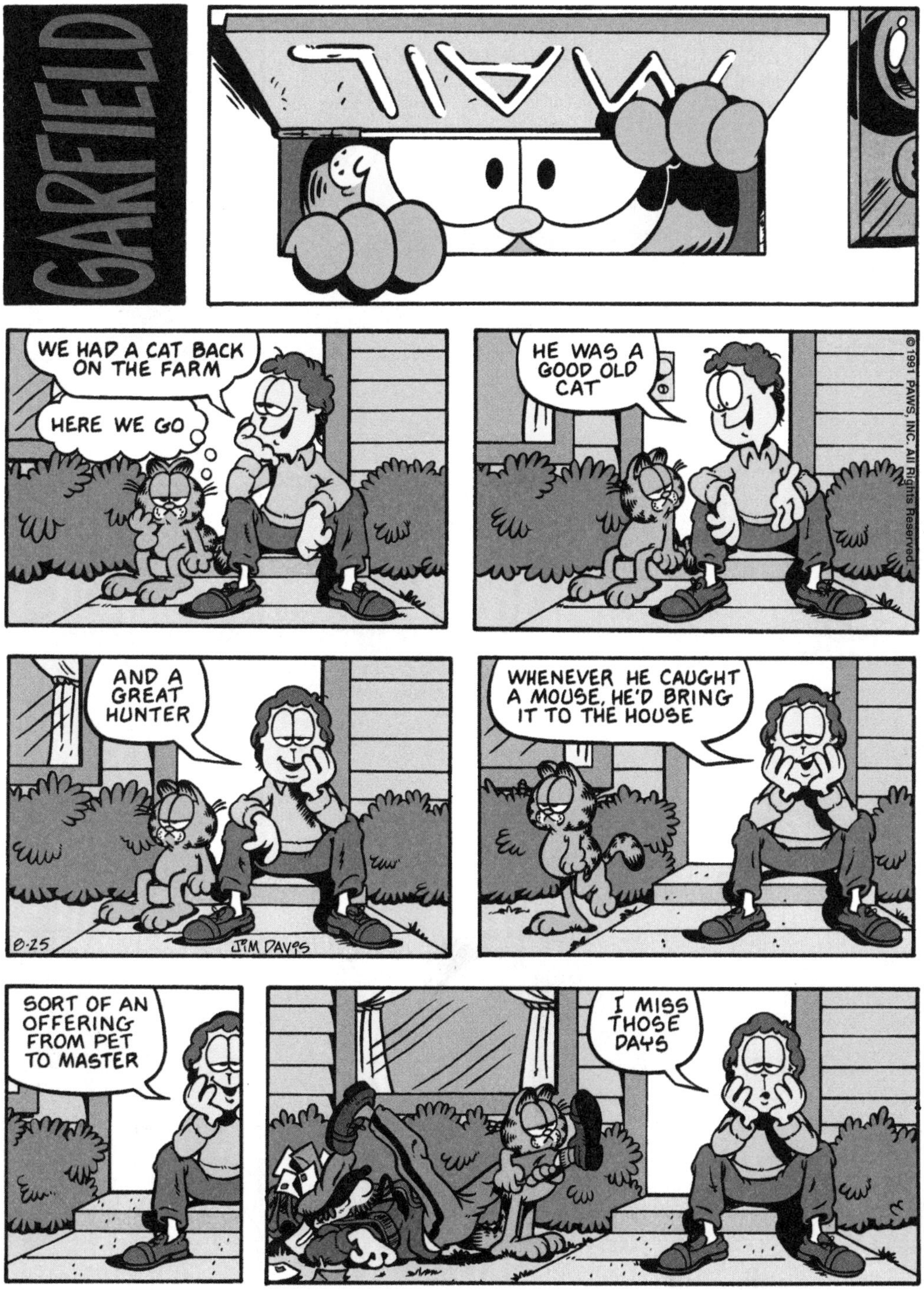
GARFIELD
MAIL
WE HAD A CAT BACK ON THE FARM
HERE WE GO
HE WAS A GOOD OLD CAT
© 1991 PAWS, INC. All Rights Reserved.
AND A GREAT HUNTER
8·25
JIM DAVIS
WHENEVER HE CAUGHT A MOUSE, HE'D BRING IT TO THE HOUSE
SORT OF AN OFFERING FROM PET TO MASTER
I MISS THOSE DAYS

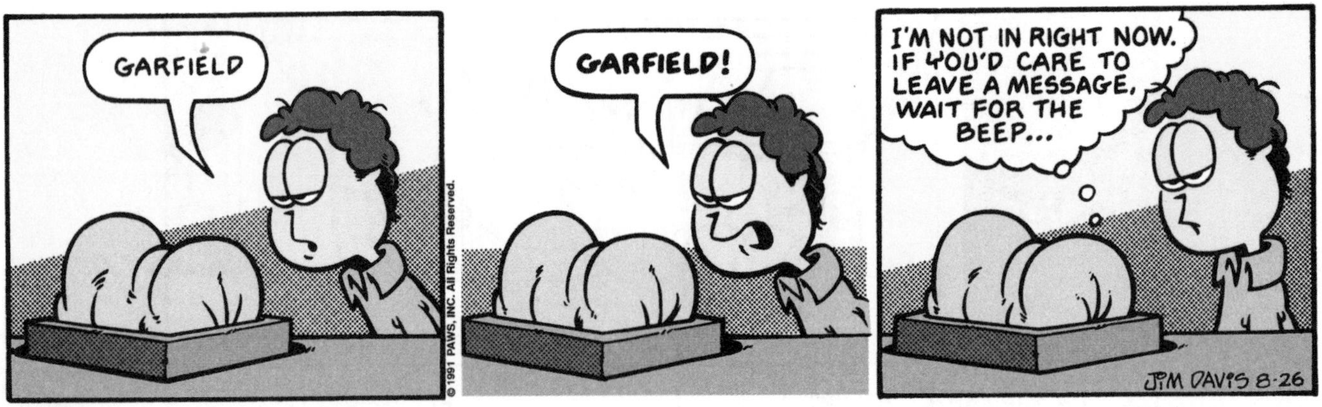
GARFIELD
GARFIELD!
I'M NOT IN RIGHT NOW. IF YOU'D CARE TO LEAVE A MESSAGE, WAIT FOR THE BEEP...
JIM DAVIS 8-26
© 1991 PAWS, INC. All Rights Reserved.

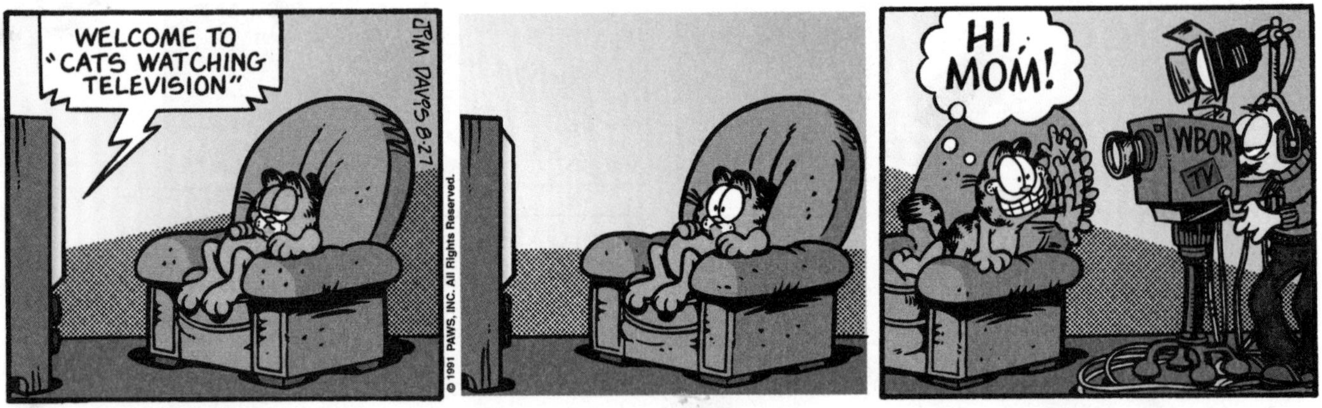
WELCOME TO "CATS WATCHING TELEVISION"
JIM DAVIS 8-27
HI, MOM!
WBOR TV
© 1991 PAWS, INC. All Rights Reserved.

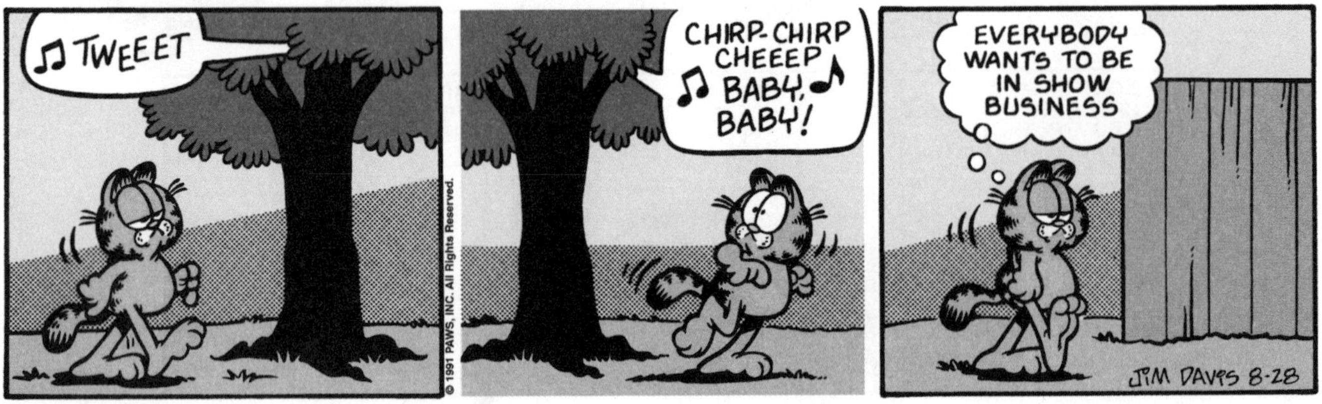
♫ TWEEET
CHIRP-CHIRP CHEEEP ♫ BABY, ♪ BABY!
EVERYBODY WANTS TO BE IN SHOW BUSINESS
JIM DAVIS 8-28
© 1991 PAWS, INC. All Rights Reserved.

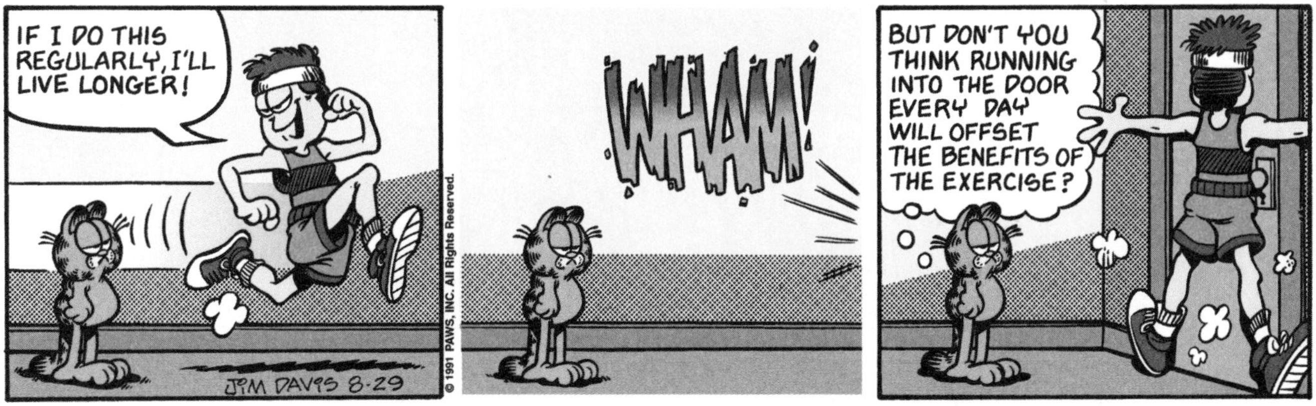
IF I DO THIS REGULARLY, I'LL LIVE LONGER!
JIM DAVIS 8-29
© 1991 PAWS, INC. All Rights Reserved.
WHAM!
BUT DON'T YOU THINK RUNNING INTO THE DOOR EVERY DAY WILL OFFSET THE BENEFITS OF THE EXERCISE?

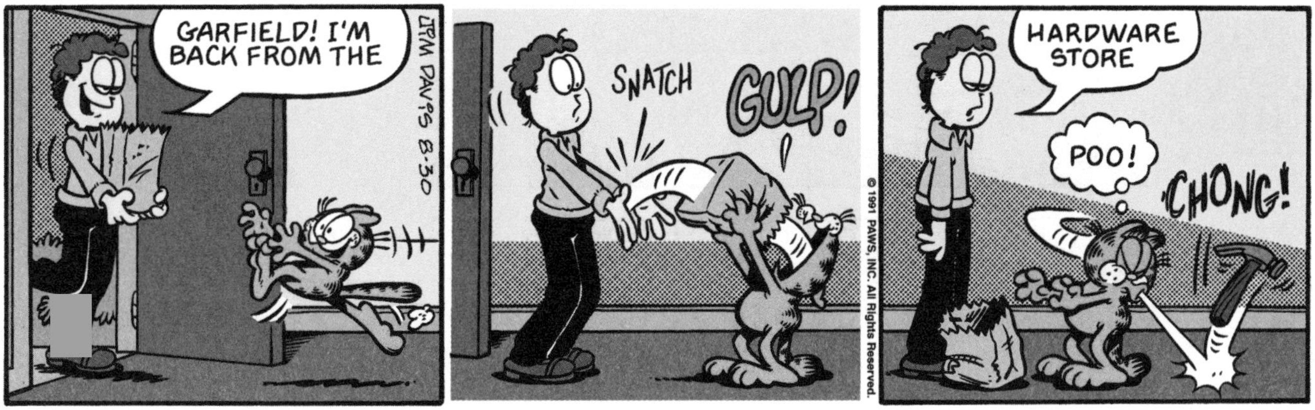
GARFIELD! I'M BACK FROM THE
JIM DAVIS 8-30
SNATCH
GULP!
© 1991 PAWS, INC. All Rights Reserved.
HARDWARE STORE
POO!
CHONG!

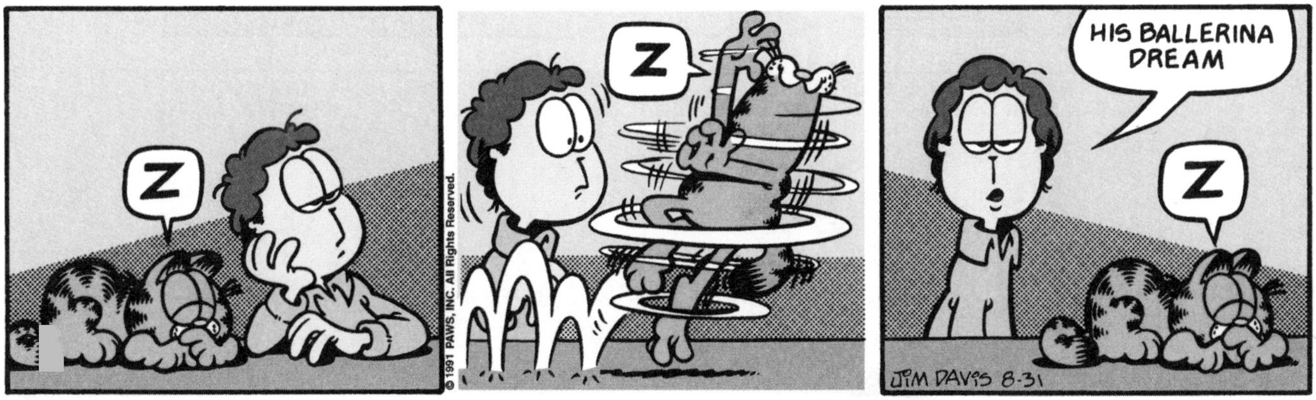
Z
© 1991 PAWS, INC. All Rights Reserved.
Z
HIS BALLERINA DREAM
Z
JIM DAVIS 8-31

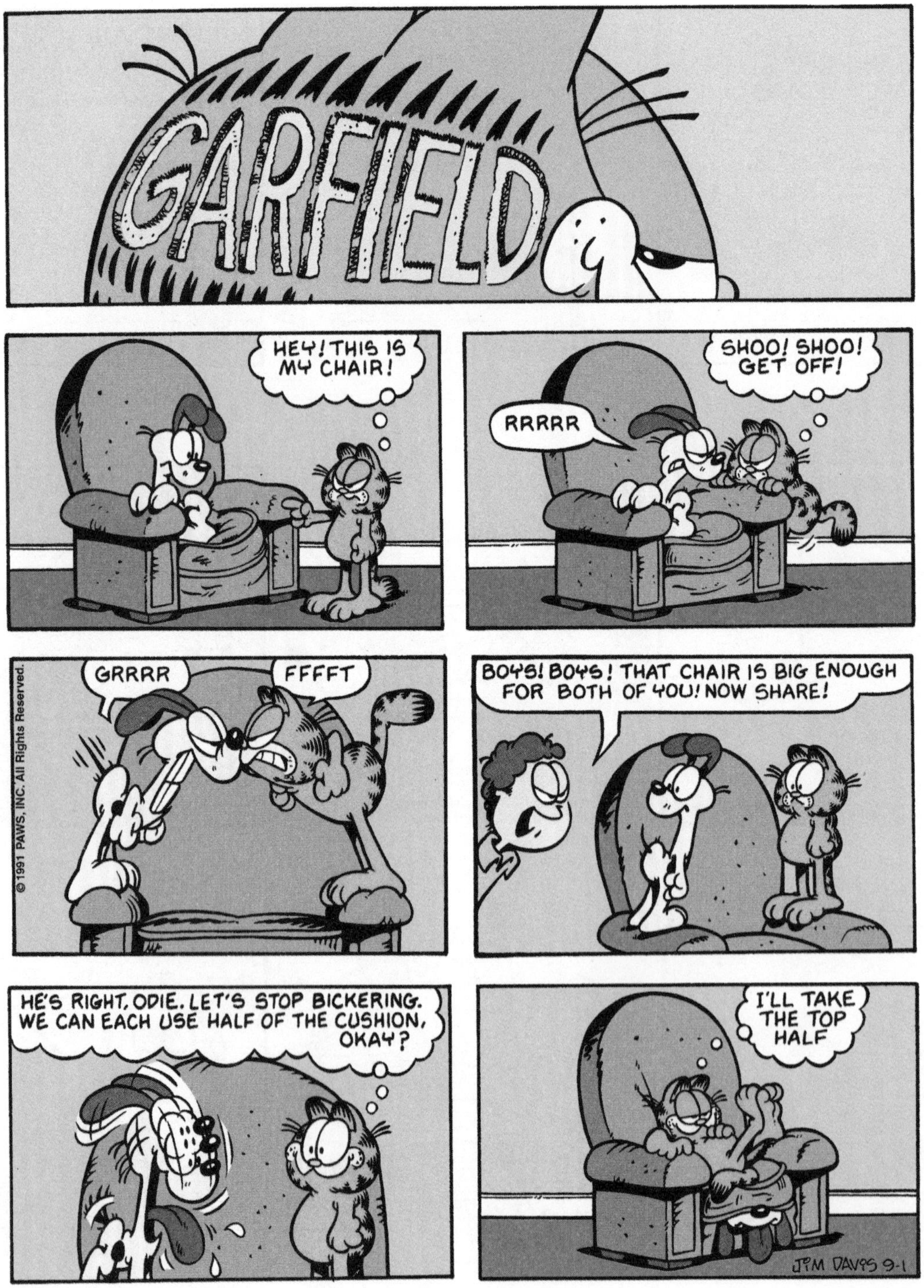
GARFIELD
HEY! THIS IS MY CHAIR!
RRRRR
SHOO! SHOO! GET OFF!
GRRRR
FFFFT
© 1991 PAWS, INC. All Rights Reserved.
BOYS! BOYS! THAT CHAIR IS BIG ENOUGH FOR BOTH OF YOU! NOW SHARE!
HE'S RIGHT, ODIE. LET'S STOP BICKERING. WE CAN EACH USE HALF OF THE CUSHION, OKAY?
I'LL TAKE THE TOP HALF
JIM DAVIS 9-1

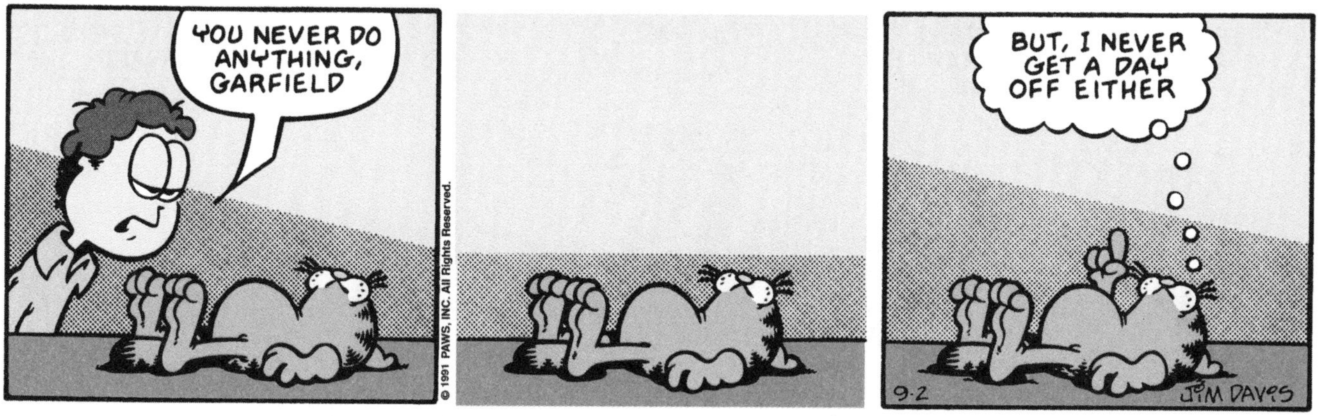
YOU NEVER DO ANYTHING, GARFIELD
© 1991 PAWS, INC. All Rights Reserved.
BUT, I NEVER GET A DAY OFF EITHER
9-2
JIM DAVIS

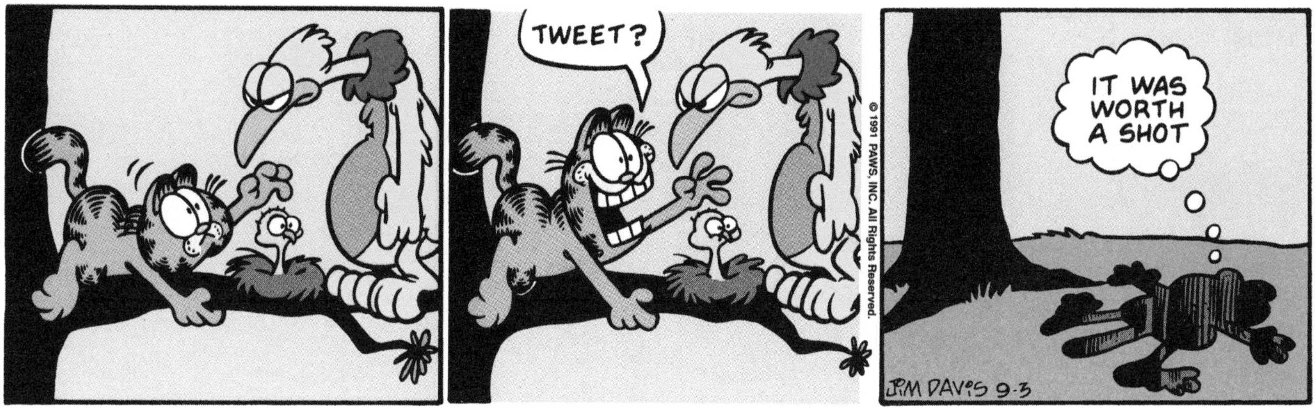
TWEET?
© 1991 PAWS, INC. All Rights Reserved.
IT WAS WORTH A SHOT
JIM DAVIS 9-3

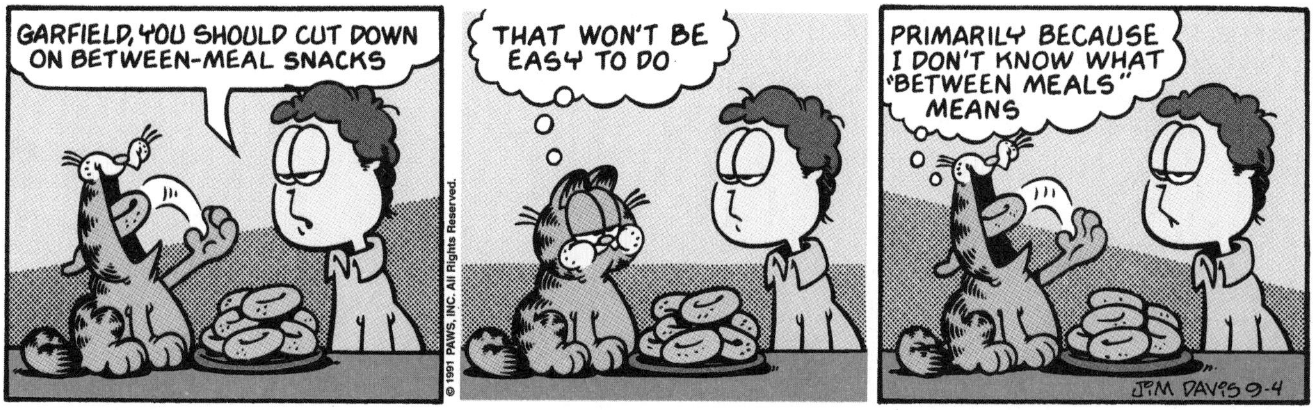
GARFIELD, YOU SHOULD CUT DOWN ON BETWEEN-MEAL SNACKS
© 1991 PAWS, INC. All Rights Reserved.
THAT WON'T BE EASY TO DO
PRIMARILY BECAUSE I DON'T KNOW WHAT "BETWEEN MEALS" MEANS
JIM DAVIS 9-4

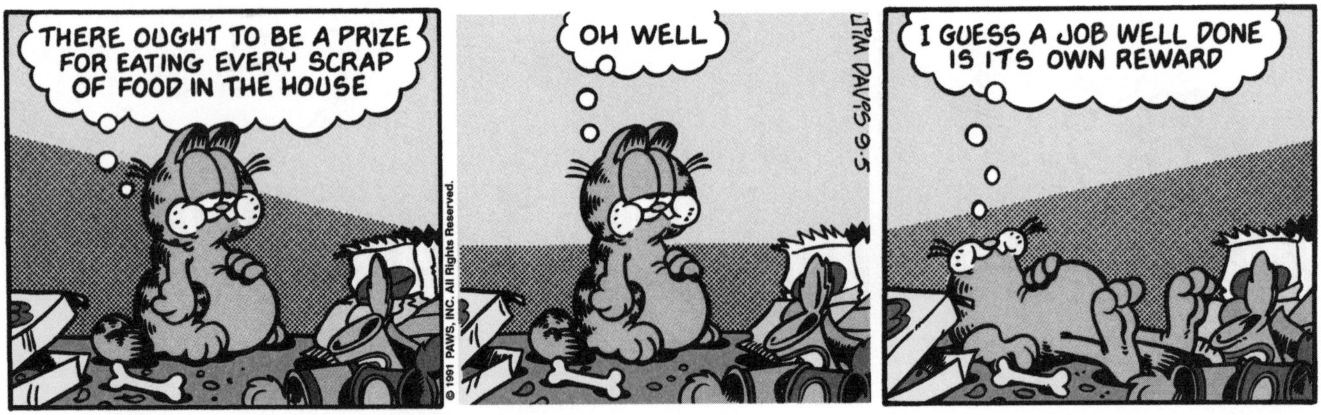
THERE OUGHT TO BE A PRIZE FOR EATING EVERY SCRAP OF FOOD IN THE HOUSE
© 1991 PAWS, INC. All Rights Reserved.
OH WELL
JIM DAVIS 9-5
I GUESS A JOB WELL DONE IS ITS OWN REWARD

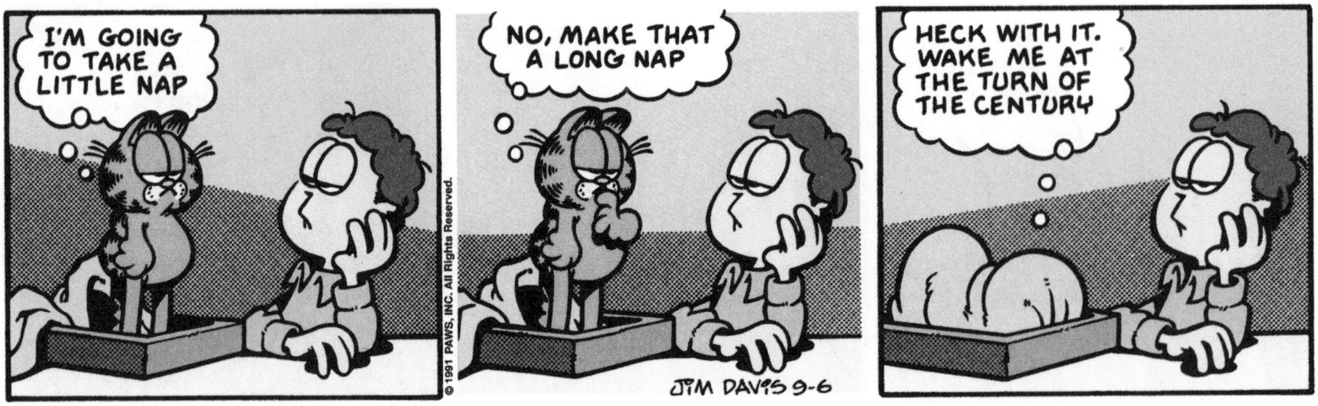
I'M GOING TO TAKE A LITTLE NAP
© 1991 PAWS, INC. All Rights Reserved.
NO, MAKE THAT A LONG NAP
JIM DAVIS 9-6
HECK WITH IT. WAKE ME AT THE TURN OF THE CENTURY

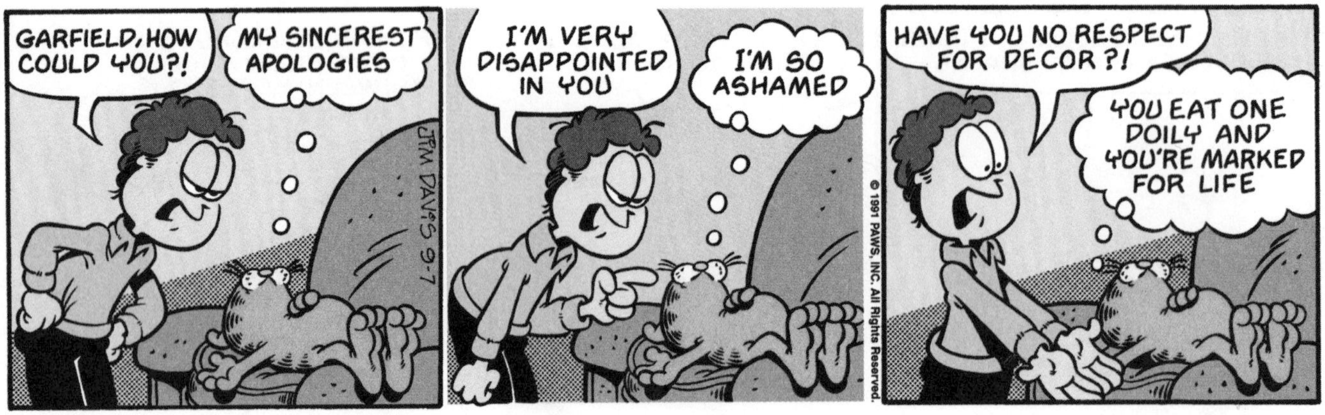
GARFIELD, HOW COULD YOU?!
MY SINCEREST APOLOGIES
JIM DAVIS 9-7
I'M VERY DISAPPOINTED IN YOU
I'M SO ASHAMED
© 1991 PAWS, INC. All Rights Reserved.
HAVE YOU NO RESPECT FOR DECOR?!
YOU EAT ONE DOILY AND YOU'RE MARKED FOR LIFE

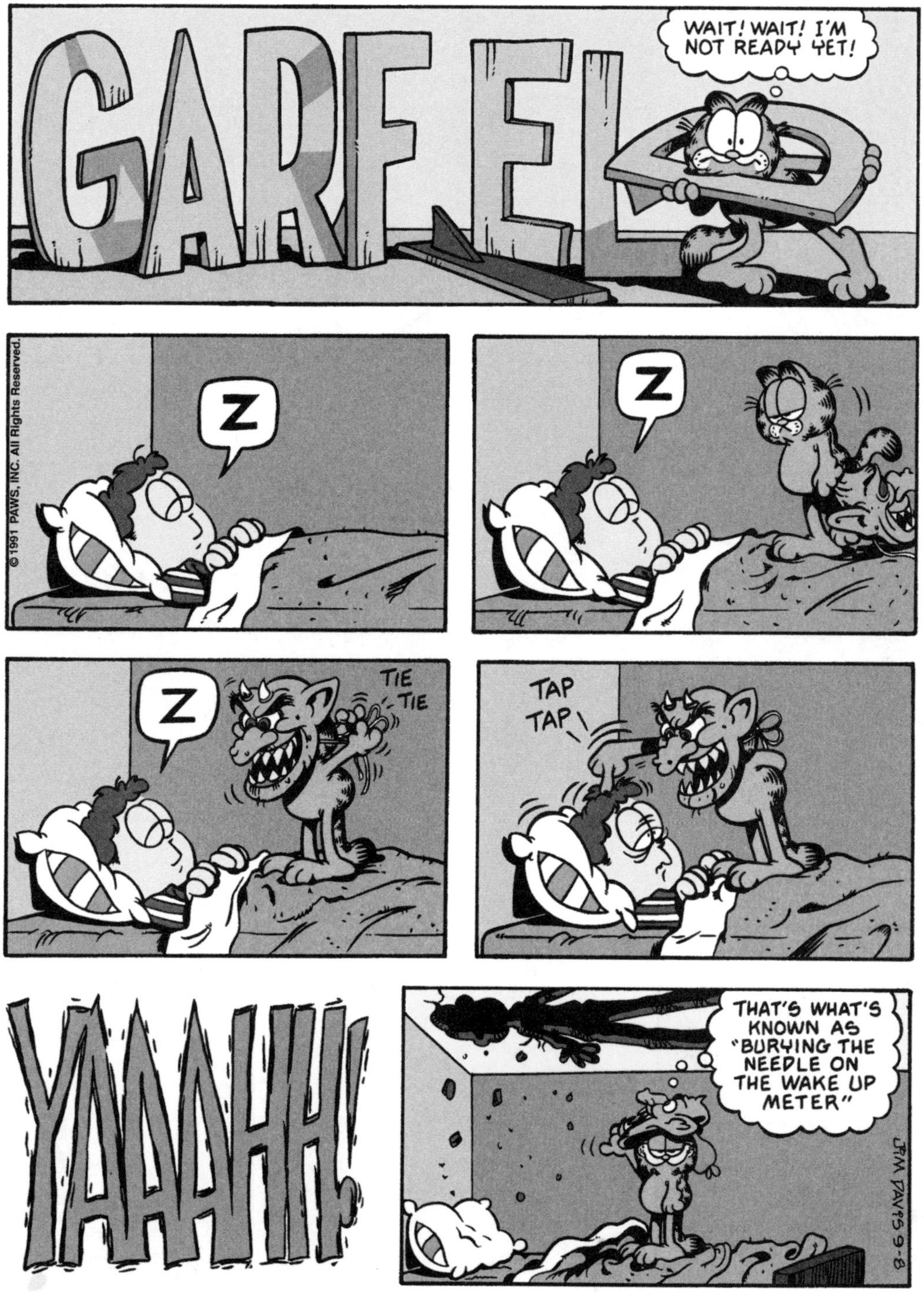
GARF EL
WAIT! WAIT! I'M NOT READY YET!
Z
Z
Z
TIE TIE
TAP TAP
YAAAHH!
THAT'S WHAT'S KNOWN AS "BURYING THE NEEDLE ON THE WAKE UP METER"
JIM DAVIS 9-8

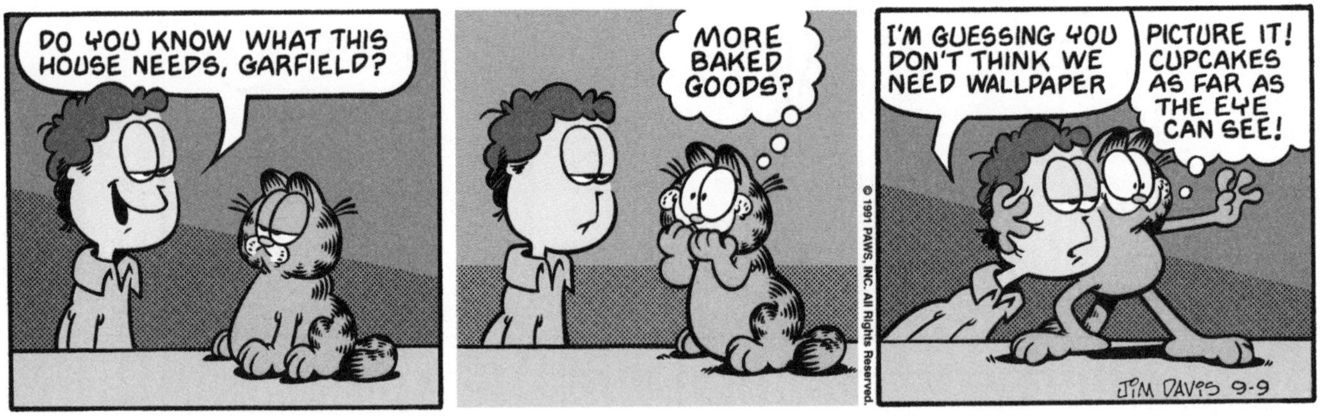
DO YOU KNOW WHAT THIS HOUSE NEEDS, GARFIELD?
MORE BAKED GOODS?
© 1991 PAWS, INC. All Rights Reserved.
I'M GUESSING YOU DON'T THINK WE NEED WALLPAPER
PICTURE IT! CUPCAKES AS FAR AS THE EYE CAN SEE!
JIM DAVIS 9-9

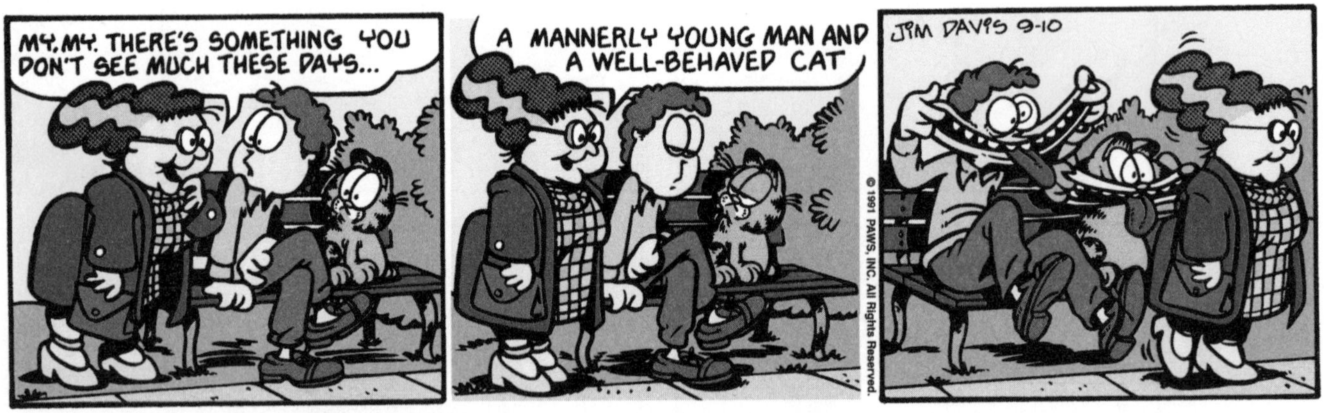
MY, MY. THERE'S SOMETHING YOU DON'T SEE MUCH THESE DAYS...
A MANNERLY YOUNG MAN AND A WELL-BEHAVED CAT
© 1991 PAWS, INC. All Rights Reserved.
JIM DAVIS 9-10

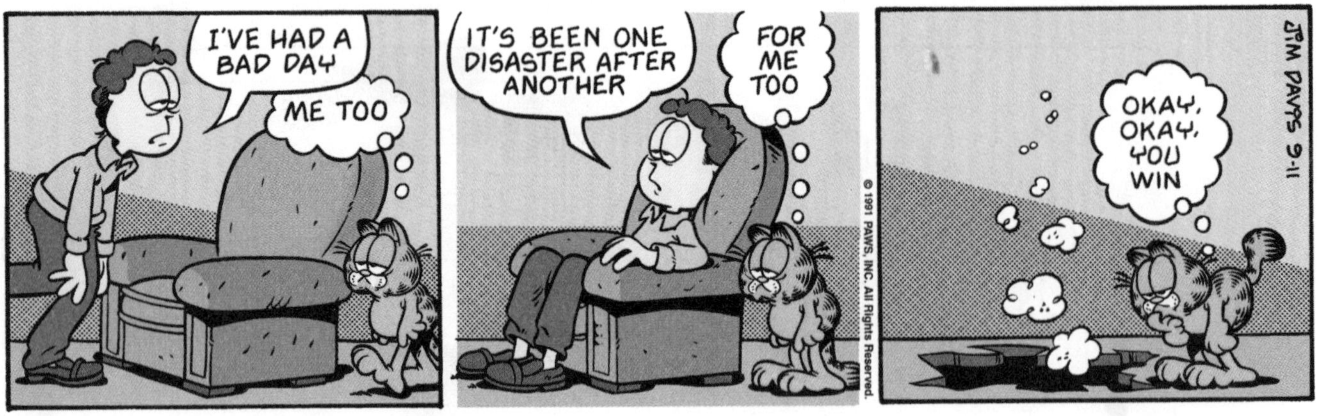
I'VE HAD A BAD DAY
ME TOO
IT'S BEEN ONE DISASTER AFTER ANOTHER
FOR ME TOO
© 1991 PAWS, INC. All Rights Reserved.
JIM DAVIS 9-11
OKAY, OKAY, YOU WIN

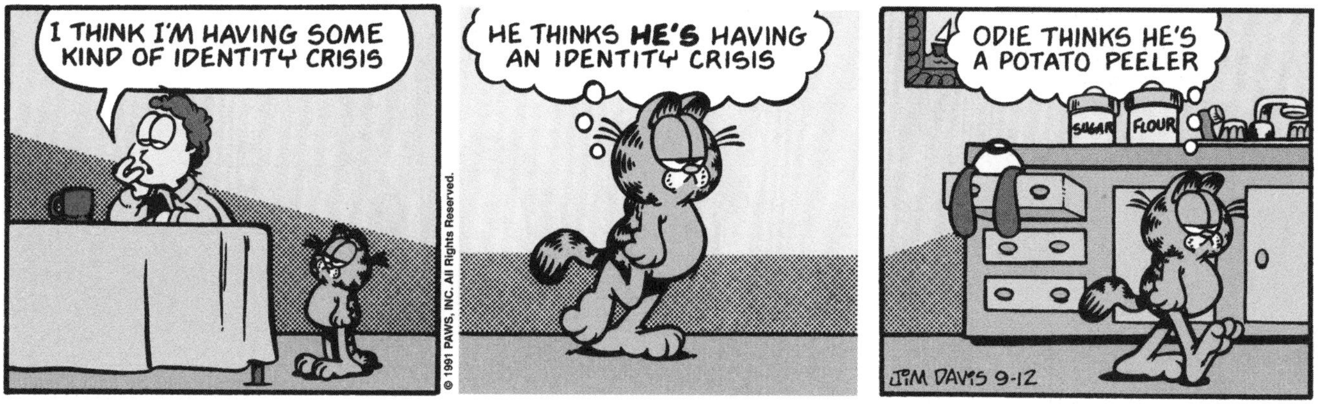
I THINK I'M HAVING SOME KIND OF IDENTITY CRISIS
HE THINKS **HE'S** HAVING AN IDENTITY CRISIS
ODIE THINKS HE'S A POTATO PEELER
SUGAR
FLOUR
JIM DAVIS 9-12

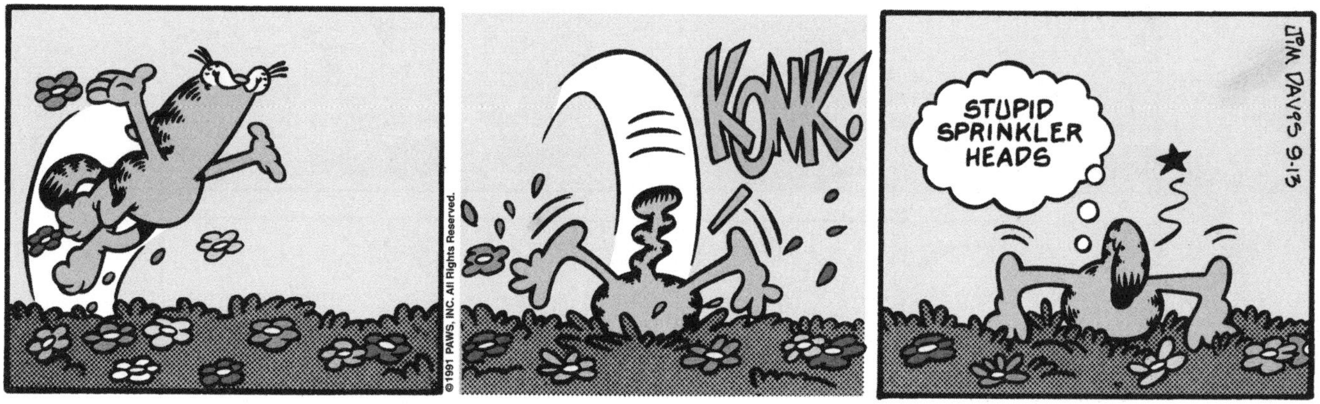
KONK!
STUPID SPRINKLER HEADS
JIM DAVIS 9-13

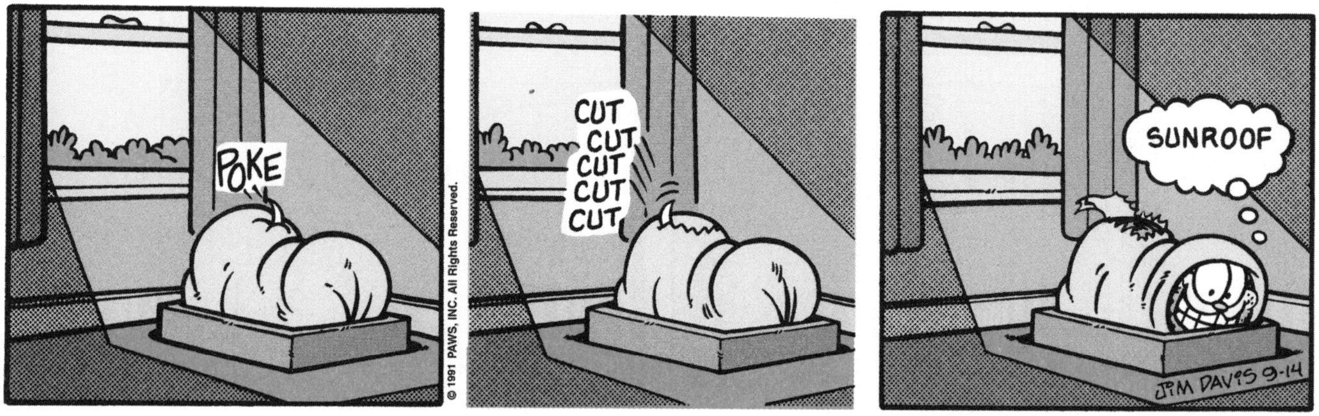
POKE
CUT
CUT
CUT
CUT
CUT
SUNROOF
JIM DAVIS 9-14

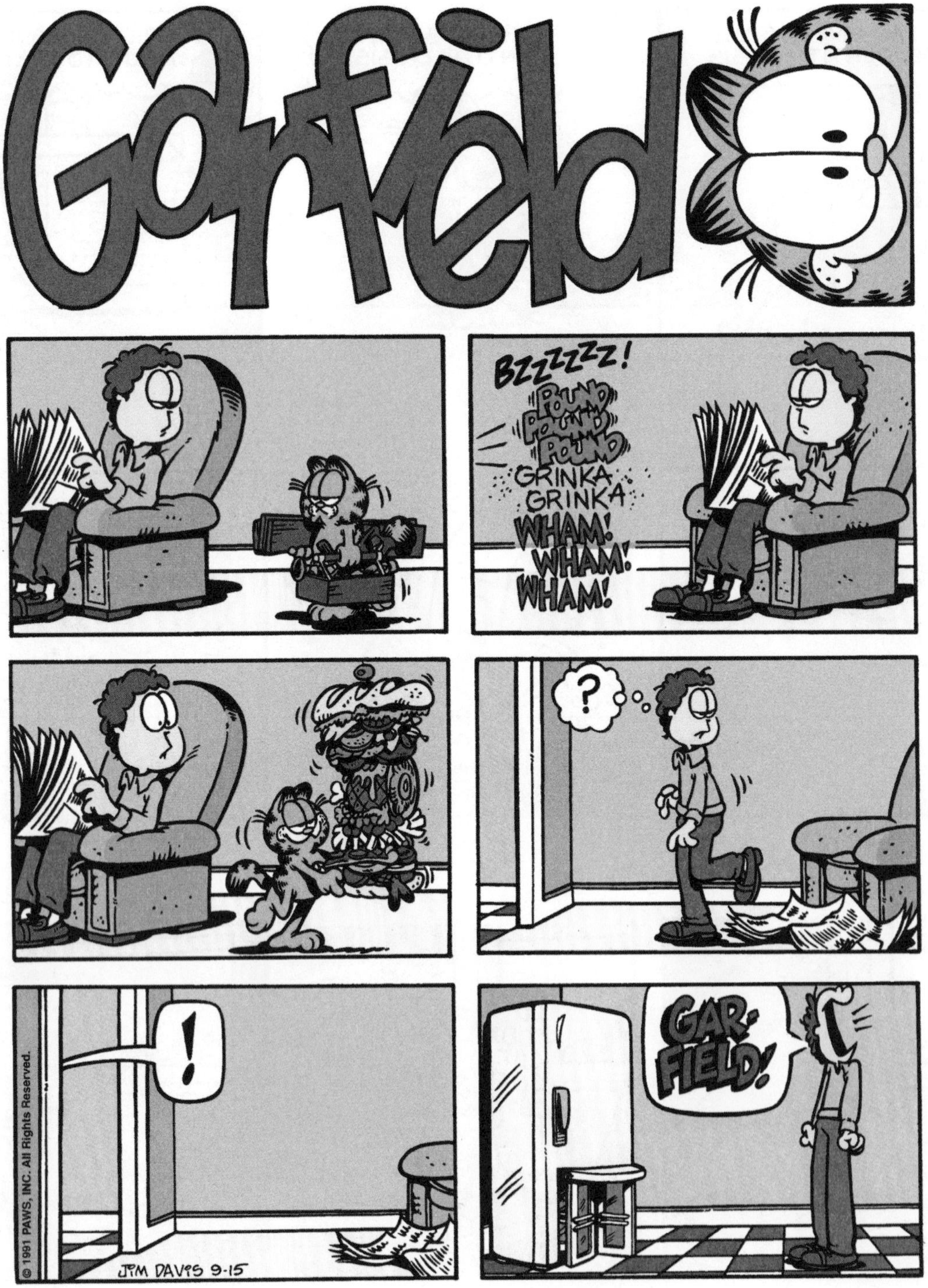
Garfield
BZZZZZZ!
POUND POUND POUND
GRINKA GRINKA
WHAM! WHAM! WHAM!
?
!
© 1991 PAWS, INC. All Rights Reserved.
JIM DAVIS 9-15
GAR-FIELD!

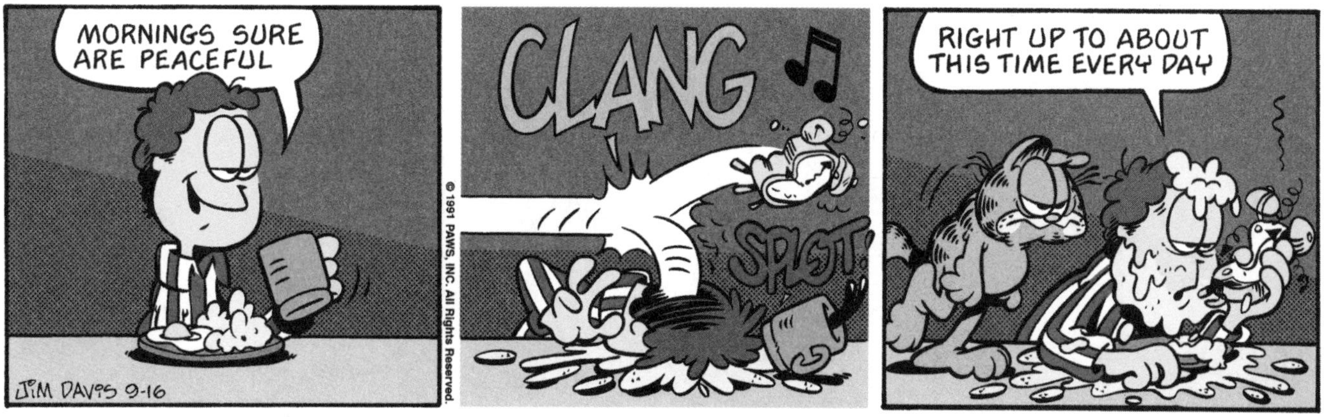
MORNINGS SURE ARE PEACEFUL
JIM DAVIS 9-16
CLANG
SPLOT
© 1991 PAWS, INC. All Rights Reserved.
RIGHT UP TO ABOUT THIS TIME EVERY DAY

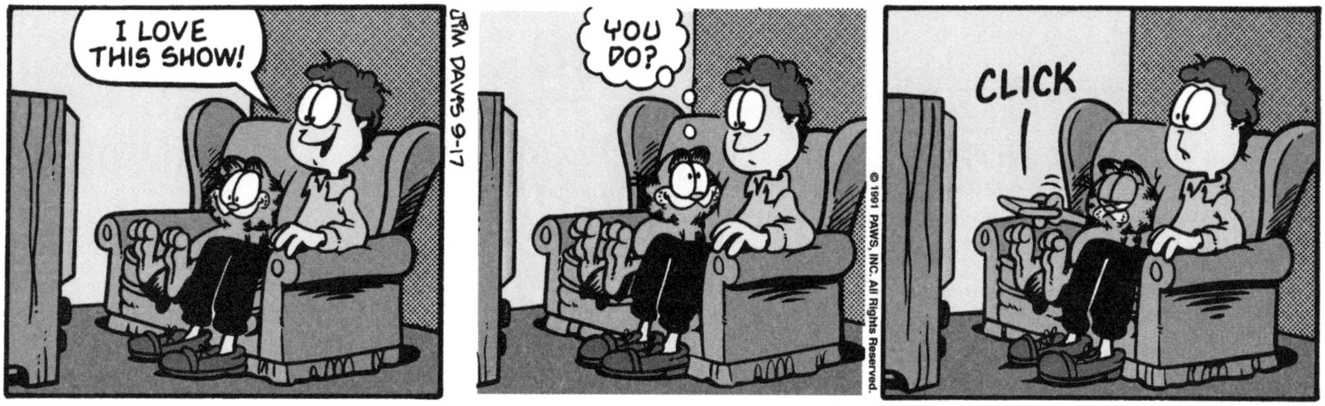
I LOVE THIS SHOW!
JIM DAVIS 9-17
YOU DO?
© 1991 PAWS, INC. All Rights Reserved.
CLICK

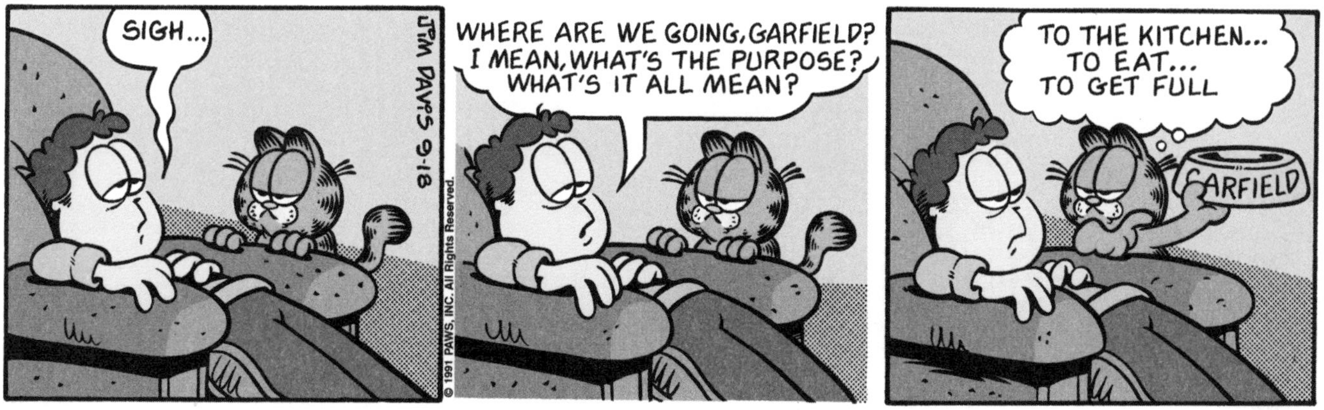
SIGH...
JIM DAVIS 9-18
© 1991 PAWS, INC. All Rights Reserved.
WHERE ARE WE GOING, GARFIELD? I MEAN, WHAT'S THE PURPOSE? WHAT'S IT ALL MEAN?
TO THE KITCHEN... TO EAT... TO GET FULL
GARFIELD

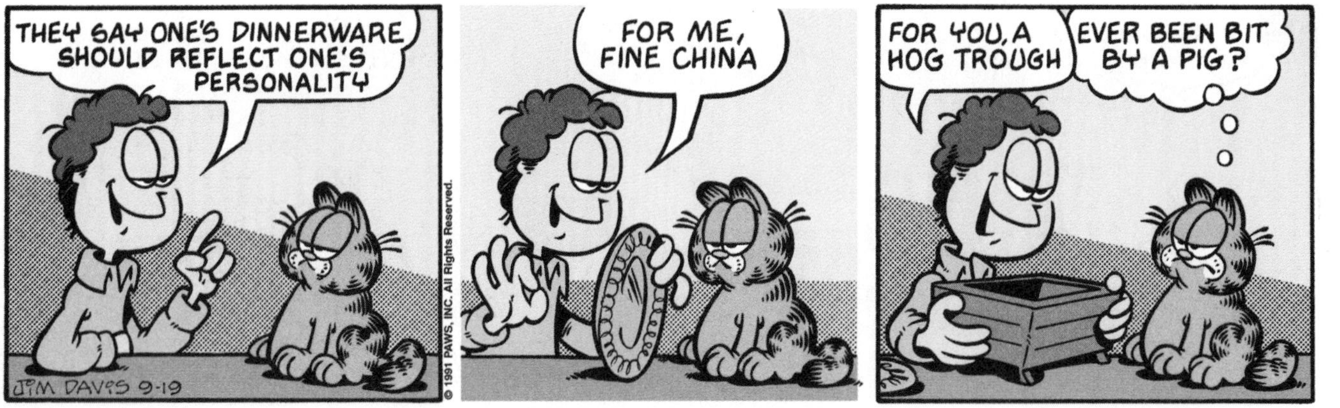
THEY SAY ONE'S DINNERWARE SHOULD REFLECT ONE'S PERSONALITY
JIM DAVIS 9-19
© 1991 PAWS, INC. All Rights Reserved.
FOR ME, FINE CHINA
FOR YOU, A HOG TROUGH
EVER BEEN BIT BY A PIG?

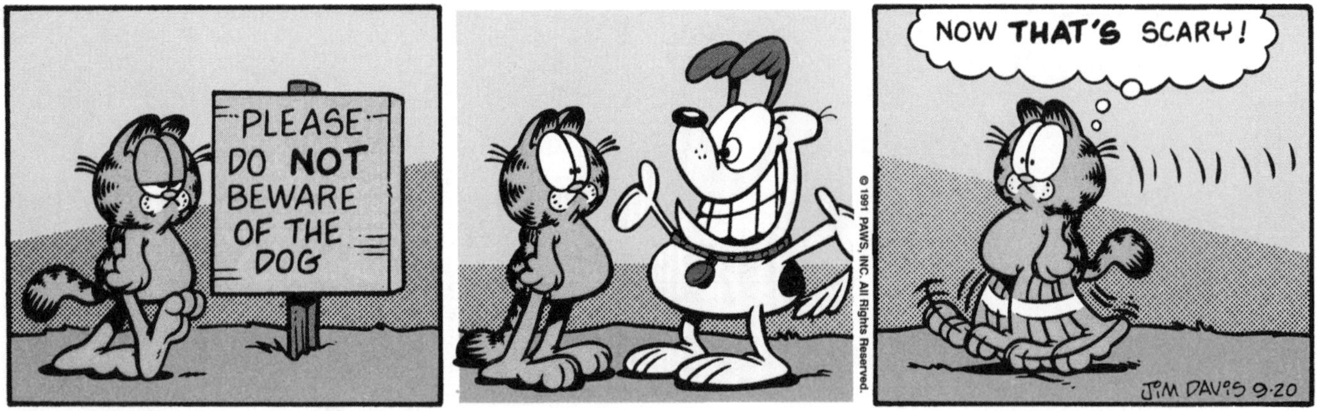
PLEASE DO NOT BEWARE OF THE DOG
© 1991 PAWS, INC. All Rights Reserved.
NOW THAT'S SCARY!
JIM DAVIS 9-20

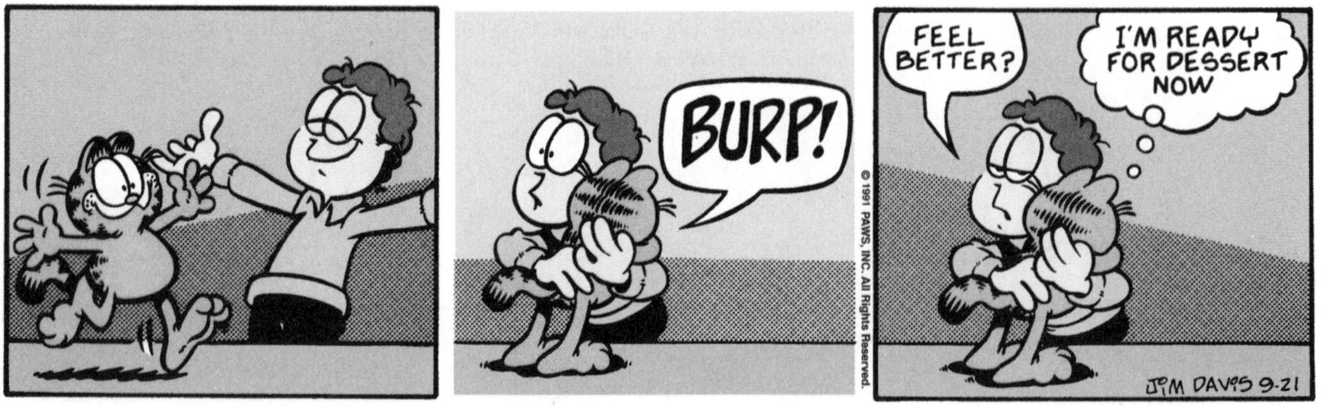
BURP!
© 1991 PAWS, INC. All Rights Reserved.
FEEL BETTER?
I'M READY FOR DESSERT NOW
JIM DAVIS 9-21

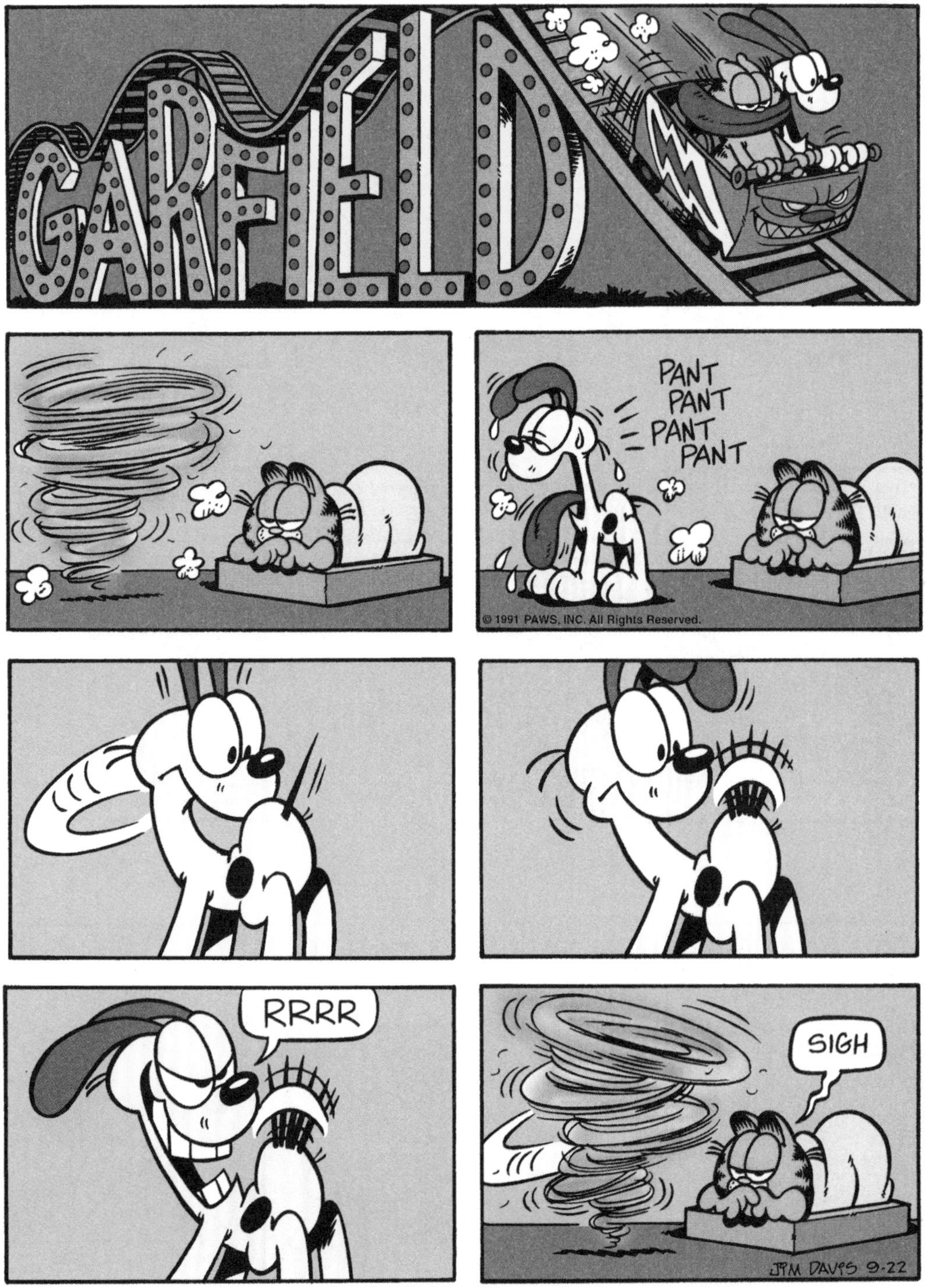
GARFIELD
PANT
PANT
PANT
PANT
© 1991 PAWS, INC. All Rights Reserved.
RRRR
SIGH
JIM DAVIS 9-22

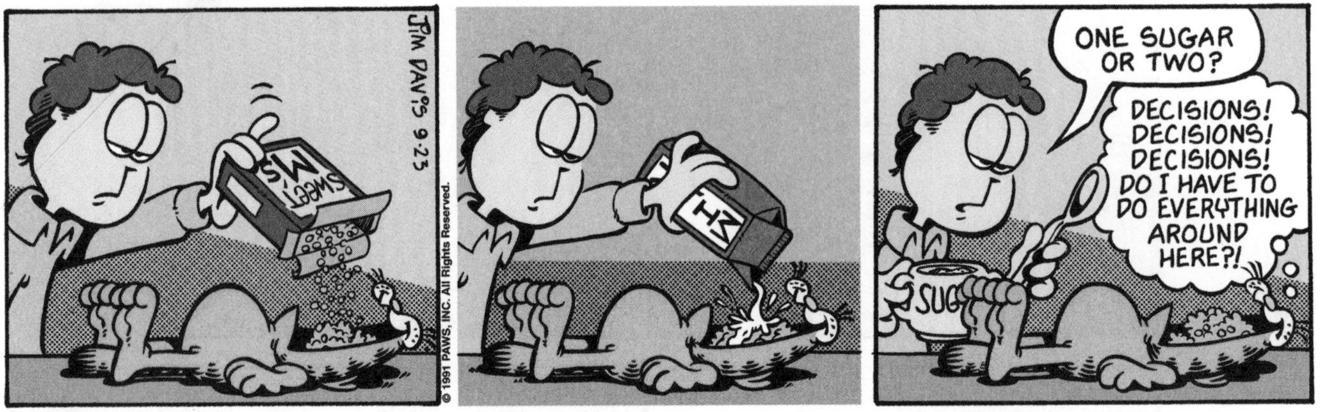
JIM DAVIS 9-23
SWEET MS
ONE SUGAR OR TWO?
DECISIONS! DECISIONS! DECISIONS! DO I HAVE TO DO EVERYTHING AROUND HERE?!
SUG
© 1991 PAWS, INC. All Rights Reserved.

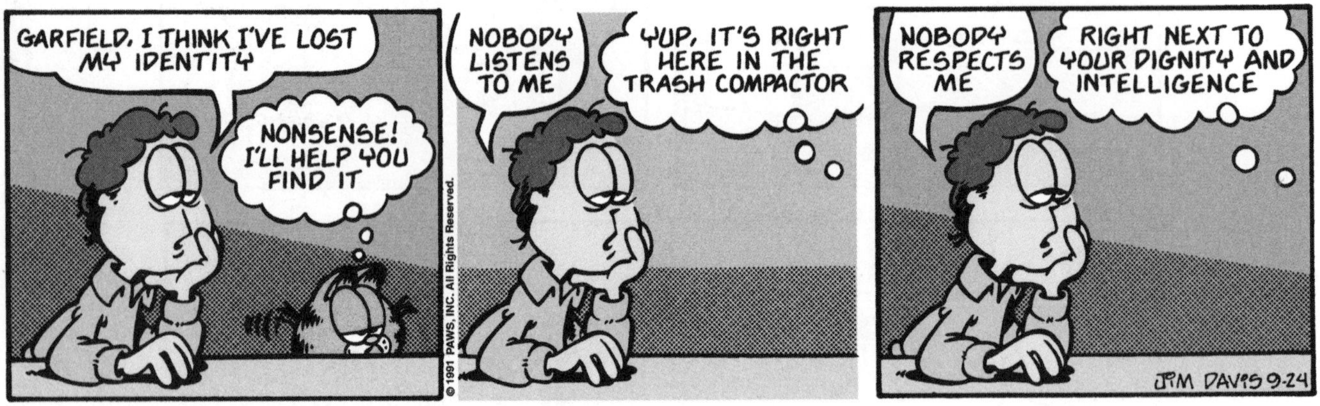
GARFIELD, I THINK I'VE LOST MY IDENTITY
NONSENSE! I'LL HELP YOU FIND IT
NOBODY LISTENS TO ME
YUP, IT'S RIGHT HERE IN THE TRASH COMPACTOR
NOBODY RESPECTS ME
RIGHT NEXT TO YOUR DIGNITY AND INTELLIGENCE
JIM DAVIS 9-24
© 1991 PAWS, INC. All Rights Reserved.

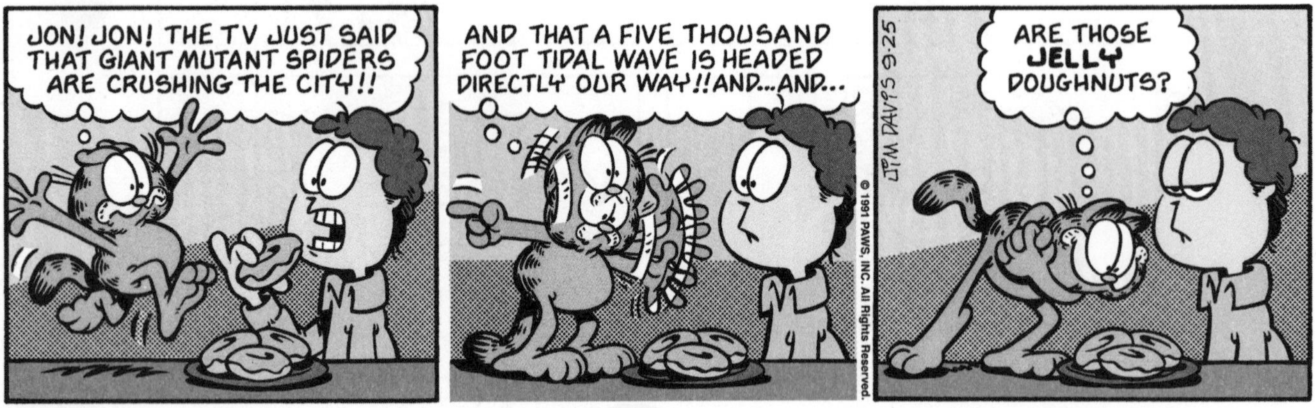
JON! JON! THE TV JUST SAID THAT GIANT MUTANT SPIDERS ARE CRUSHING THE CITY!!
AND THAT A FIVE THOUSAND FOOT TIDAL WAVE IS HEADED DIRECTLY OUR WAY!! AND...AND...
ARE THOSE JELLY DOUGHNUTS?
JIM DAVIS 9-25
© 1991 PAWS, INC. All Rights Reserved.

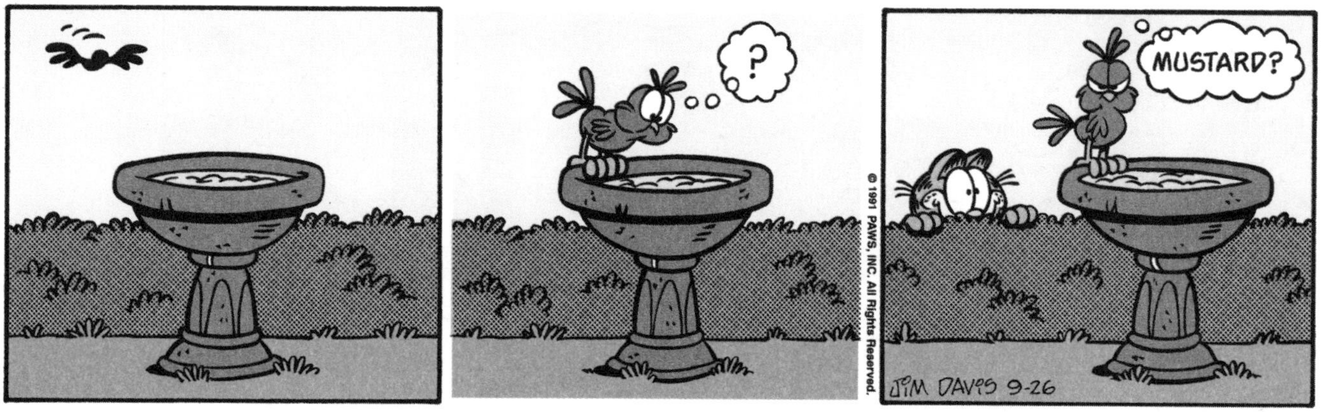
?
MUSTARD?
© 1991 PAWS, INC. All Rights Reserved.
JIM DAVIS 9-26

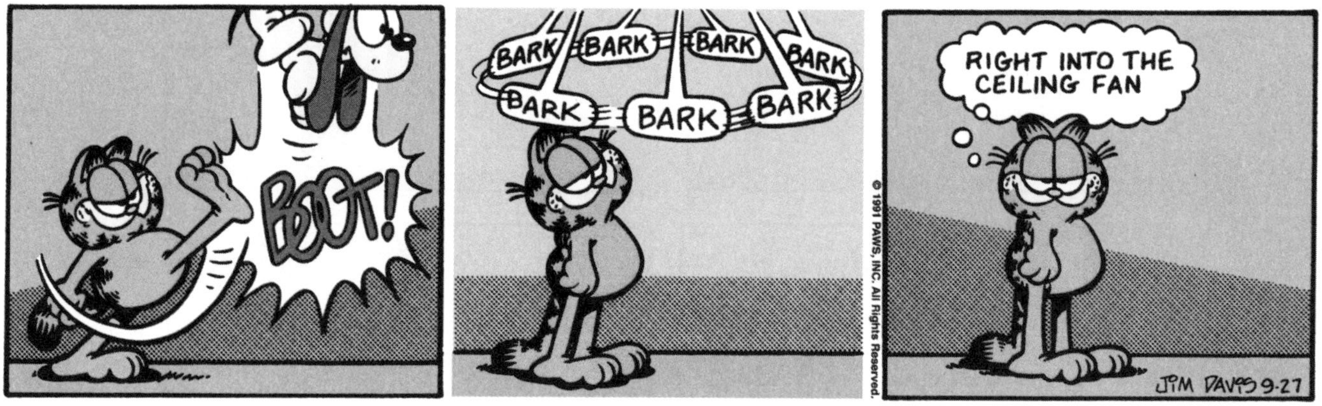
BOOT!
BARK BARK BARK BARK
BARK BARK BARK
RIGHT INTO THE CEILING FAN
© 1991 PAWS, INC. All Rights Reserved.
JIM DAVIS 9-27

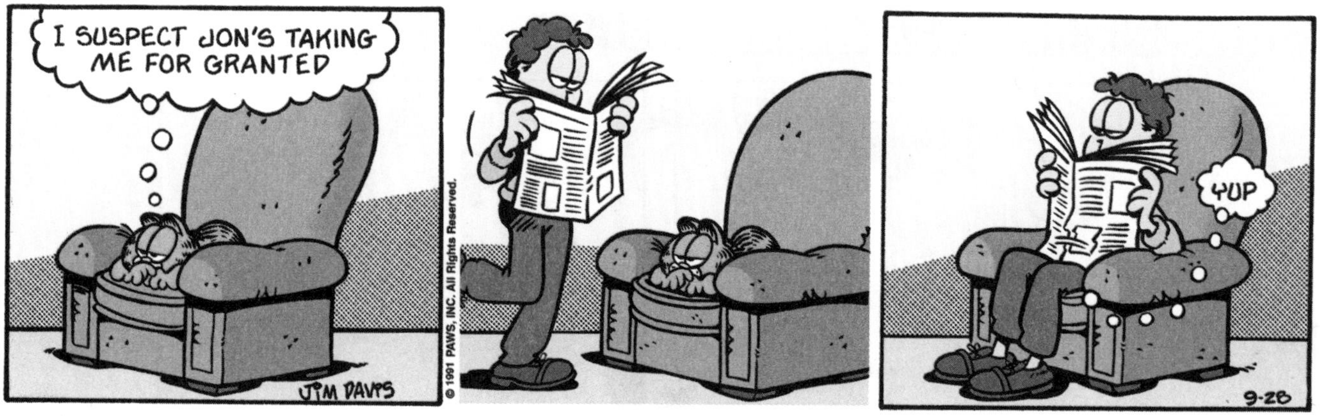
I SUSPECT JON'S TAKING ME FOR GRANTED
JIM DAVIS
© 1991 PAWS, INC. All Rights Reserved.
YUP
9-28

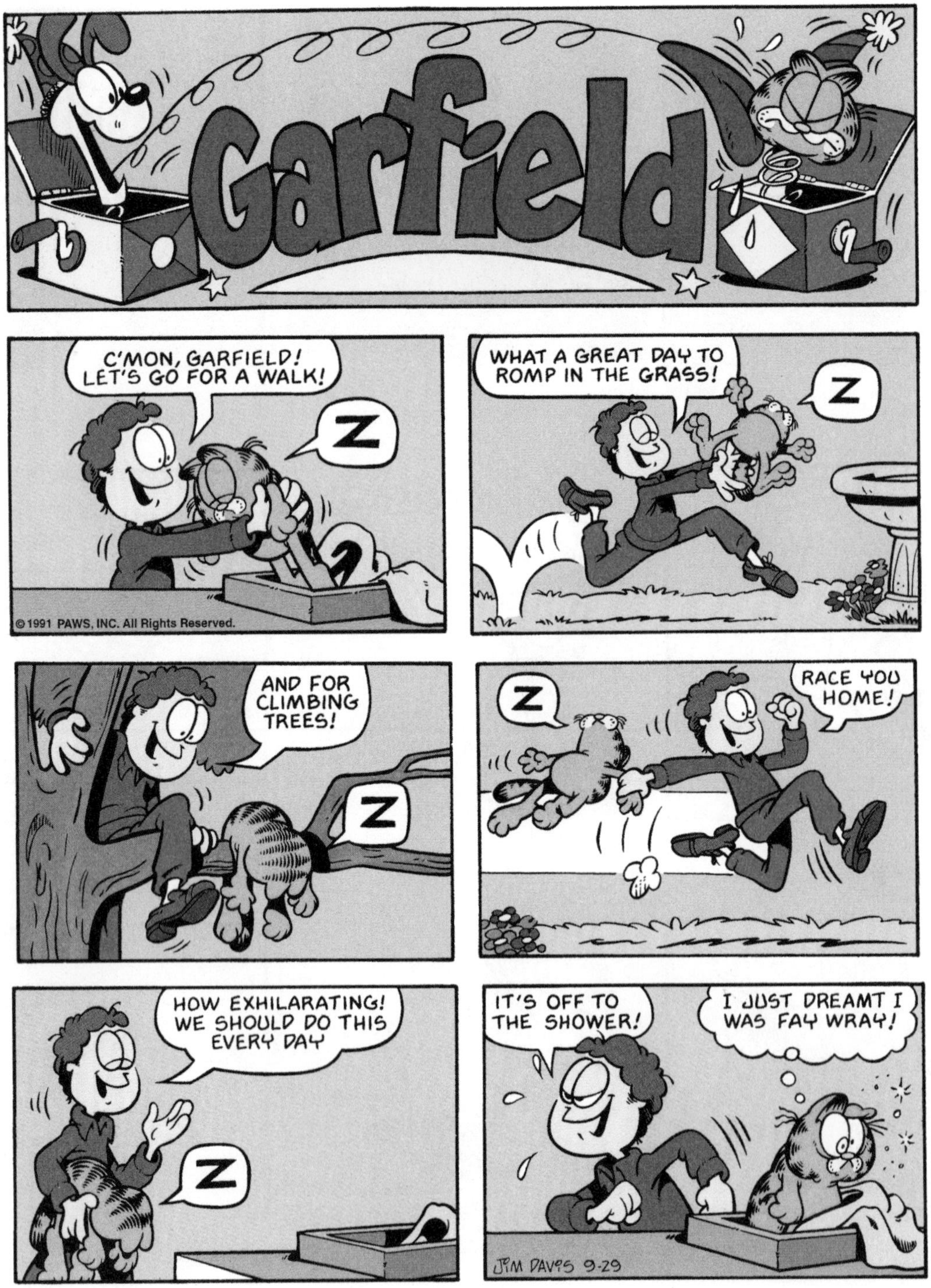
Garfield
C'MON, GARFIELD! LET'S GO FOR A WALK!
Z
©1991 PAWS, INC. All Rights Reserved.
WHAT A GREAT DAY TO ROMP IN THE GRASS!
Z
AND FOR CLIMBING TREES!
Z
Z
RACE YOU HOME!
HOW EXHILARATING! WE SHOULD DO THIS EVERY DAY
Z
IT'S OFF TO THE SHOWER!
I JUST DREAMT I WAS FAY WRAY!
JIM DAVIS 9-29

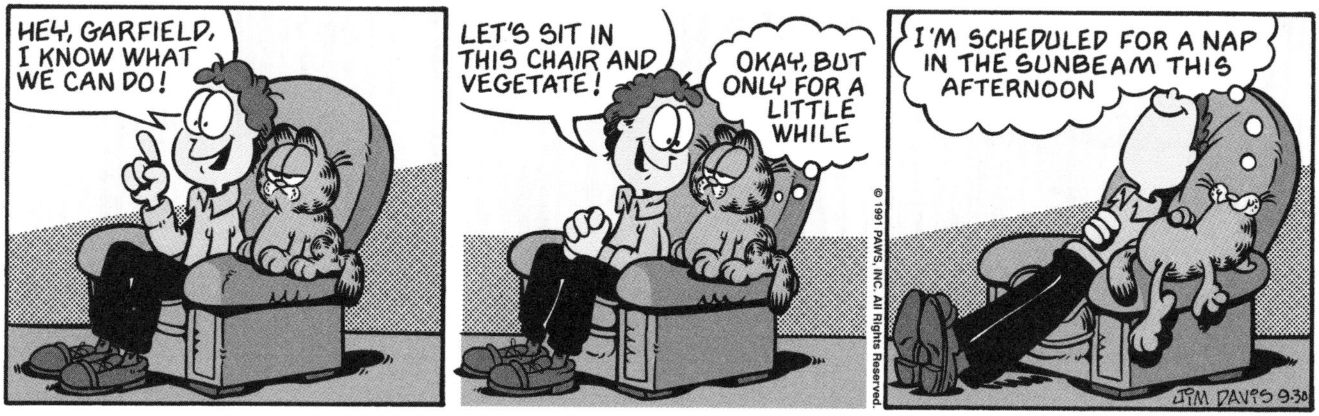
HEY, GARFIELD, I KNOW WHAT WE CAN DO!
LET'S SIT IN THIS CHAIR AND VEGETATE!
OKAY, BUT ONLY FOR A LITTLE WHILE
I'M SCHEDULED FOR A NAP IN THE SUNBEAM THIS AFTERNOON
© 1991 PAWS, INC. All Rights Reserved.
JIM DAVIS 9-30

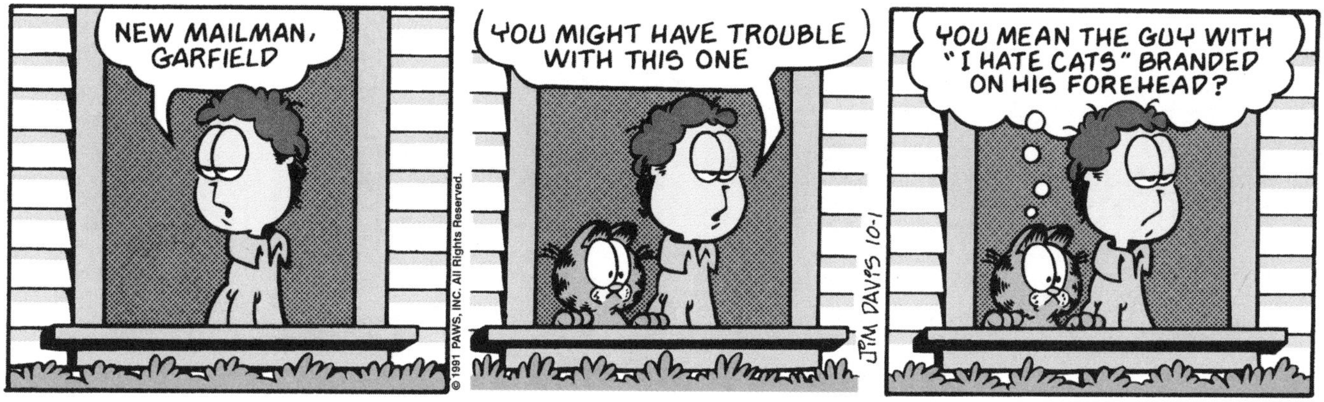
NEW MAILMAN, GARFIELD
YOU MIGHT HAVE TROUBLE WITH THIS ONE
YOU MEAN THE GUY WITH "I HATE CATS" BRANDED ON HIS FOREHEAD?
© 1991 PAWS, INC. All Rights Reserved.
JIM DAVIS 10-1

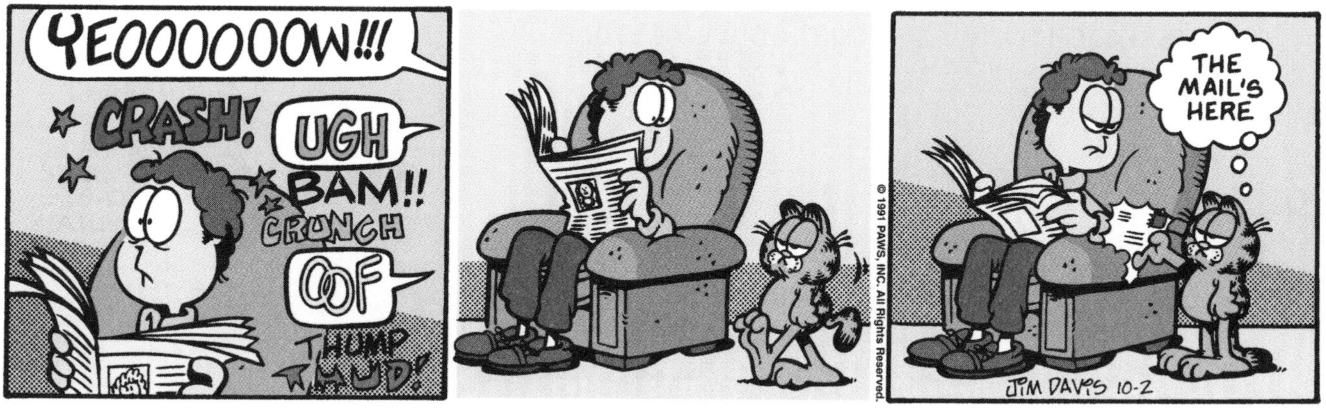
YEOOOOOOW!!!
CRASH!
UGH
BAM!!
CRUNCH
OOF
THUMP
THUD!
THE MAIL'S HERE
© 1991 PAWS, INC. All Rights Reserved.
JIM DAVIS 10-2

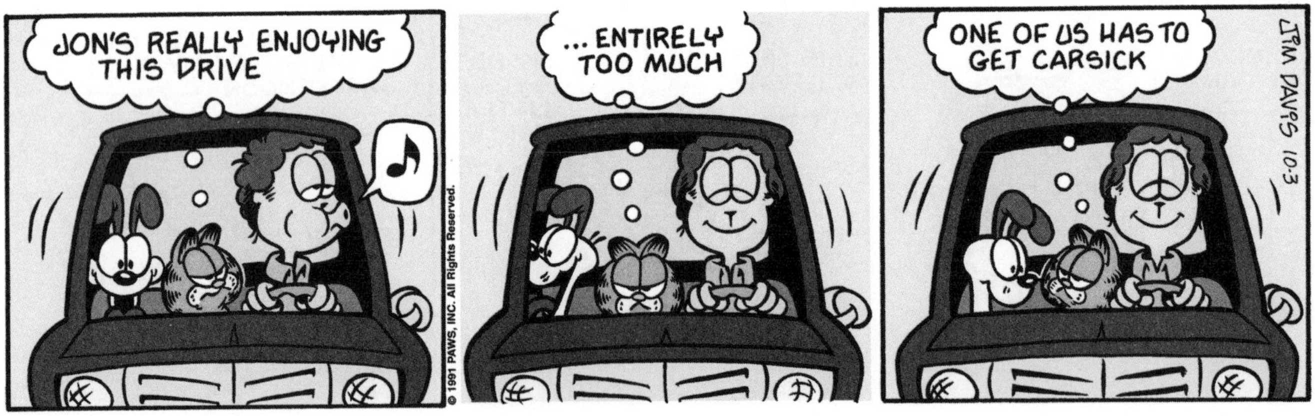
JON'S REALLY ENJOYING THIS DRIVE
♪
... ENTIRELY TOO MUCH
ONE OF US HAS TO GET CARSICK
JIM DAVIS 10-3
© 1991 PAWS, INC. All Rights Reserved.

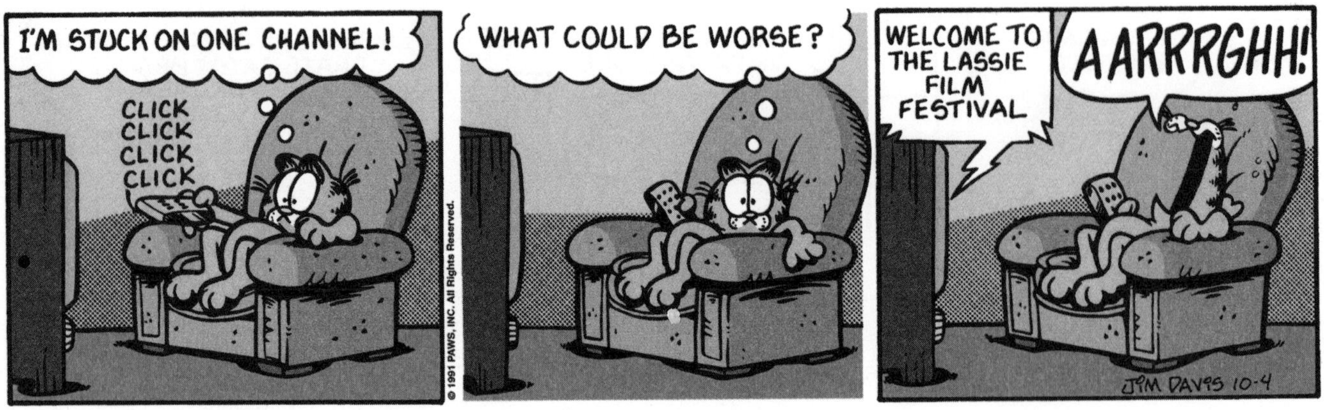
I'M STUCK ON ONE CHANNEL!
CLICK CLICK CLICK CLICK
WHAT COULD BE WORSE?
WELCOME TO THE LASSIE FILM FESTIVAL
AARRRGHH!
JIM DAVIS 10-4
© 1991 PAWS, INC. All Rights Reserved.

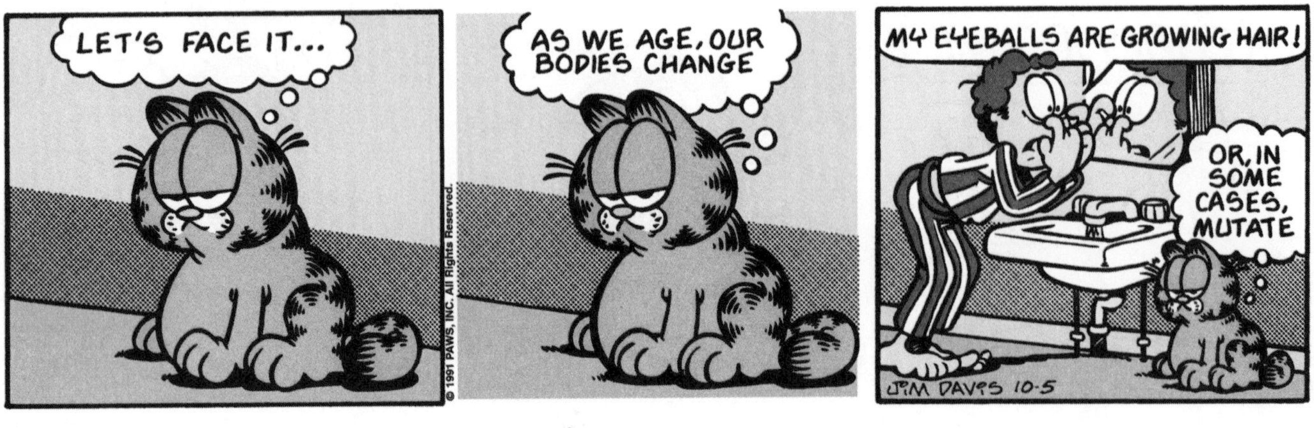
LET'S FACE IT...
AS WE AGE, OUR BODIES CHANGE
MY EYEBALLS ARE GROWING HAIR!
OR, IN SOME CASES, MUTATE
JIM DAVIS 10-5
© 1991 PAWS, INC. All Rights Reserved.

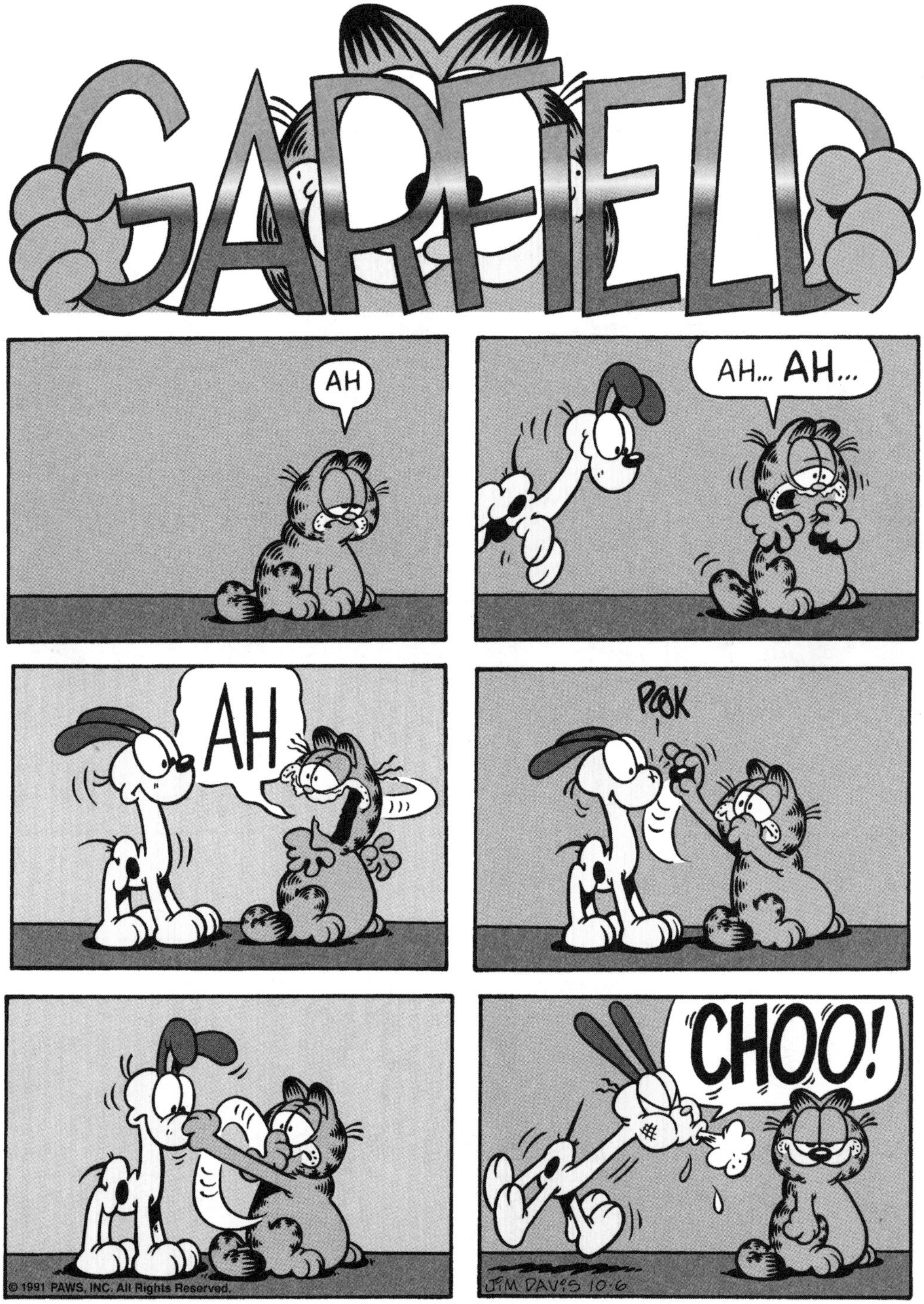
GARFIELD
AH
AH... AH...
AH
POOK
CHOO!
© 1991 PAWS, INC. All Rights Reserved.
JIM DAVIS 10-6

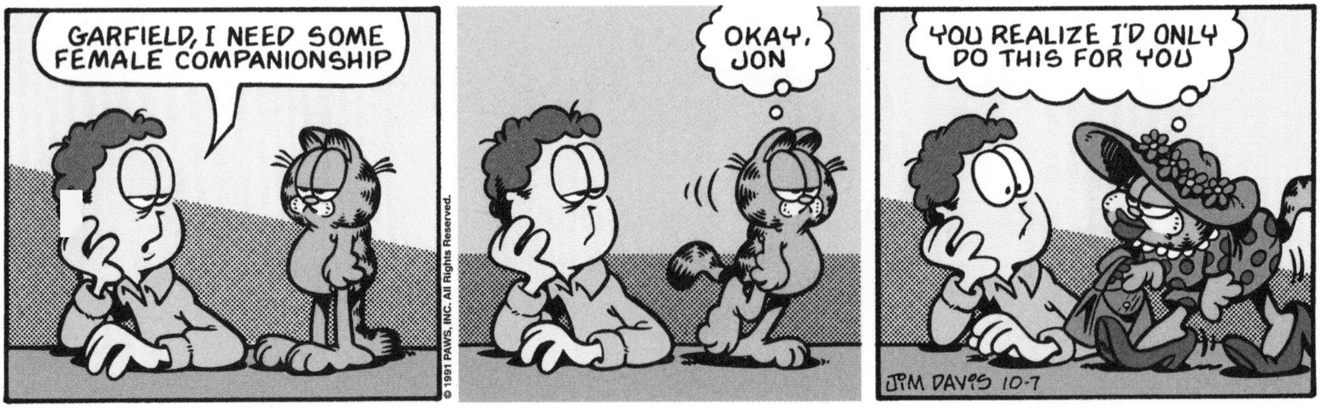
GARFIELD, I NEED SOME FEMALE COMPANIONSHIP
© 1991 PAWS, INC. All Rights Reserved.
OKAY, JON
YOU REALIZE I'D ONLY DO THIS FOR YOU
JIM DAVIS 10-7

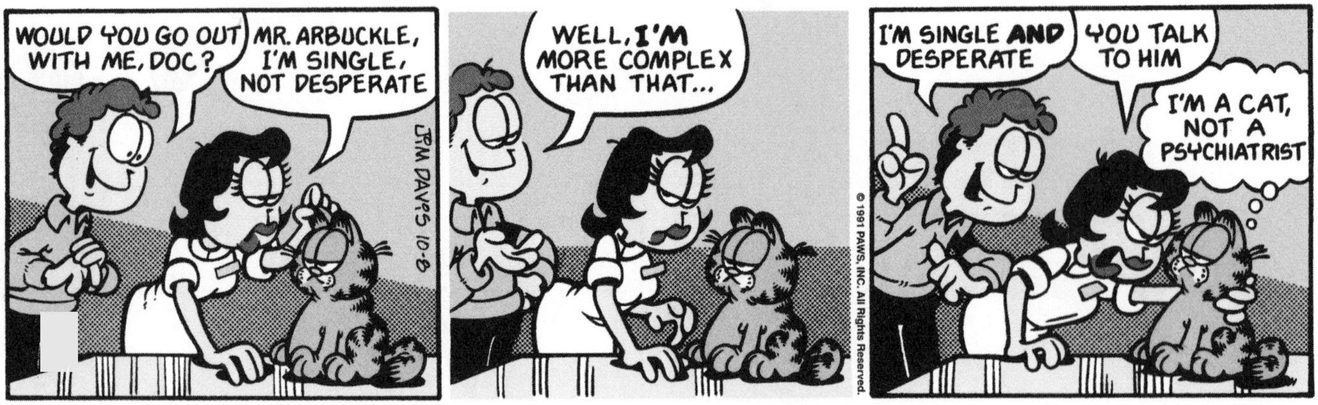
WOULD YOU GO OUT WITH ME, DOC?
MR. ARBUCKLE, I'M SINGLE, NOT DESPERATE
JIM DAVIS 10-8
WELL, **I'M** MORE COMPLEX THAN THAT...
© 1991 PAWS, INC. All Rights Reserved.
I'M SINGLE **AND** DESPERATE
YOU TALK TO HIM
I'M A CAT, NOT A PSYCHIATRIST

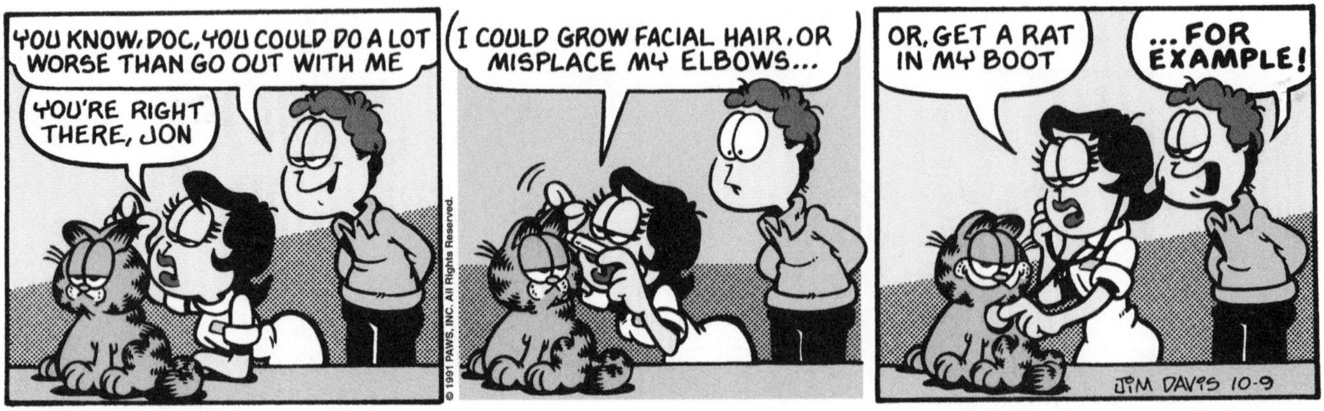
YOU KNOW, DOC, YOU COULD DO A LOT WORSE THAN GO OUT WITH ME
YOU'RE RIGHT THERE, JON
© 1991 PAWS, INC. All Rights Reserved.
I COULD GROW FACIAL HAIR, OR MISPLACE MY ELBOWS...
OR, GET A RAT IN MY BOOT
...**FOR EXAMPLE!**
JIM DAVIS 10-9

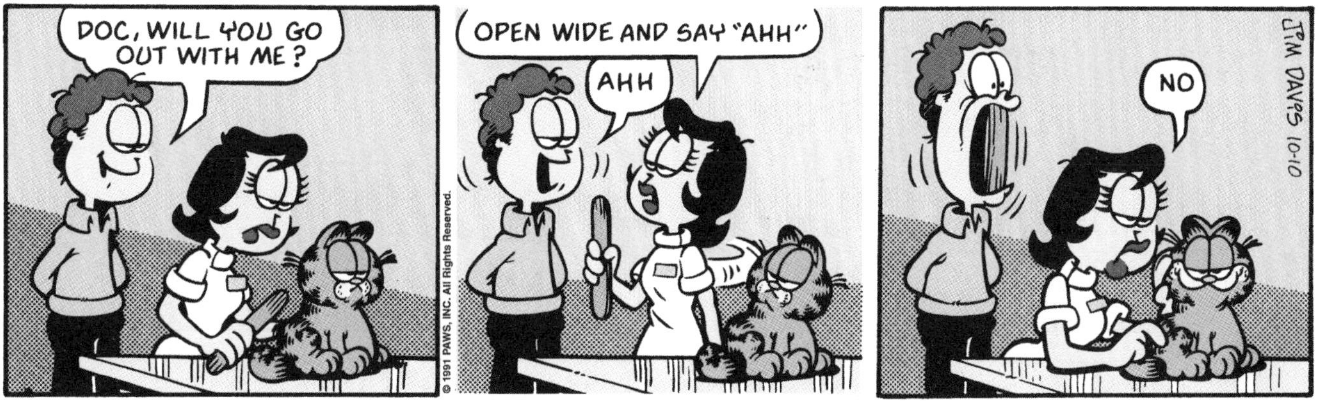
DOC, WILL YOU GO OUT WITH ME?
OPEN WIDE AND SAY "AHH"
AHH
© 1991 PAWS, INC. All Rights Reserved.
NO
JIM DAVIS 10-10

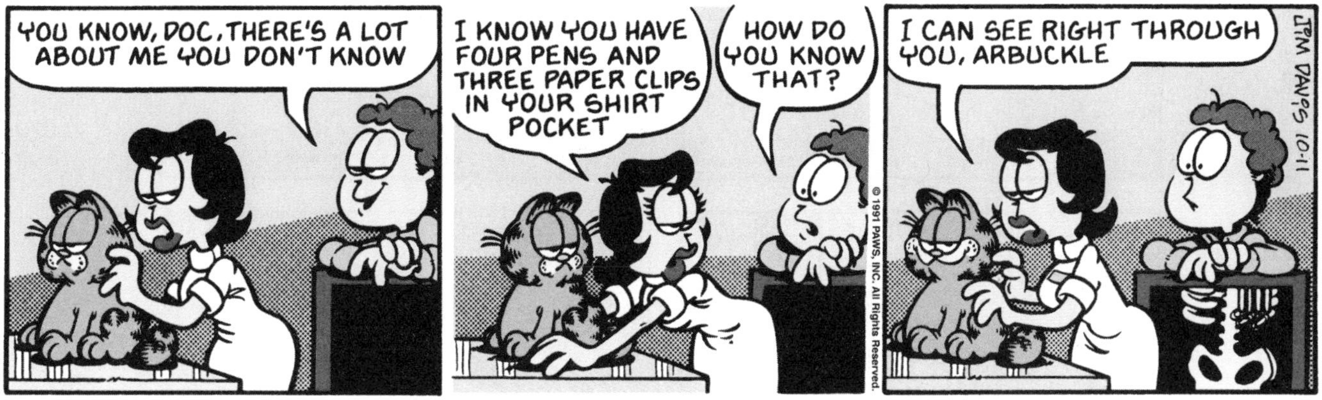
YOU KNOW, DOC, THERE'S A LOT ABOUT ME YOU DON'T KNOW
I KNOW YOU HAVE FOUR PENS AND THREE PAPER CLIPS IN YOUR SHIRT POCKET
HOW DO YOU KNOW THAT?
© 1991 PAWS, INC. All Rights Reserved.
I CAN SEE RIGHT THROUGH YOU, ARBUCKLE
JIM DAVIS 10-11

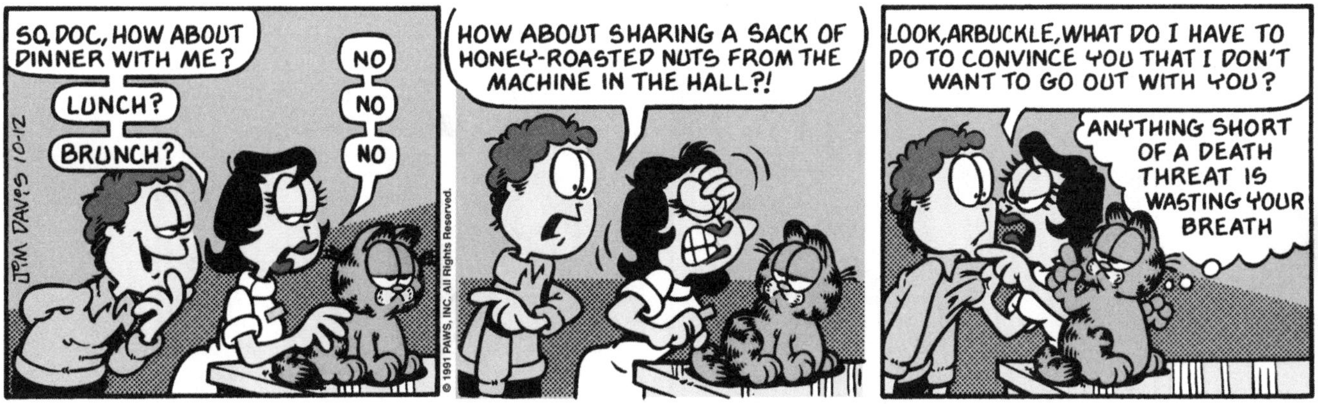
SO, DOC, HOW ABOUT DINNER WITH ME?
NO
LUNCH?
NO
BRUNCH?
NO
JIM DAVIS 10-12
© 1991 PAWS, INC. All Rights Reserved.
HOW ABOUT SHARING A SACK OF HONEY-ROASTED NUTS FROM THE MACHINE IN THE HALL?!
LOOK, ARBUCKLE, WHAT DO I HAVE TO DO TO CONVINCE YOU THAT I DON'T WANT TO GO OUT WITH YOU?
ANYTHING SHORT OF A DEATH THREAT IS WASTING YOUR BREATH

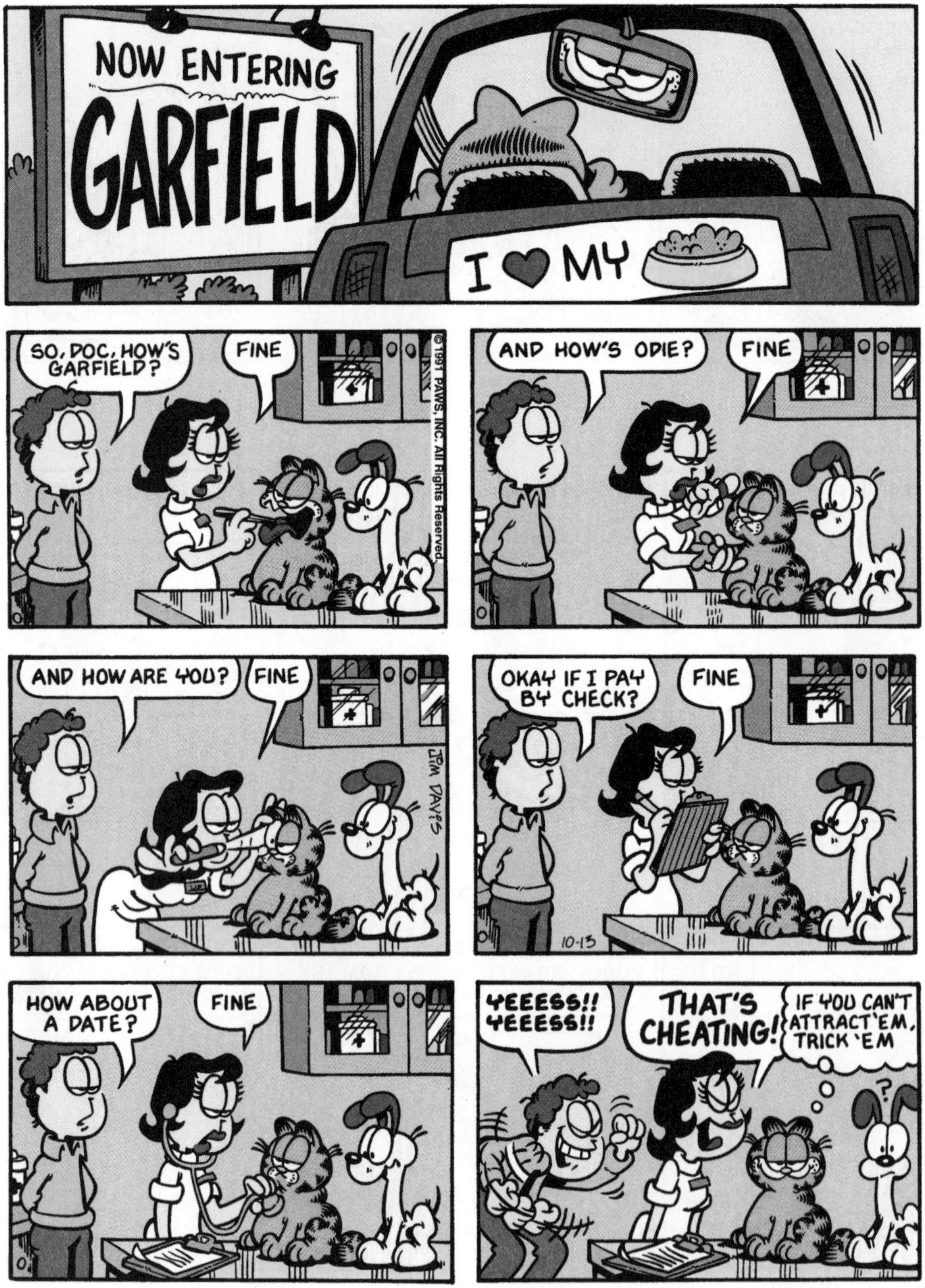
NOW ENTERING
GARFIELD
I ♥ MY
SO, DOC, HOW'S GARFIELD?
FINE
© 1991 PAWS, INC. All Rights Reserved.
AND HOW'S ODIE?
FINE
AND HOW ARE YOU?
FINE
JIM DAVIS
OKAY IF I PAY BY CHECK?
FINE
10-13
HOW ABOUT A DATE?
FINE
YEEESS!! YEEESS!!
THAT'S CHEATING!
IF YOU CAN'T ATTRACT 'EM, TRICK 'EM
?

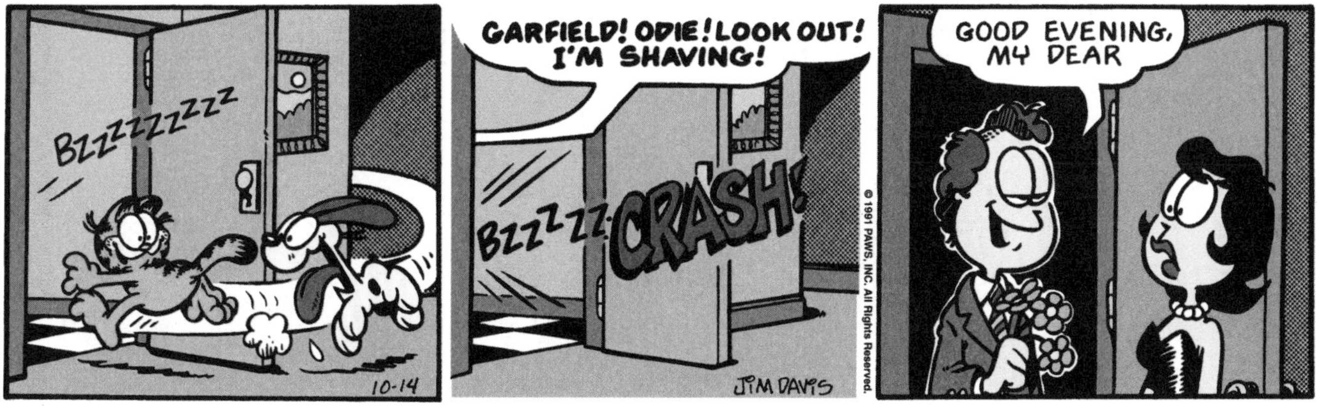
BZZZZZZZZZ
10-14
GARFIELD! ODIE! LOOK OUT!
I'M SHAVING!
BZZZZZ
CRASH!
JIM DAVIS
© 1991 PAWS, INC. All Rights Reserved.
GOOD EVENING, MY DEAR

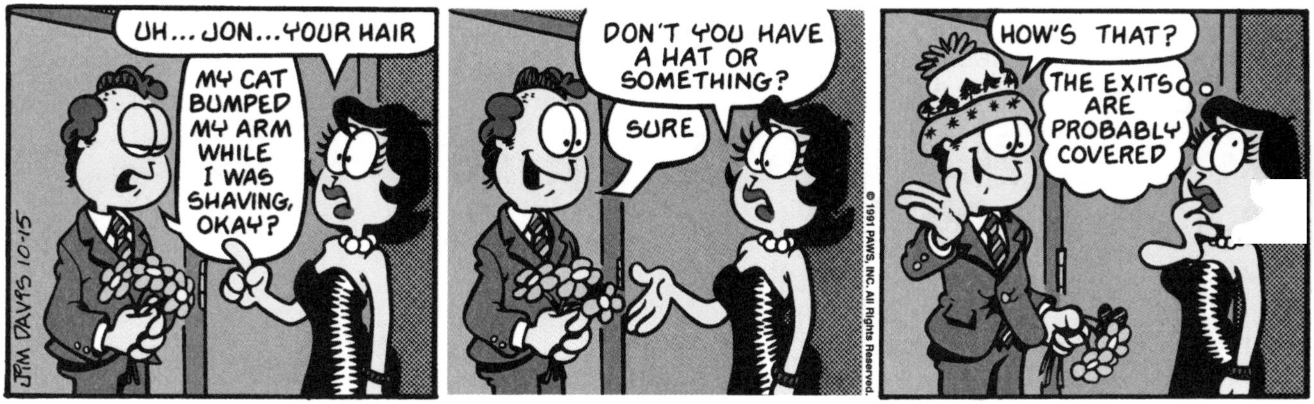
UH... JON... YOUR HAIR
MY CAT BUMPED MY ARM WHILE I WAS SHAVING, OKAY?
JIM DAVIS 10-15
DON'T YOU HAVE A HAT OR SOMETHING?
SURE
© 1991 PAWS, INC. All Rights Reserved.
HOW'S THAT?
THE EXITS ARE PROBABLY COVERED

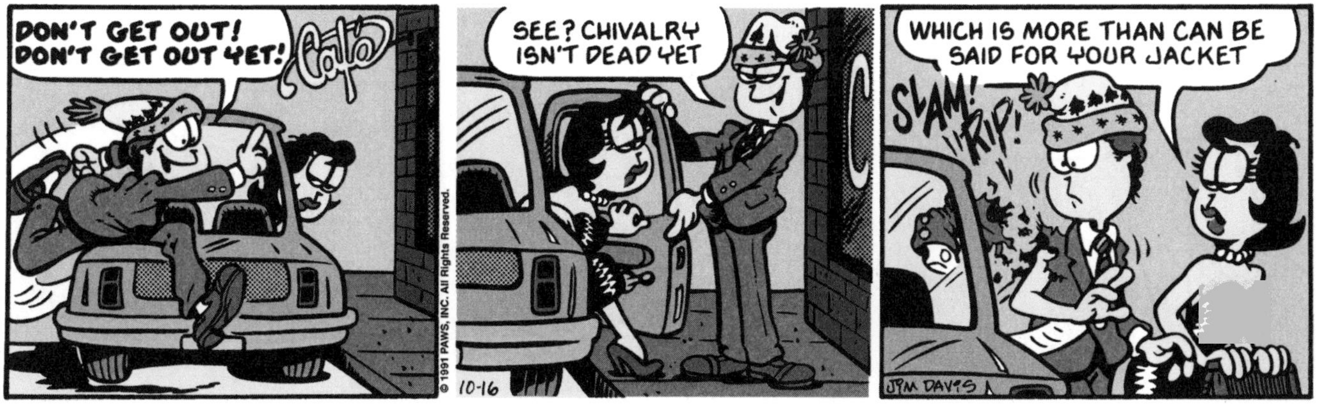
DON'T GET OUT!
DON'T GET OUT YET!
© 1991 PAWS, INC. All Rights Reserved.
SEE? CHIVALRY ISN'T DEAD YET
10-16
WHICH IS MORE THAN CAN BE SAID FOR YOUR JACKET
SLAM!
RIP!
JIM DAVIS

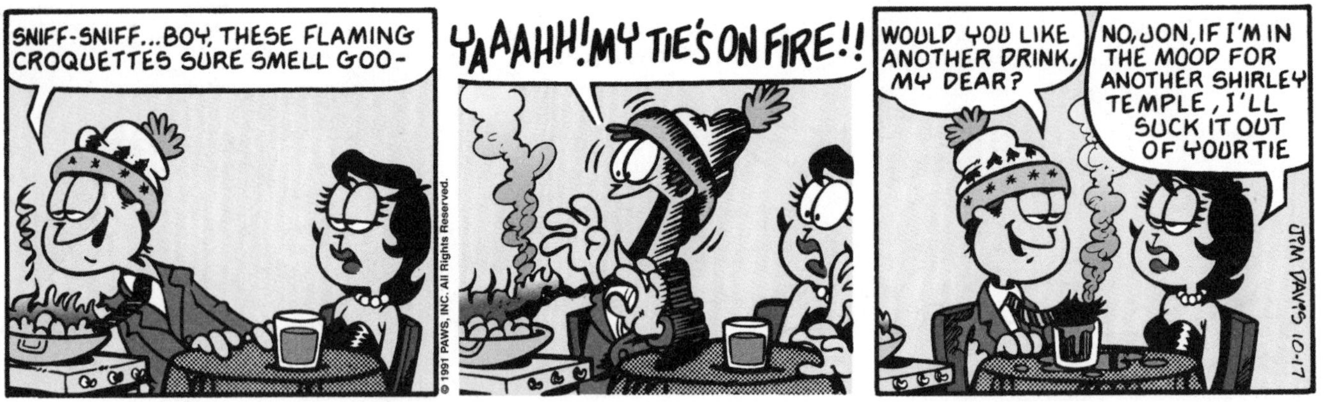
SNIFF-SNIFF...BOY, THESE FLAMING CROQUETTES SURE SMELL GOO-
YAAAHH! MY TIE'S ON FIRE!!
WOULD YOU LIKE ANOTHER DRINK, MY DEAR?
NO, JON, IF I'M IN THE MOOD FOR ANOTHER SHIRLEY TEMPLE, I'LL SUCK IT OUT OF YOUR TIE
JIM DAVIS 10-17

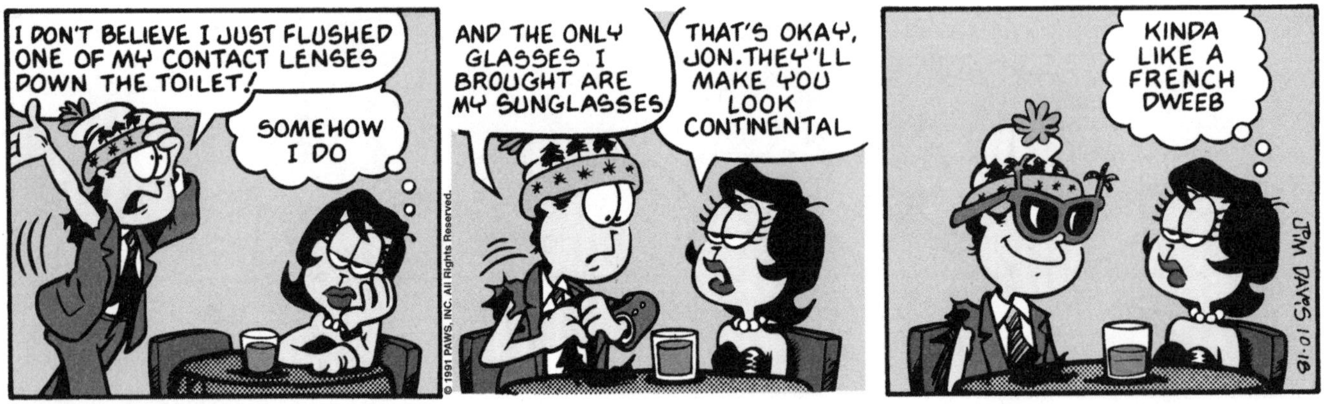
I DON'T BELIEVE I JUST FLUSHED ONE OF MY CONTACT LENSES DOWN THE TOILET!
SOMEHOW I DO
AND THE ONLY GLASSES I BROUGHT ARE MY SUNGLASSES
THAT'S OKAY, JON. THEY'LL MAKE YOU LOOK CONTINENTAL
KINDA LIKE A FRENCH DWEEB
JIM DAVIS 10-18

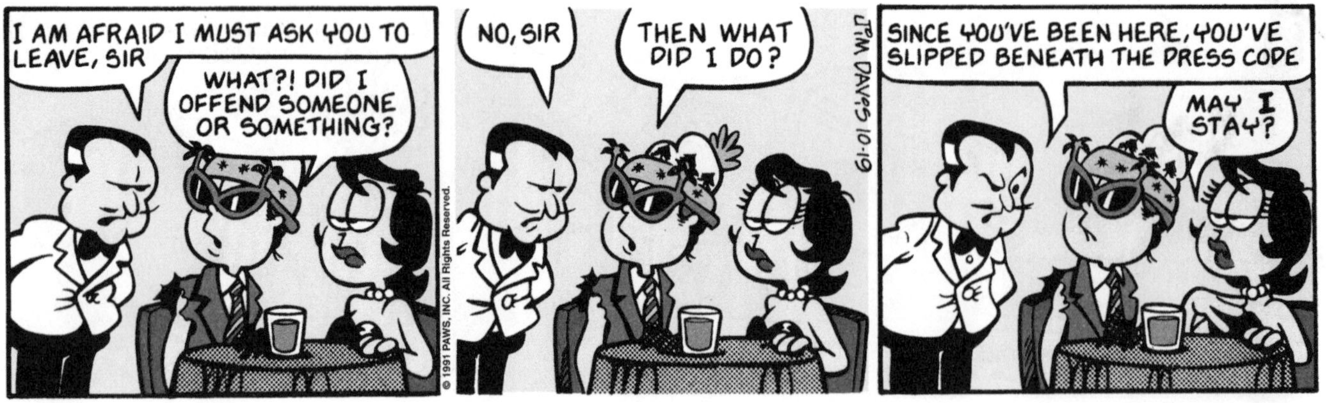
I AM AFRAID I MUST ASK YOU TO LEAVE, SIR
WHAT?! DID I OFFEND SOMEONE OR SOMETHING?
NO, SIR
THEN WHAT DID I DO?
JIM DAVIS 10-19
SINCE YOU'VE BEEN HERE, YOU'VE SLIPPED BENEATH THE DRESS CODE
MAY I STAY?

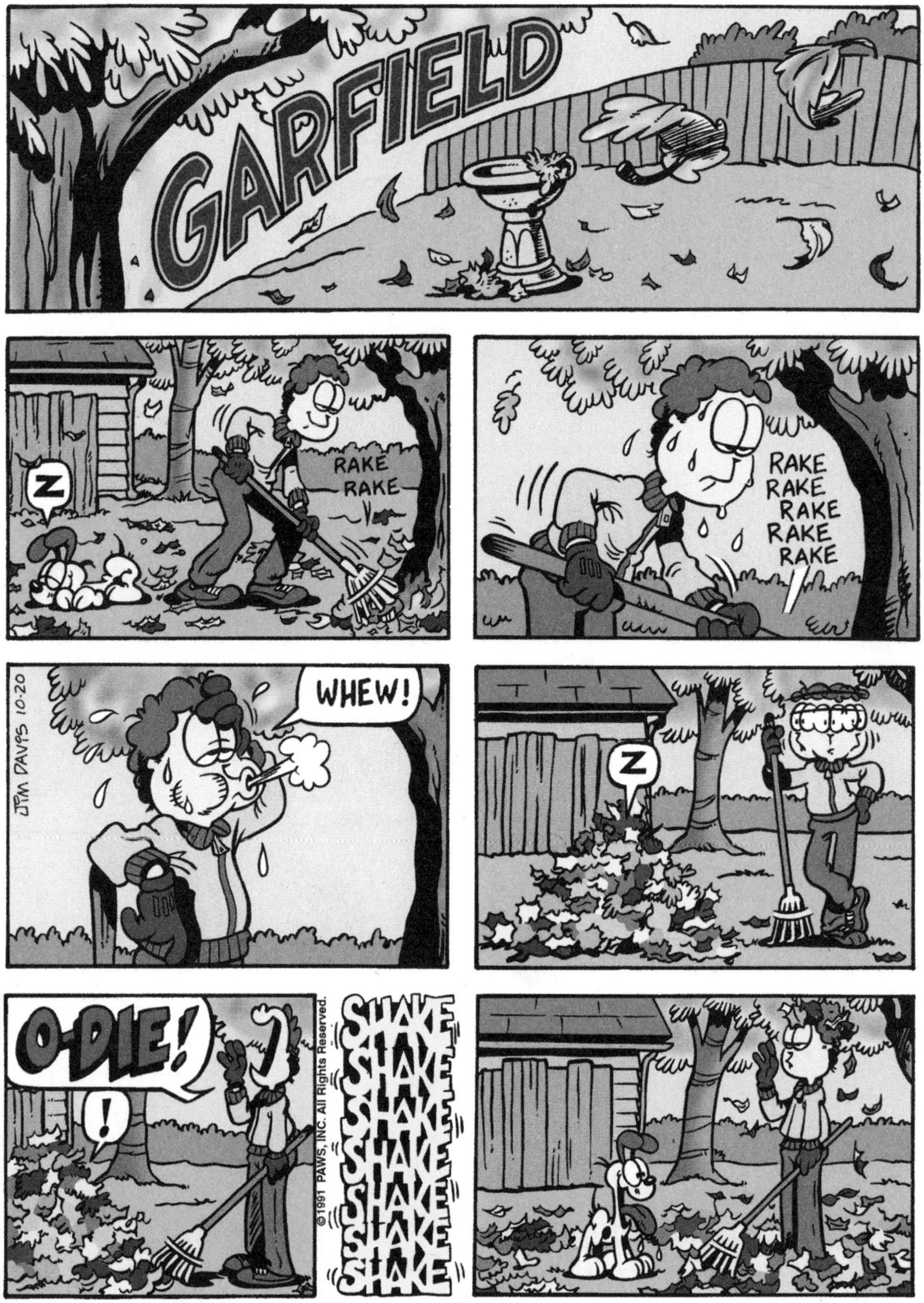
GARFIELD
Z
RAKE
RAKE
RAKE
RAKE
RAKE
RAKE
RAKE
JPM DAVPS 10-20
WHEW!
Z
O-DIE!
!
©1991 PAWS, INC. All Rights Reserved.
SHAKE
SHAKE
SHAKE
SHAKE
SHAKE
SHAKE
SHAKE
SHAKE
SHAKE

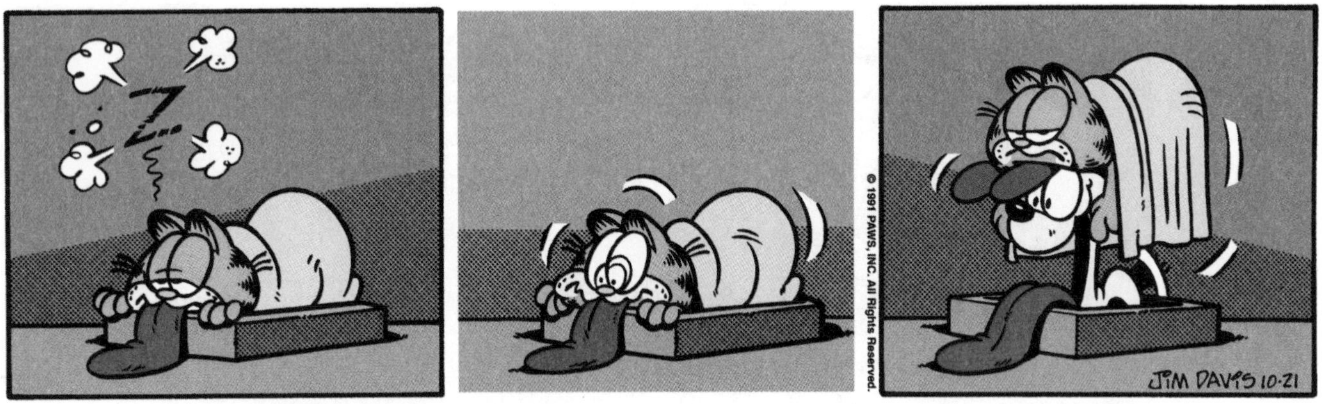
© 1991 PAWS, INC. All Rights Reserved.
JIM DAVIS 10-21

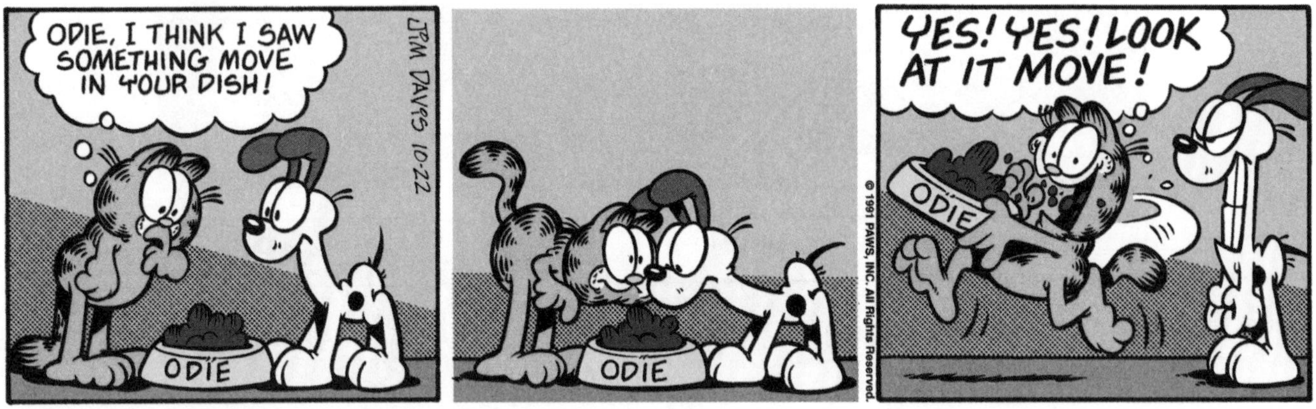
ODIE, I THINK I SAW SOMETHING MOVE IN YOUR DISH!
JIM DAVIS 10-22
ODIE
ODIE
© 1991 PAWS, INC. All Rights Reserved.
YES! YES! LOOK AT IT MOVE!
ODIE

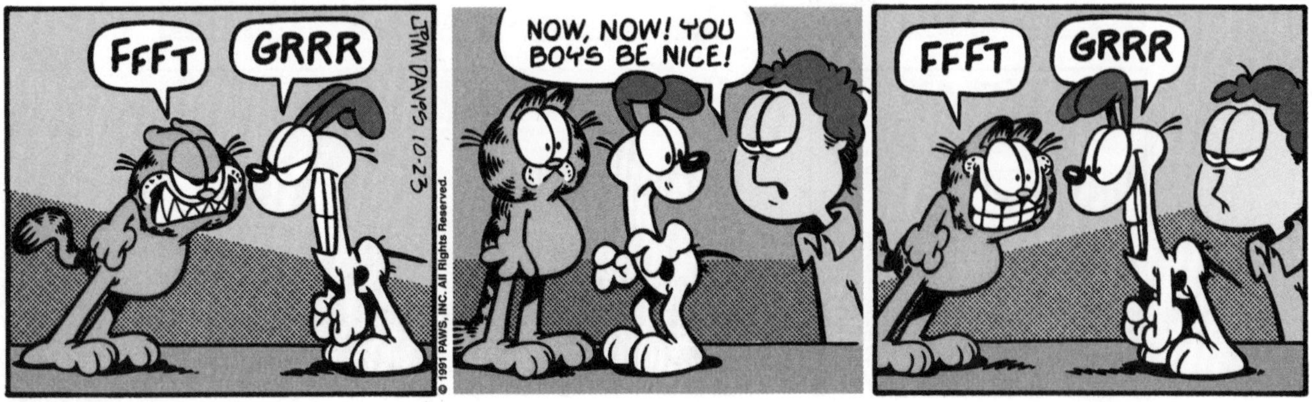
FFFT
GRRR
JIM DAVIS 10-23
© 1991 PAWS, INC. All Rights Reserved.
NOW, NOW! YOU BOYS BE NICE!
FFFT
GRRR

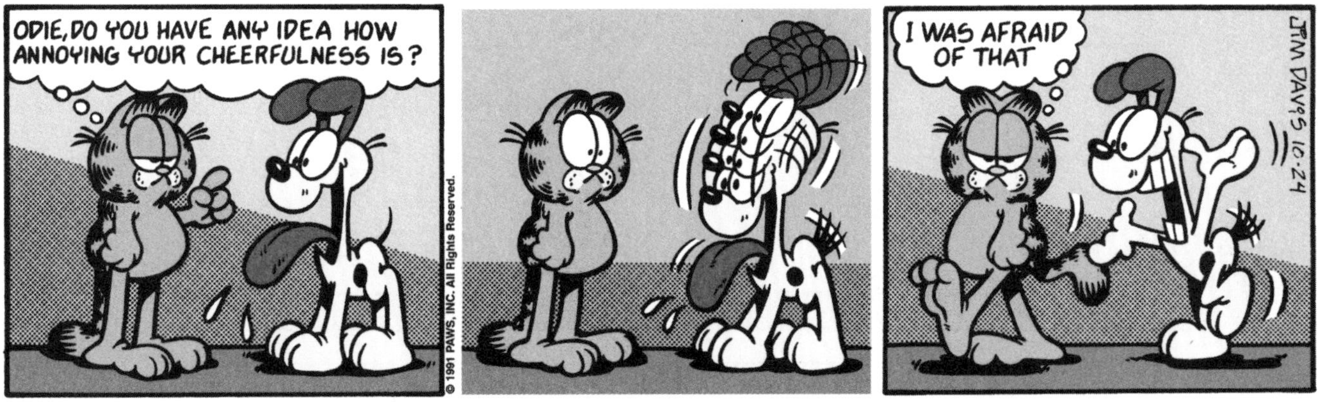
ODIE, DO YOU HAVE ANY IDEA HOW ANNOYING YOUR CHEERFULNESS IS?
© 1991 PAWS, INC. All Rights Reserved.
I WAS AFRAID OF THAT
JIM DAVIS 10-24

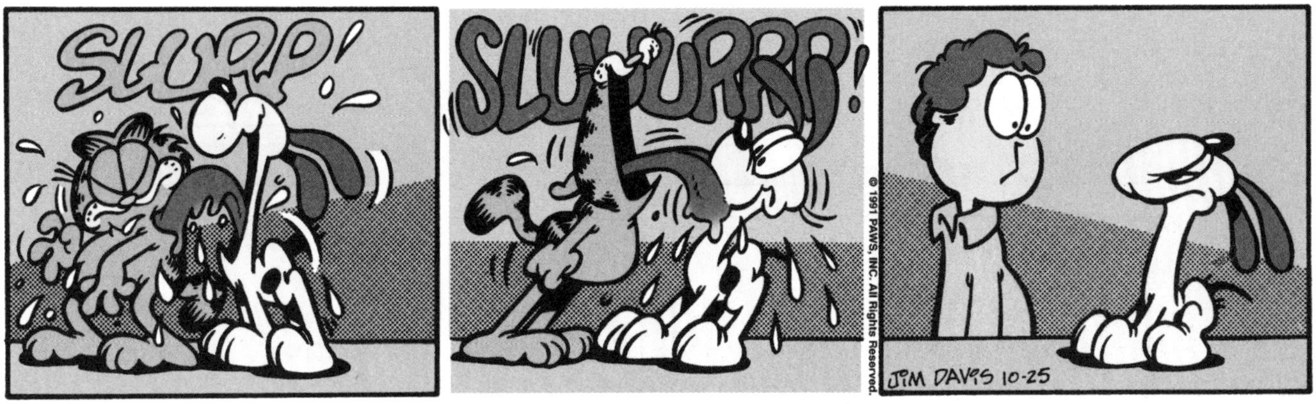
SLURP!
SLURRRP!
© 1991 PAWS, INC. All Rights Reserved.
JIM DAVIS 10-25

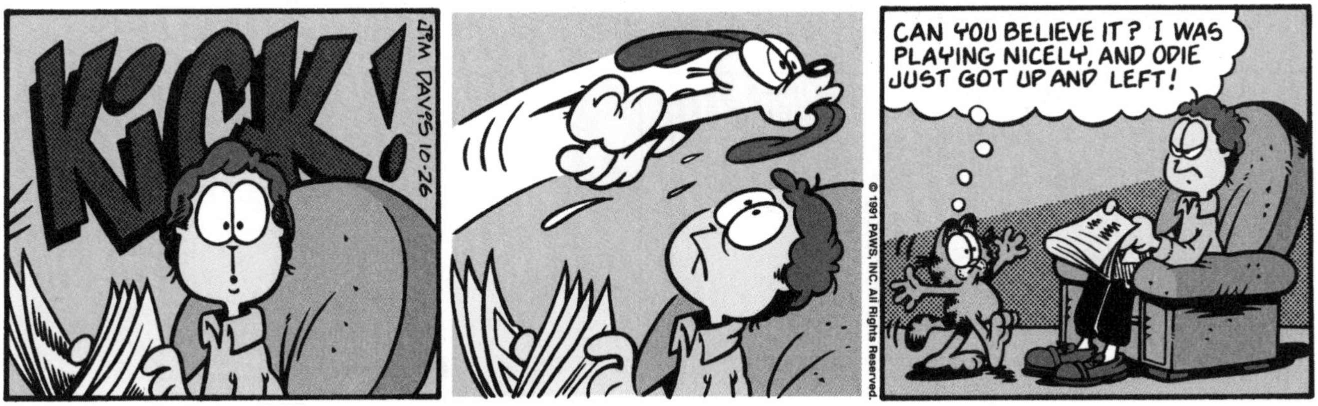
KICK!
JIM DAVIS 10-26
© 1991 PAWS, INC. All Rights Reserved.
CAN YOU BELIEVE IT? I WAS PLAYING NICELY, AND ODIE JUST GOT UP AND LEFT!

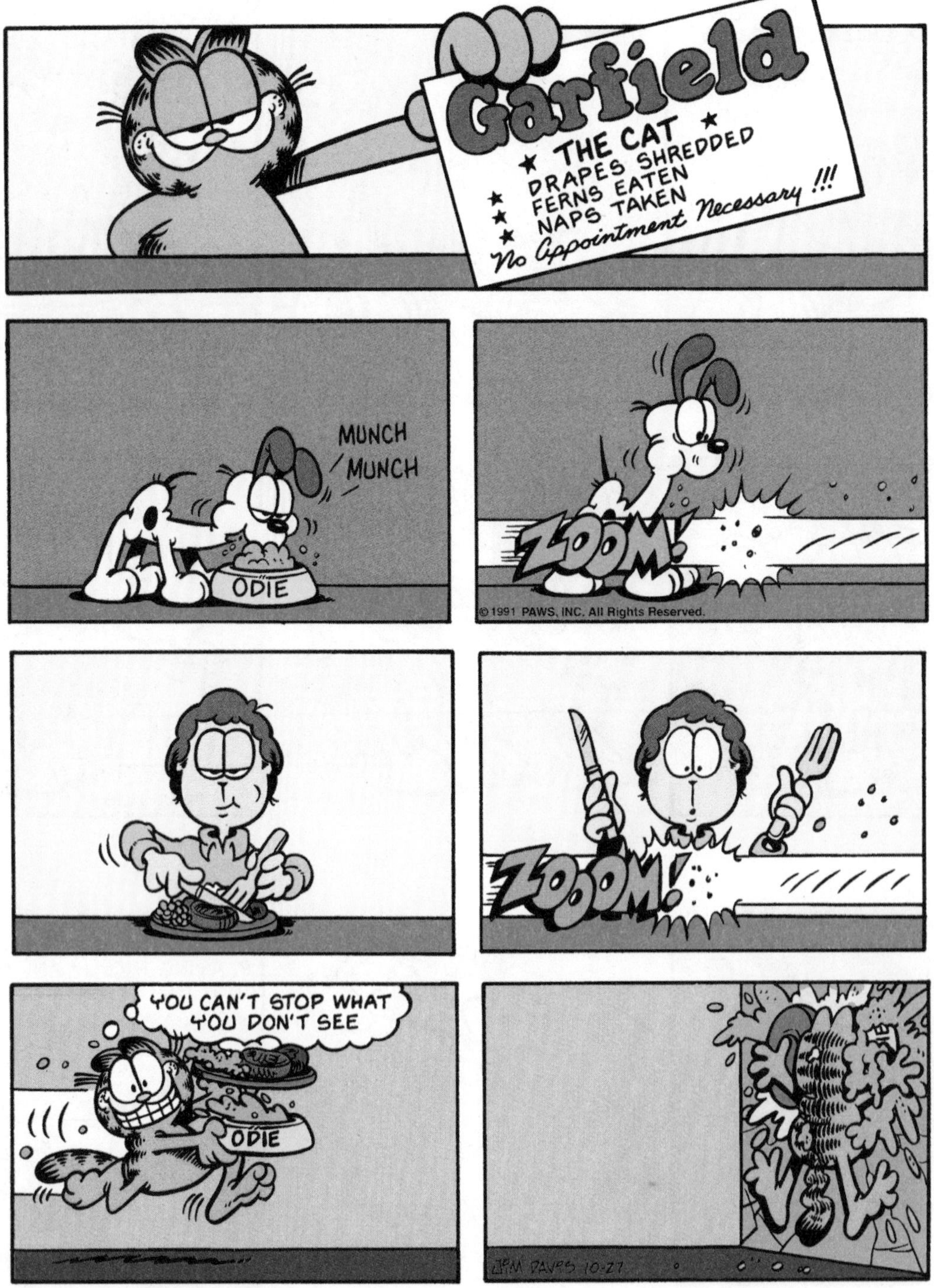
Garfield
★ THE CAT ★
DRAPES SHREDDED
★ FERNS EATEN
★ NAPS TAKEN
★ No Appointment Necessary !!!
MUNCH
MUNCH
ODIE
ZOOM!
© 1991 PAWS, INC. All Rights Reserved.
ZOOOM!
YOU CAN'T STOP WHAT YOU DON'T SEE
ODIE
JPM DAVPS 10-27

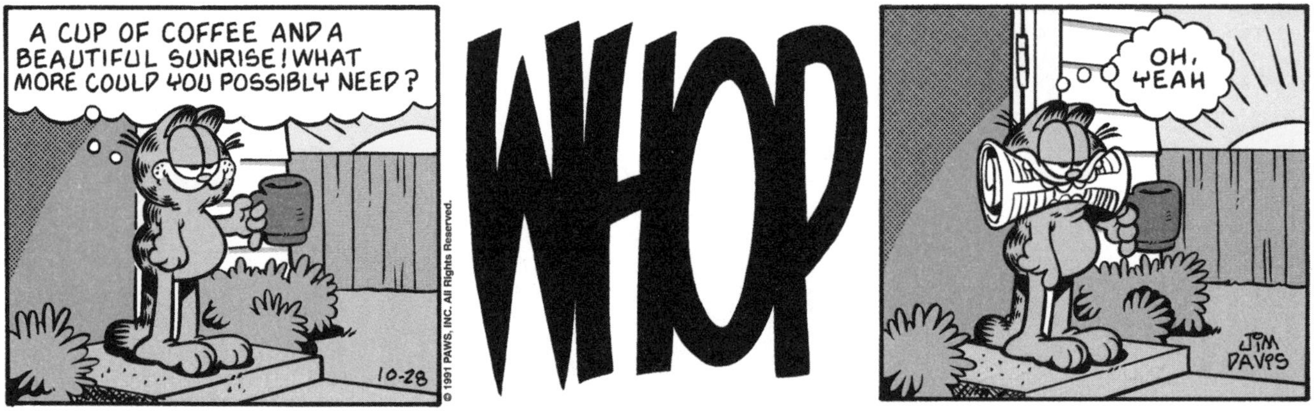
A CUP OF COFFEE AND A BEAUTIFUL SUNRISE! WHAT MORE COULD YOU POSSIBLY NEED?
10-28
© 1991 PAWS, INC. All Rights Reserved.
WHOP
OH, YEAH
JIM DAVIS

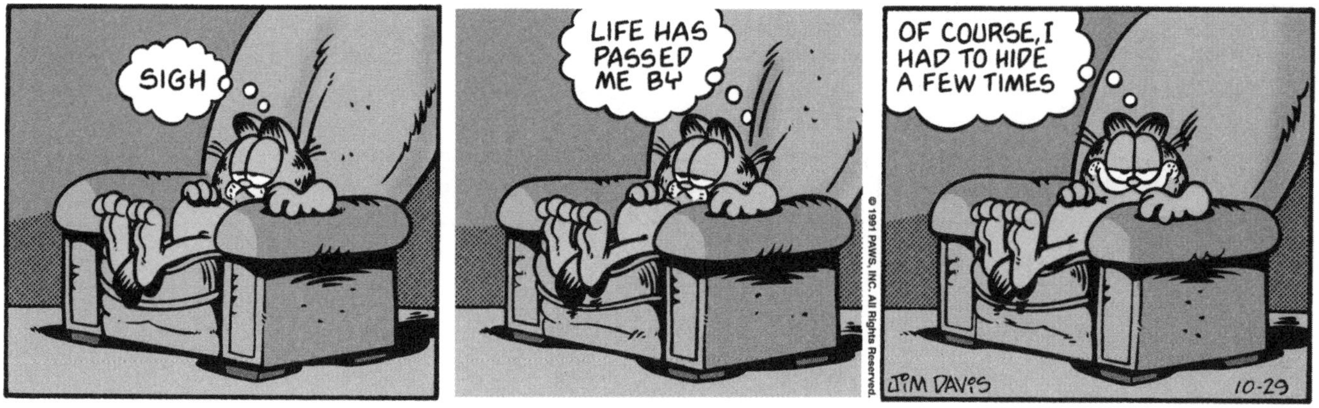
SIGH
LIFE HAS PASSED ME BY
© 1991 PAWS, INC. All Rights Reserved.
OF COURSE, I HAD TO HIDE A FEW TIMES
JIM DAVIS
10-29

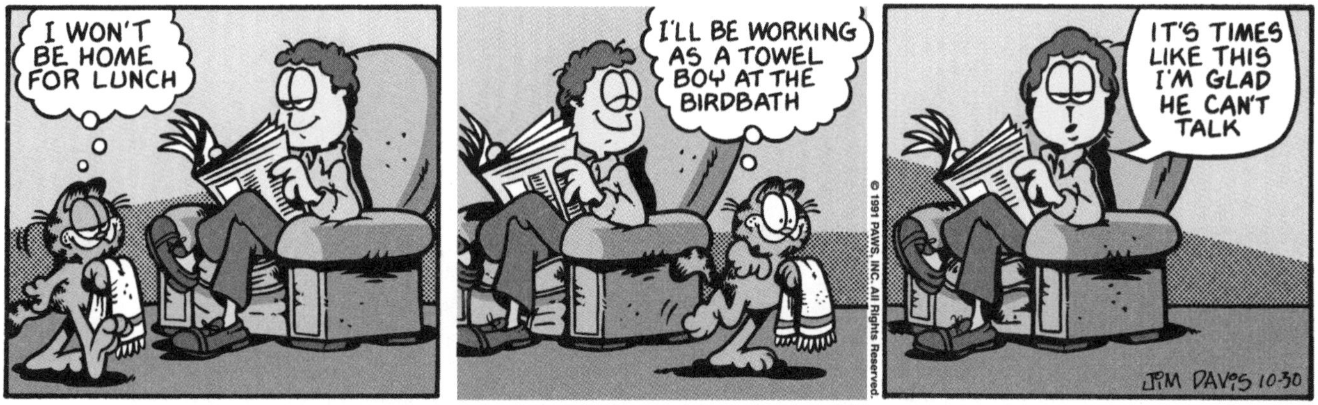
I WON'T BE HOME FOR LUNCH
I'LL BE WORKING AS A TOWEL BOY AT THE BIRDBATH
© 1991 PAWS, INC. All Rights Reserved.
IT'S TIMES LIKE THIS I'M GLAD HE CAN'T TALK
JIM DAVIS 10-30

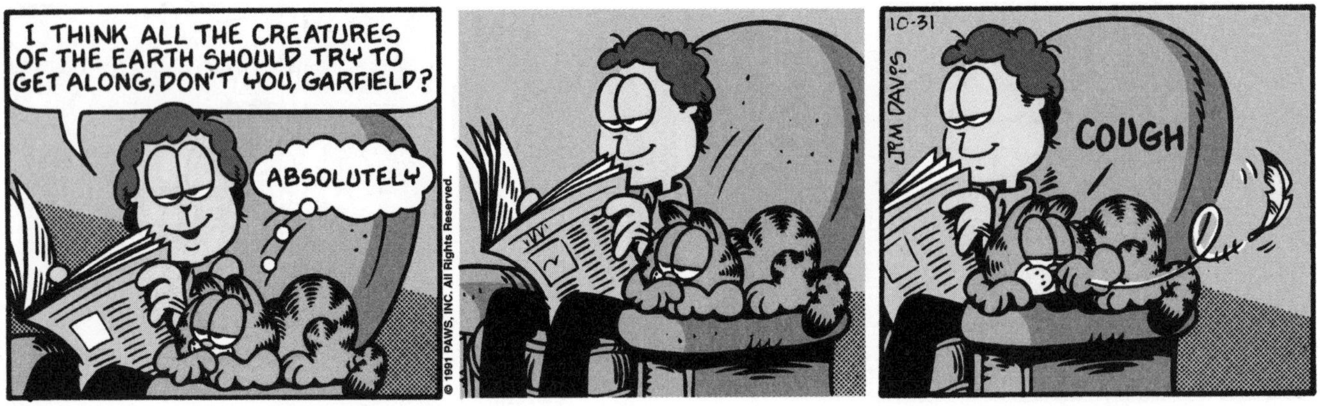
I THINK ALL THE CREATURES OF THE EARTH SHOULD TRY TO GET ALONG, DON'T YOU, GARFIELD?
ABSOLUTELY
COUGH
10-31
JIM DAVIS
© 1991 PAWS, INC. All Rights Reserved.

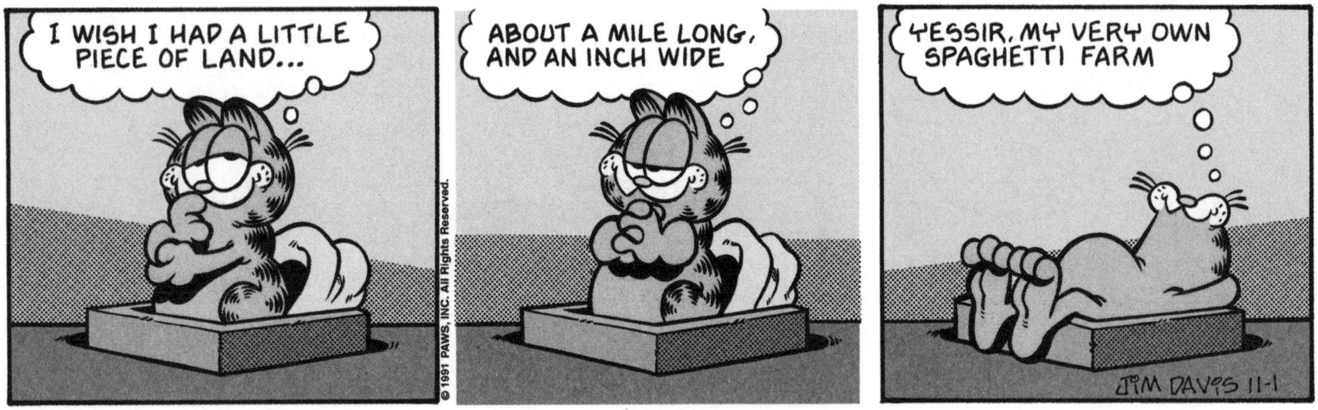
I WISH I HAD A LITTLE PIECE OF LAND...
ABOUT A MILE LONG, AND AN INCH WIDE
YESSIR, MY VERY OWN SPAGHETTI FARM
JIM DAVIS 11-1
© 1991 PAWS, INC. All Rights Reserved.

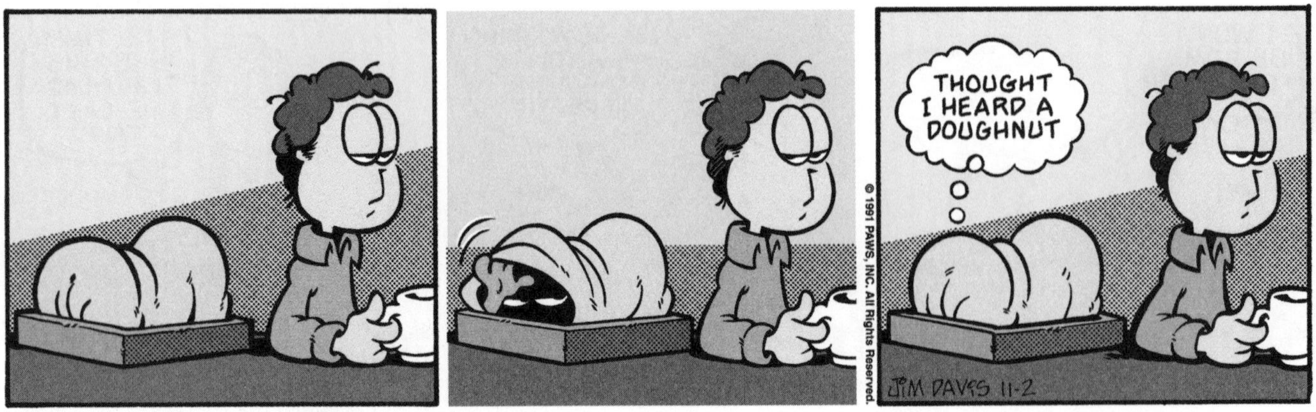
THOUGHT I HEARD A DOUGHNUT
JIM DAVIS 11-2
© 1991 PAWS, INC. All Rights Reserved.

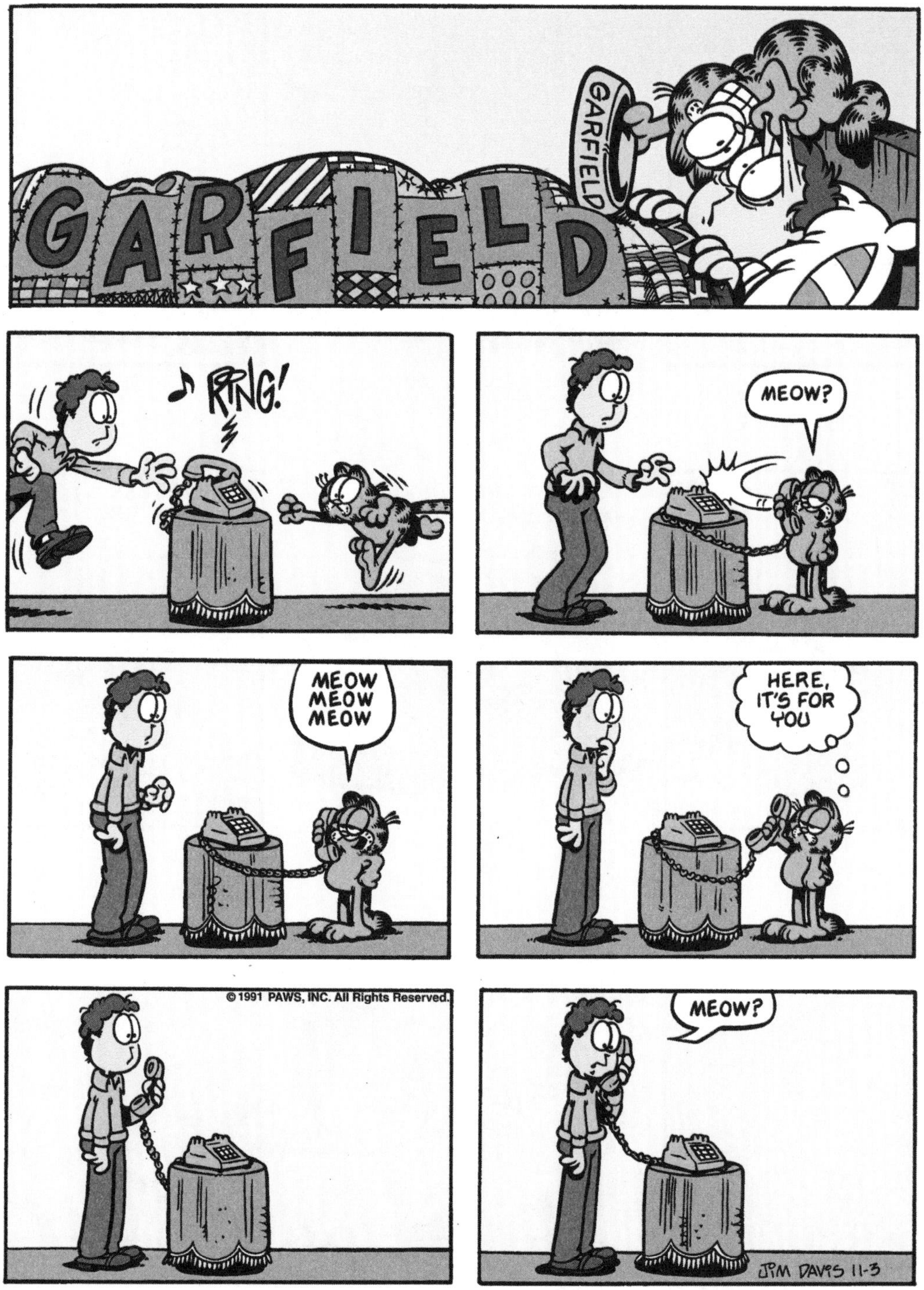
GARFIELD
GARFIELD
♪ RING!
MEOW?
MEOW MEOW MEOW
HERE, IT'S FOR YOU
© 1991 PAWS, INC. All Rights Reserved.
MEOW?
JIM DAVIS 11-3

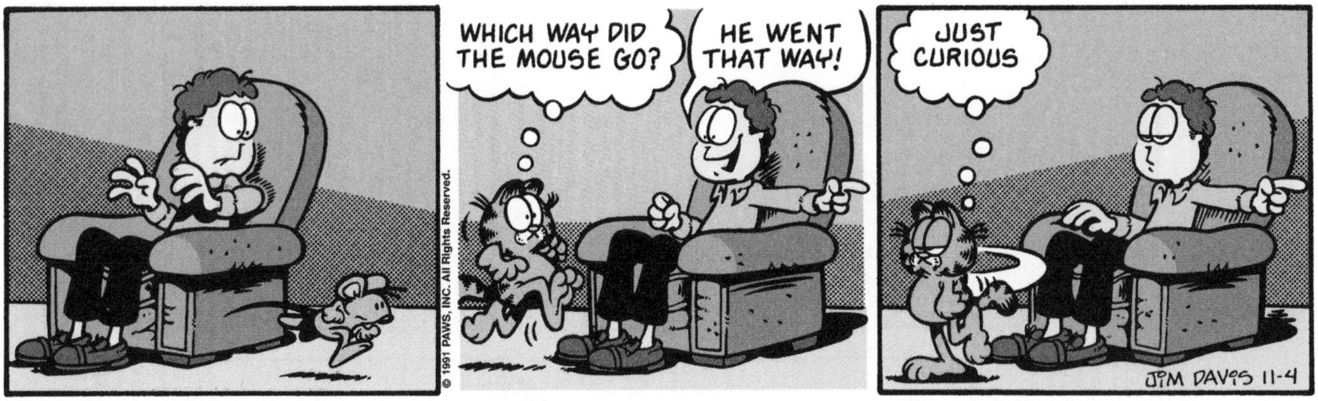
WHICH WAY DID THE MOUSE GO?
HE WENT THAT WAY!
JUST CURIOUS
© 1991 PAWS, INC. All Rights Reserved.
JIM DAVIS 11-4

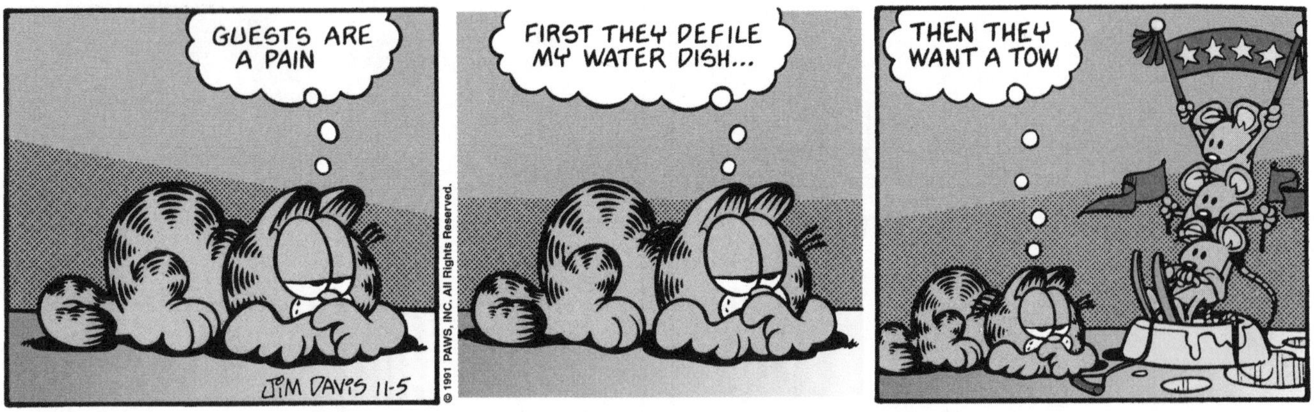
GUESTS ARE A PAIN
JIM DAVIS 11-5
© 1991 PAWS, INC. All Rights Reserved.
FIRST THEY DEFILE MY WATER DISH...
THEN THEY WANT A TOW

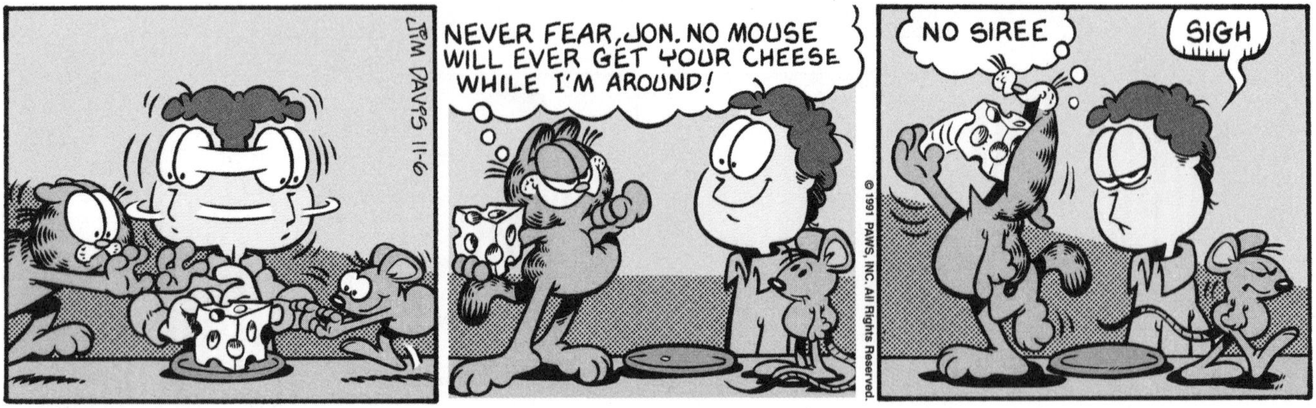
JIM DAVIS 11-6
NEVER FEAR, JON. NO MOUSE WILL EVER GET YOUR CHEESE WHILE I'M AROUND!
© 1991 PAWS, INC. All Rights Reserved.
NO SIREE
SIGH

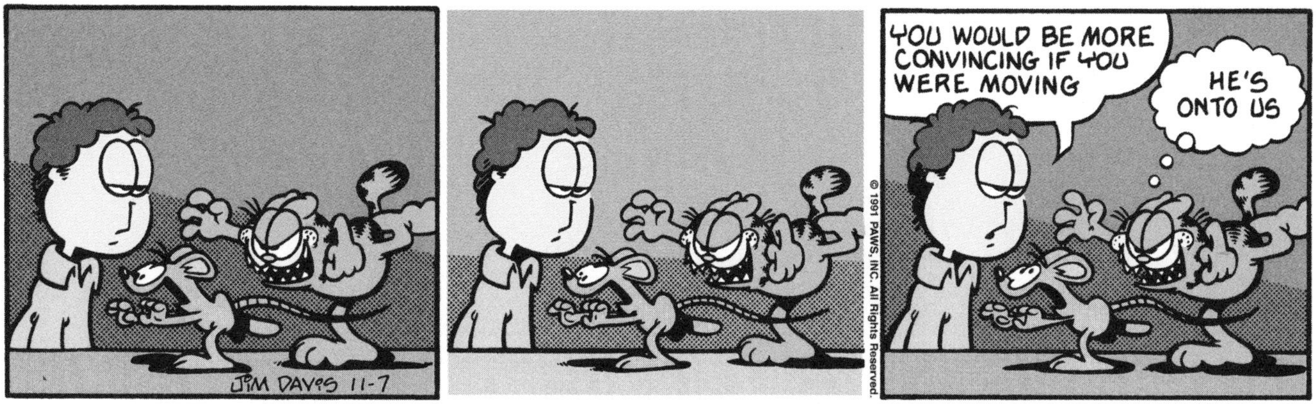
JIM DAVIS 11-7
© 1991 PAWS, INC. All Rights Reserved.
YOU WOULD BE MORE CONVINCING IF YOU WERE MOVING
HE'S ONTO US

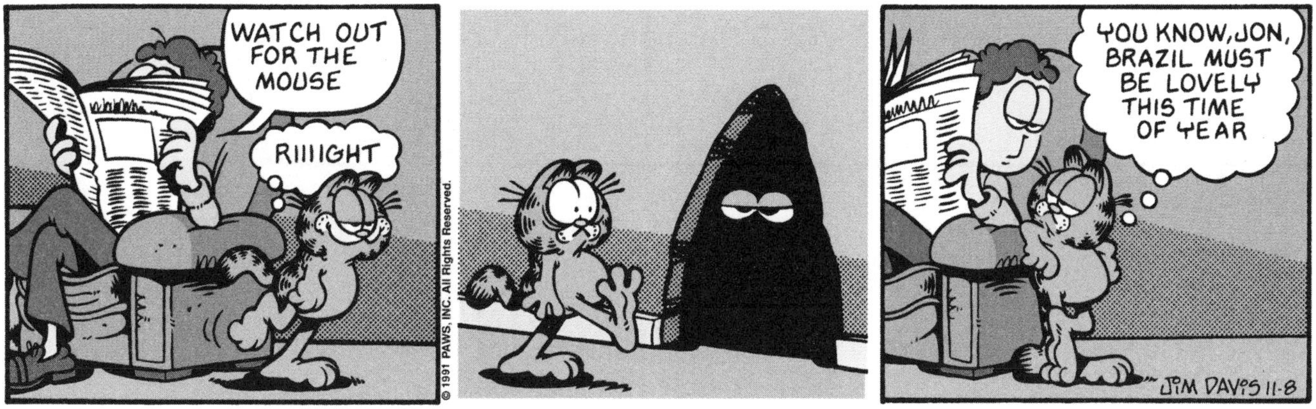
WATCH OUT FOR THE MOUSE
RIIIIGHT
© 1991 PAWS, INC. All Rights Reserved.
YOU KNOW, JON, BRAZIL MUST BE LOVELY THIS TIME OF YEAR
JIM DAVIS 11-8

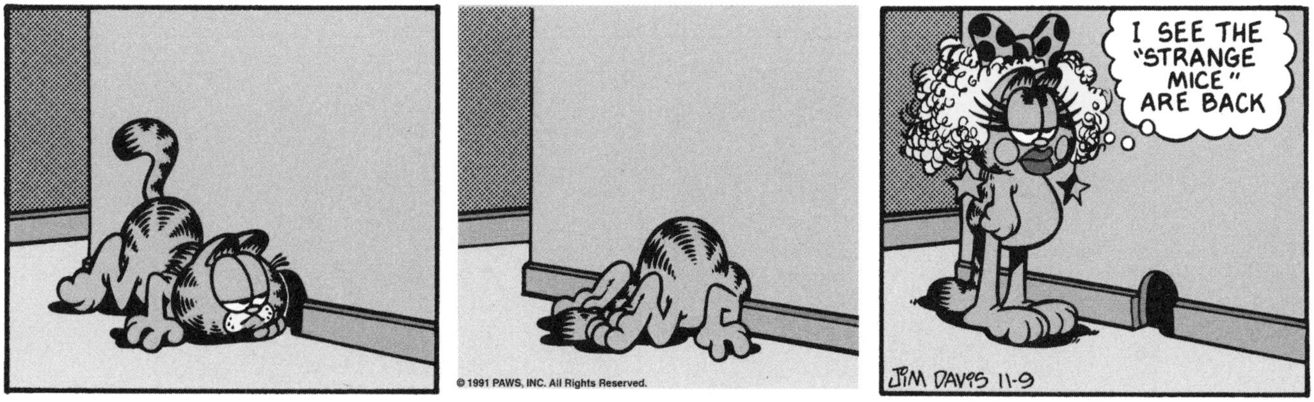
© 1991 PAWS, INC. All Rights Reserved.
I SEE THE "STRANGE MICE" ARE BACK
JIM DAVIS 11-9

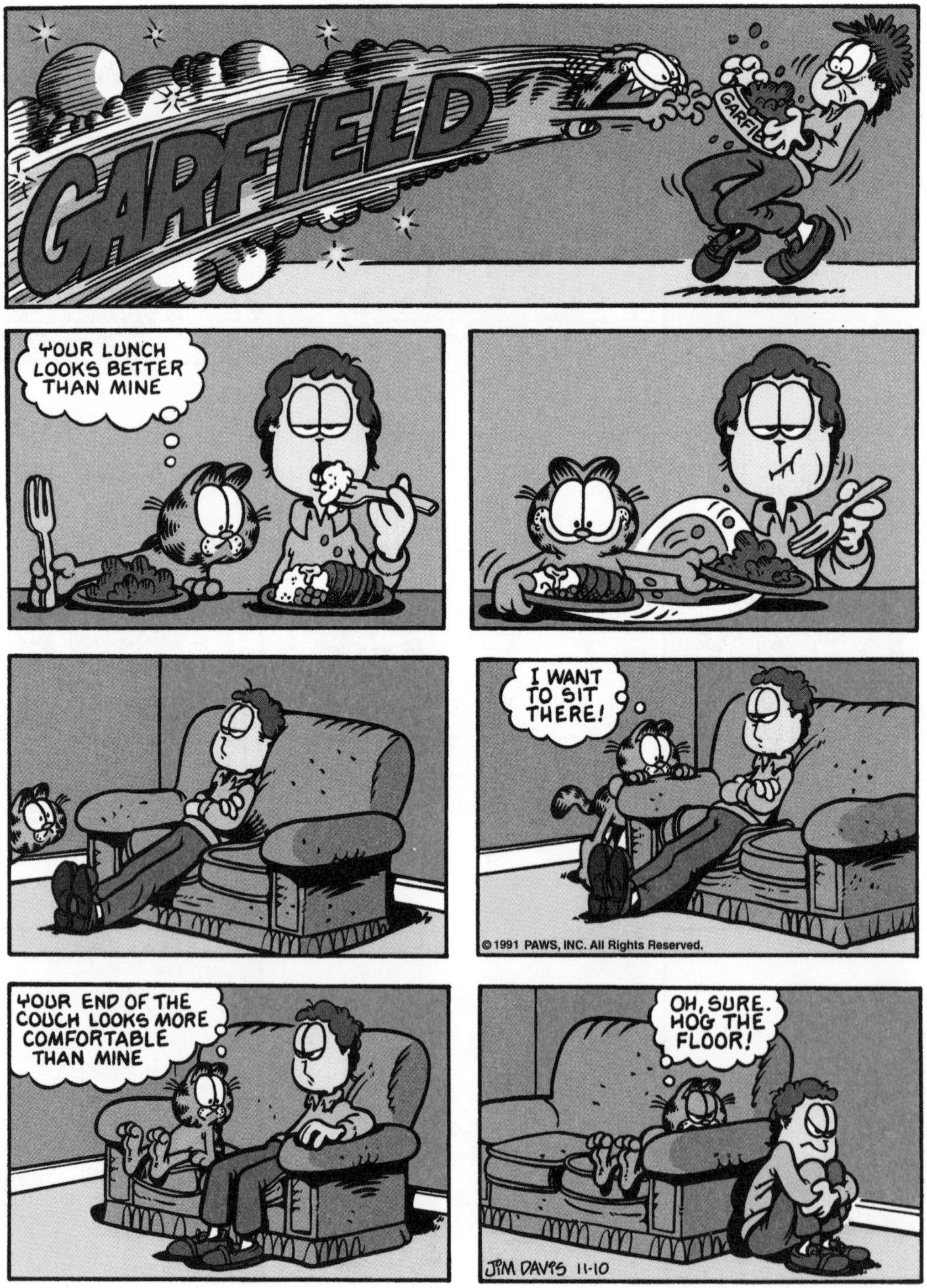
GARFIELD
YOUR LUNCH LOOKS BETTER THAN MINE
I WANT TO SIT THERE!
© 1991 PAWS, INC. All Rights Reserved.
YOUR END OF THE COUCH LOOKS MORE COMFORTABLE THAN MINE
OH, SURE. HOG THE FLOOR!
JIM DAVIS 11-10

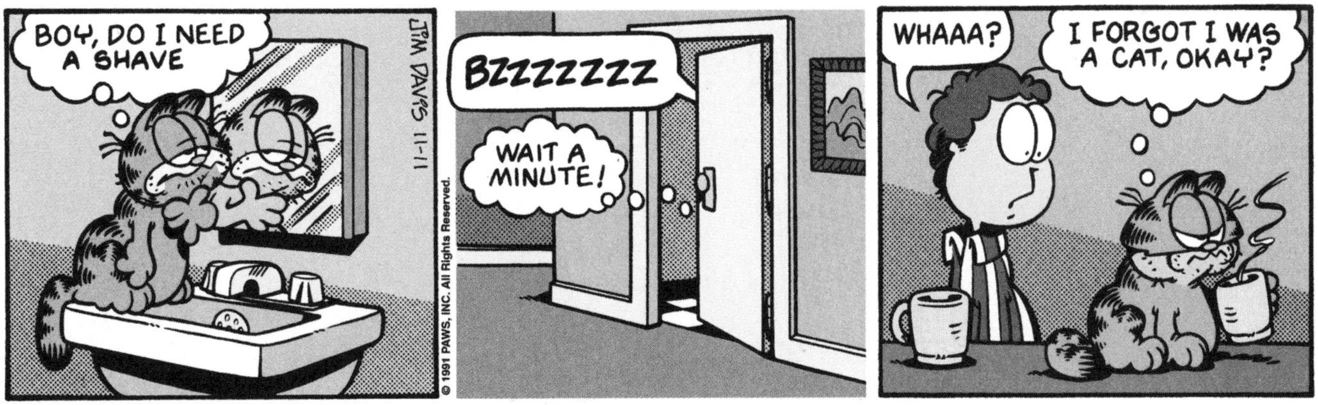
BOY, DO I NEED A SHAVE
JIM DAVIS 11-11
© 1991 PAWS, INC. All Rights Reserved.
BZZZZZZZ
WAIT A MINUTE!
WHAAA?
I FORGOT I WAS A CAT, OKAY?

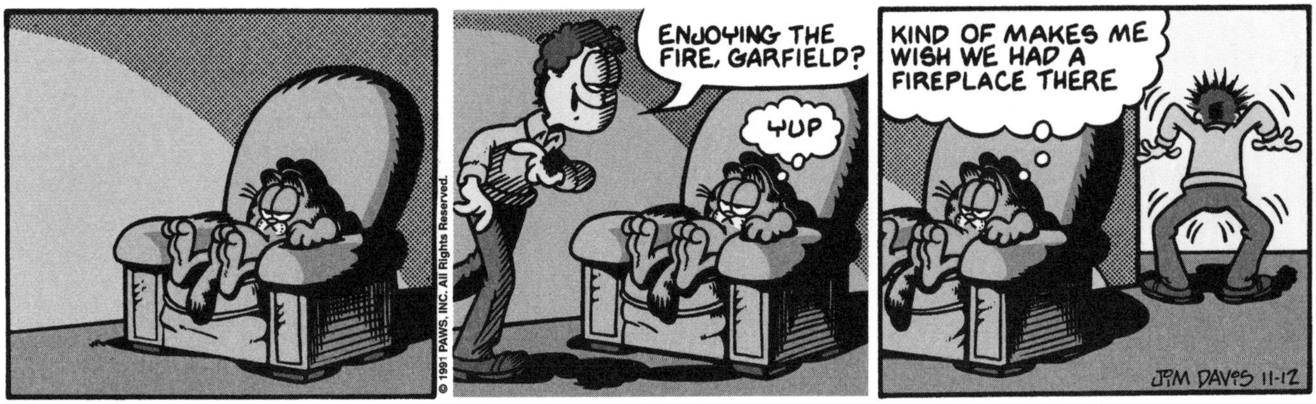
© 1991 PAWS, INC. All Rights Reserved.
ENJOYING THE FIRE, GARFIELD?
YUP
KIND OF MAKES ME WISH WE HAD A FIREPLACE THERE
JIM DAVIS 11-12

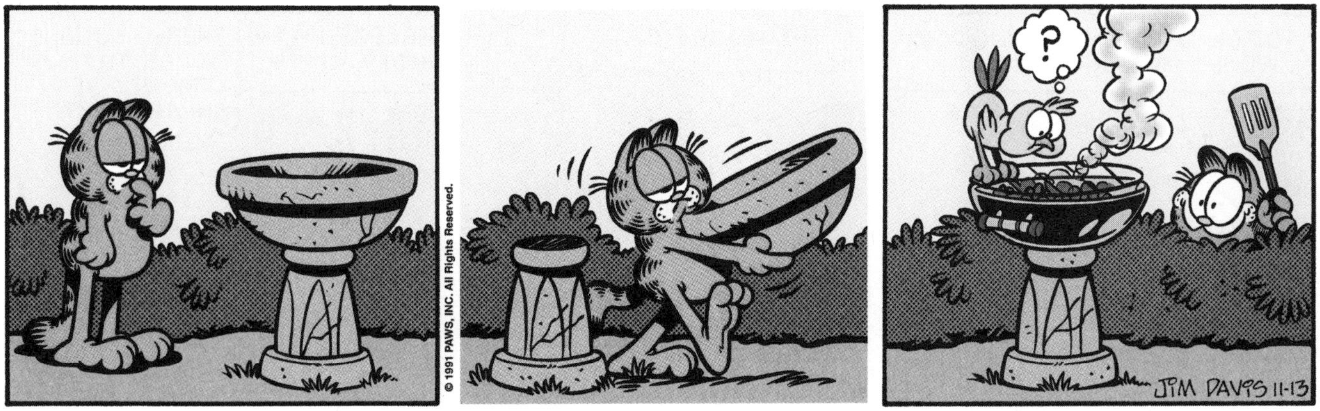
© 1991 PAWS, INC. All Rights Reserved.
?
JIM DAVIS 11-13

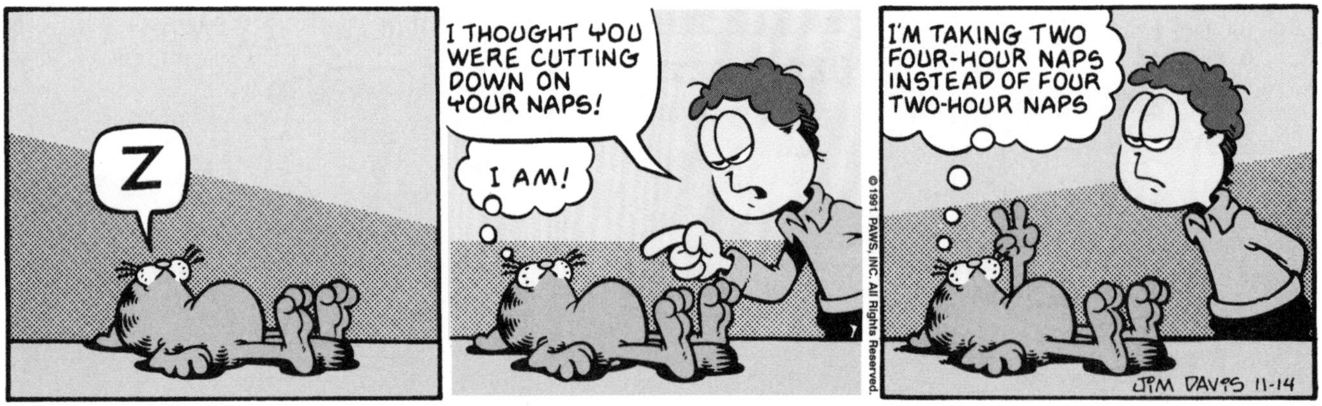
Z
I THOUGHT YOU WERE CUTTING DOWN ON YOUR NAPS!
I AM!
© 1991 PAWS, INC. All Rights Reserved.
I'M TAKING TWO FOUR-HOUR NAPS INSTEAD OF FOUR TWO-HOUR NAPS
JIM DAVIS 11-14

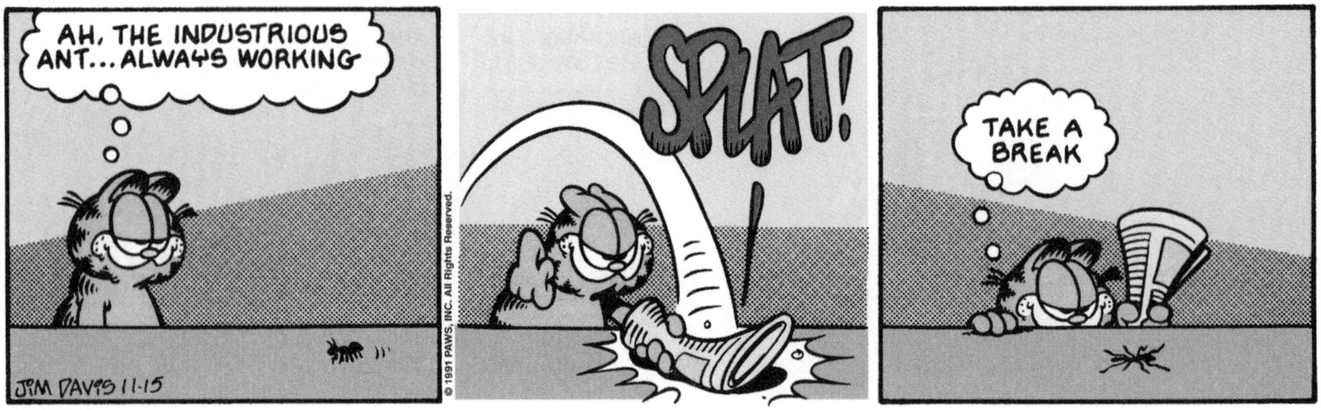
AH, THE INDUSTRIOUS ANT... ALWAYS WORKING
JIM DAVIS 11-15
© 1991 PAWS, INC. All Rights Reserved.
SPLAT!
TAKE A BREAK

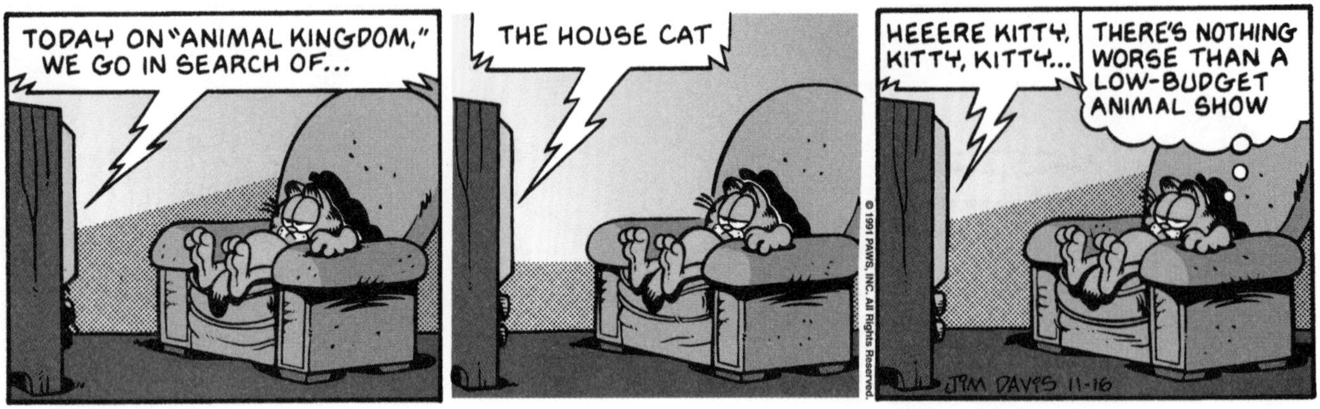
TODAY ON "ANIMAL KINGDOM," WE GO IN SEARCH OF...
THE HOUSE CAT
© 1991 PAWS, INC. All Rights Reserved.
HEEERE KITTY, KITTY, KITTY...
THERE'S NOTHING WORSE THAN A LOW-BUDGET ANIMAL SHOW
JIM DAVIS 11-16

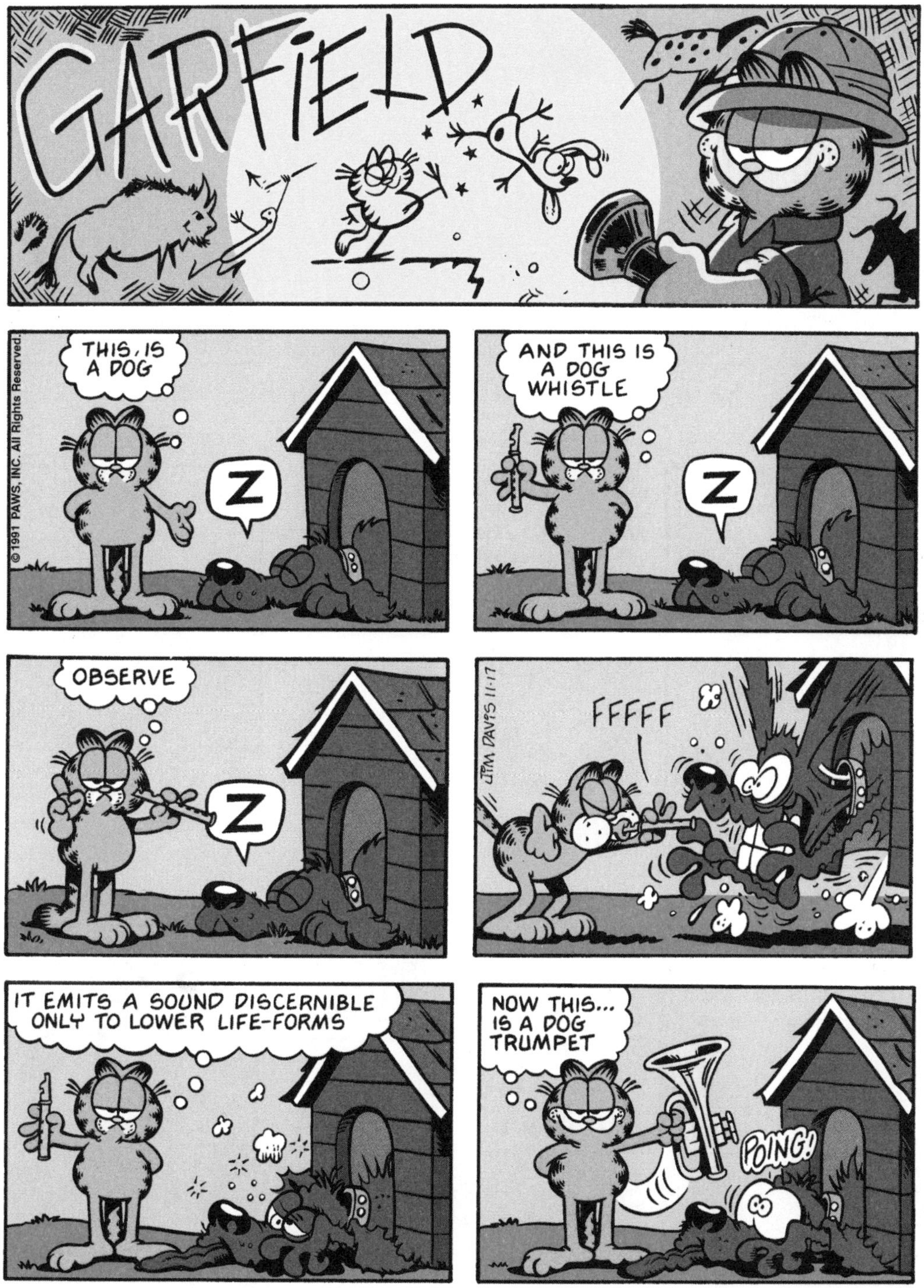
GARFIELD
© 1991 PAWS, INC. All Rights Reserved.
THIS, IS A DOG
Z
AND THIS IS A DOG WHISTLE
Z
OBSERVE
Z
JIM DAVIS 11-17
FFFFF
IT EMITS A SOUND DISCERNIBLE ONLY TO LOWER LIFE-FORMS
NOW THIS... IS A DOG TRUMPET
POING!

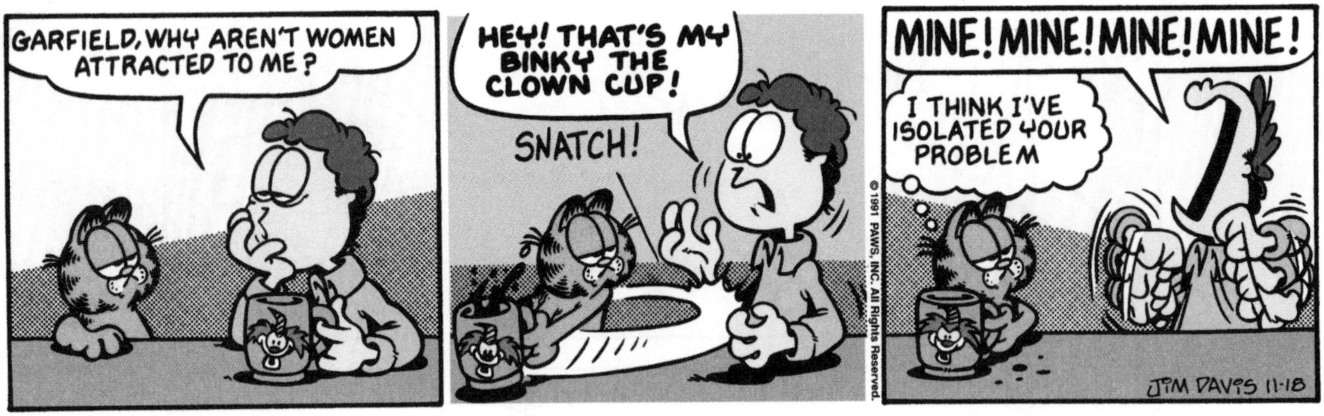
GARFIELD, WHY AREN'T WOMEN ATTRACTED TO ME?
HEY! THAT'S MY BINKY THE CLOWN CUP!
SNATCH!
© 1991 PAWS, INC. All Rights Reserved.
MINE! MINE! MINE! MINE!
I THINK I'VE ISOLATED YOUR PROBLEM
JIM DAVIS 11-18

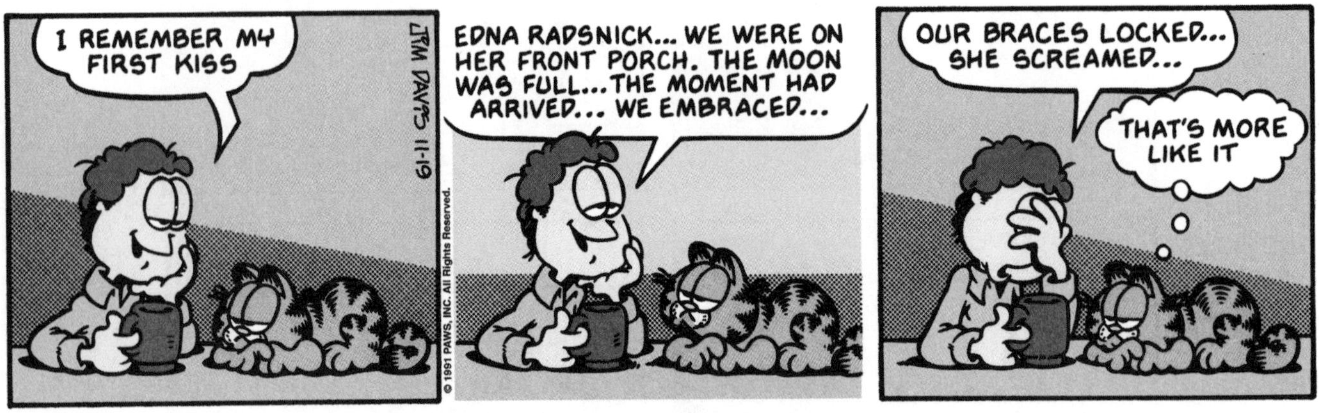
I REMEMBER MY FIRST KISS
JIM DAVIS 11-19
© 1991 PAWS, INC. All Rights Reserved.
EDNA RADSNICK... WE WERE ON HER FRONT PORCH. THE MOON WAS FULL... THE MOMENT HAD ARRIVED... WE EMBRACED...
OUR BRACES LOCKED... SHE SCREAMED...
THAT'S MORE LIKE IT

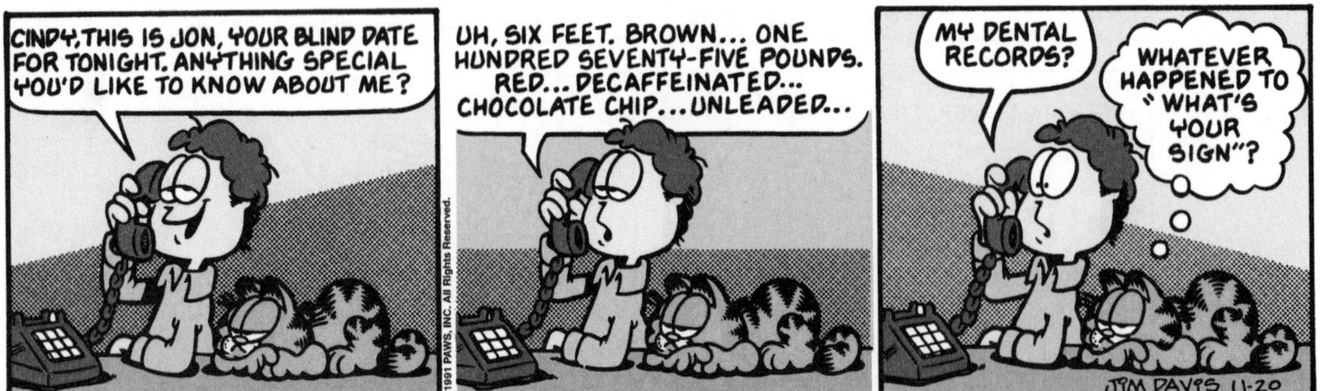
CINDY, THIS IS JON, YOUR BLIND DATE FOR TONIGHT. ANYTHING SPECIAL YOU'D LIKE TO KNOW ABOUT ME?
© 1991 PAWS, INC. All Rights Reserved.
UH, SIX FEET. BROWN... ONE HUNDRED SEVENTY-FIVE POUNDS. RED... DECAFFEINATED... CHOCOLATE CHIP... UNLEADED...
MY DENTAL RECORDS?
WHATEVER HAPPENED TO "WHAT'S YOUR SIGN"?
JIM DAVIS 11-20

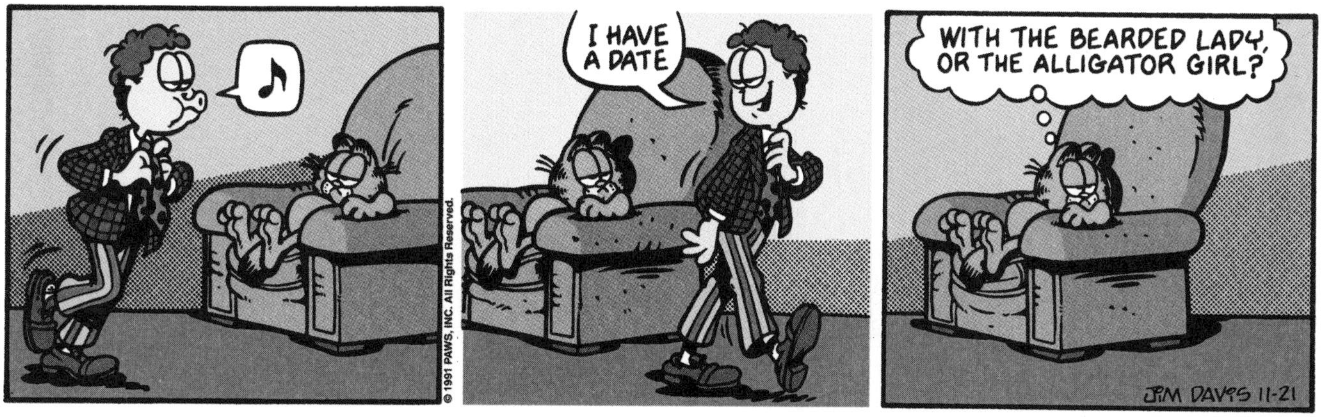
♪
© 1991 PAWS, INC. All Rights Reserved.
I HAVE A DATE
WITH THE BEARDED LADY, OR THE ALLIGATOR GIRL?
JIM DAVIS 11-21

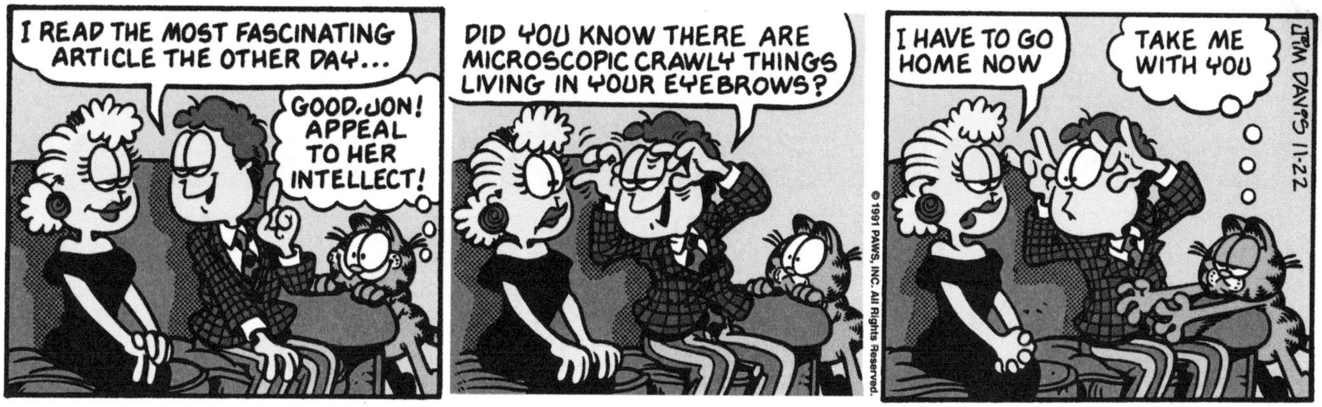
I READ THE MOST FASCINATING ARTICLE THE OTHER DAY...
GOOD, JON! APPEAL TO HER INTELLECT!
DID YOU KNOW THERE ARE MICROSCOPIC CRAWLY THINGS LIVING IN YOUR EYEBROWS?
© 1991 PAWS, INC. All Rights Reserved.
I HAVE TO GO HOME NOW
TAKE ME WITH YOU
JIM DAVIS 11-22

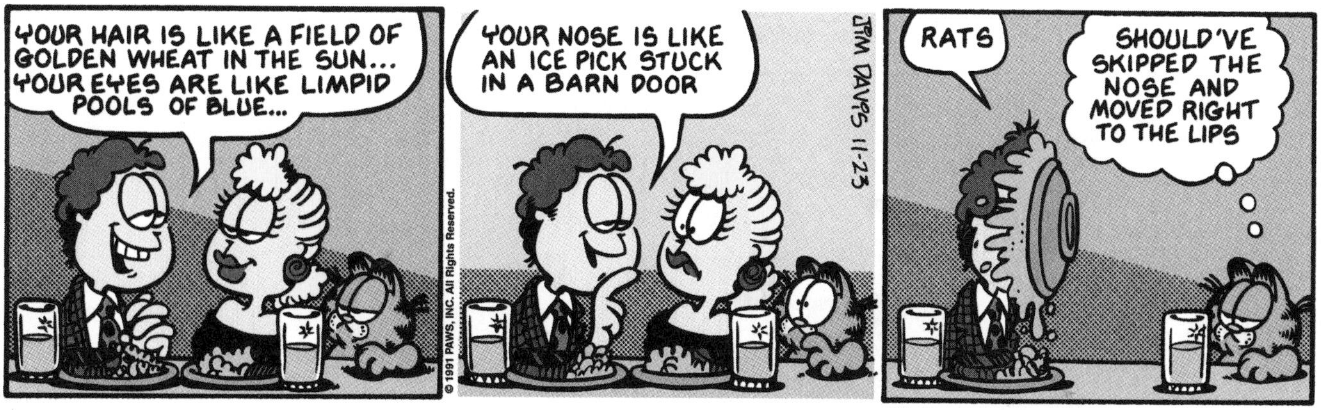
YOUR HAIR IS LIKE A FIELD OF GOLDEN WHEAT IN THE SUN... YOUR EYES ARE LIKE LIMPID POOLS OF BLUE...
© 1991 PAWS, INC. All Rights Reserved.
YOUR NOSE IS LIKE AN ICE PICK STUCK IN A BARN DOOR
JIM DAVIS 11-23
RATS
SHOULD'VE SKIPPED THE NOSE AND MOVED RIGHT TO THE LIPS

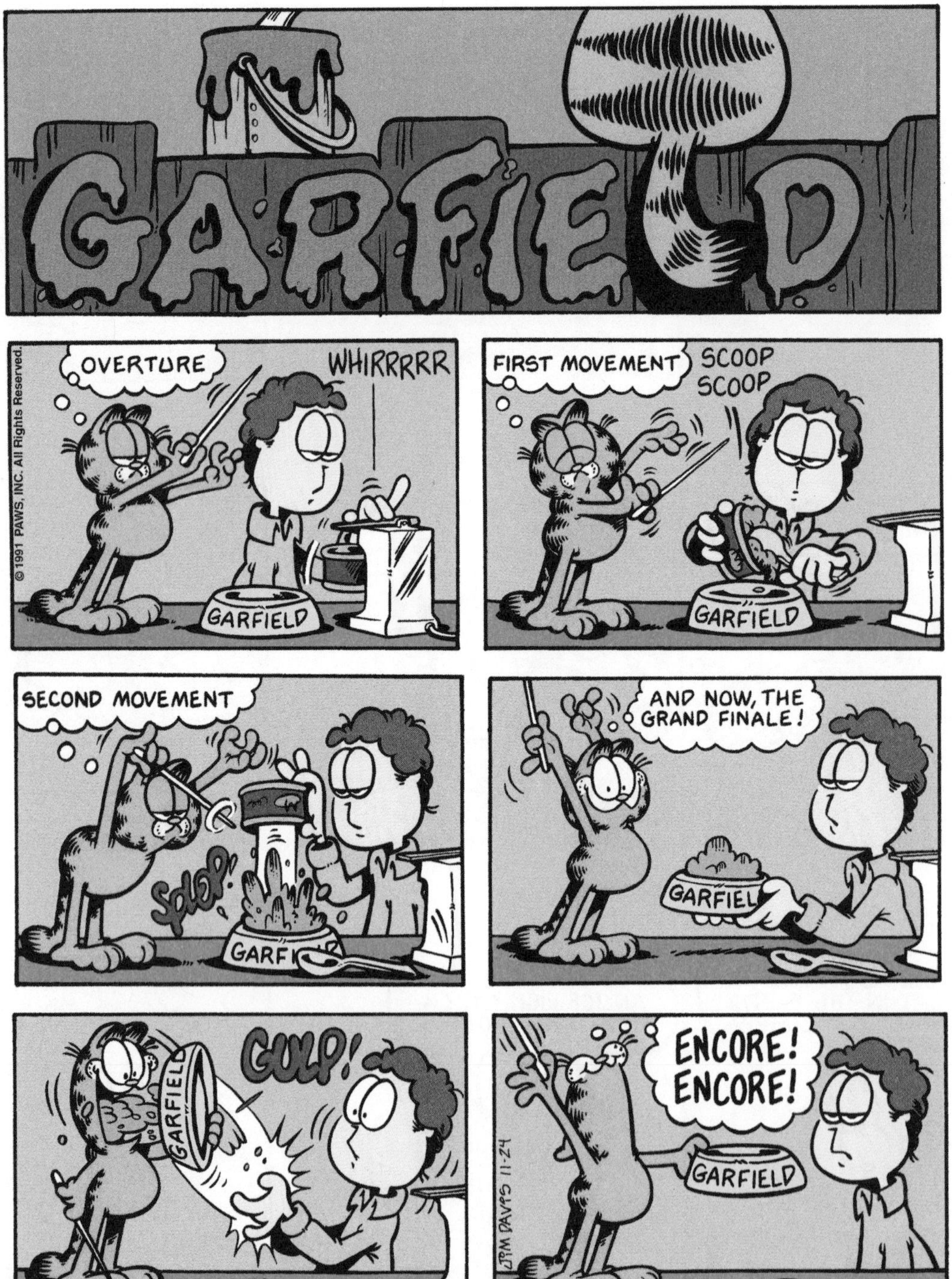
GARFIELD
© 1991 PAWS, INC. All Rights Reserved.
OVERTURE
WHIRRRRR
GARFIELD
FIRST MOVEMENT
SCOOP
SCOOP
GARFIELD
SECOND MOVEMENT
SPLOP!
AND NOW, THE GRAND FINALE!
GULP!
ENCORE! ENCORE!
JPM DAVIS 11-24
GARFIELD

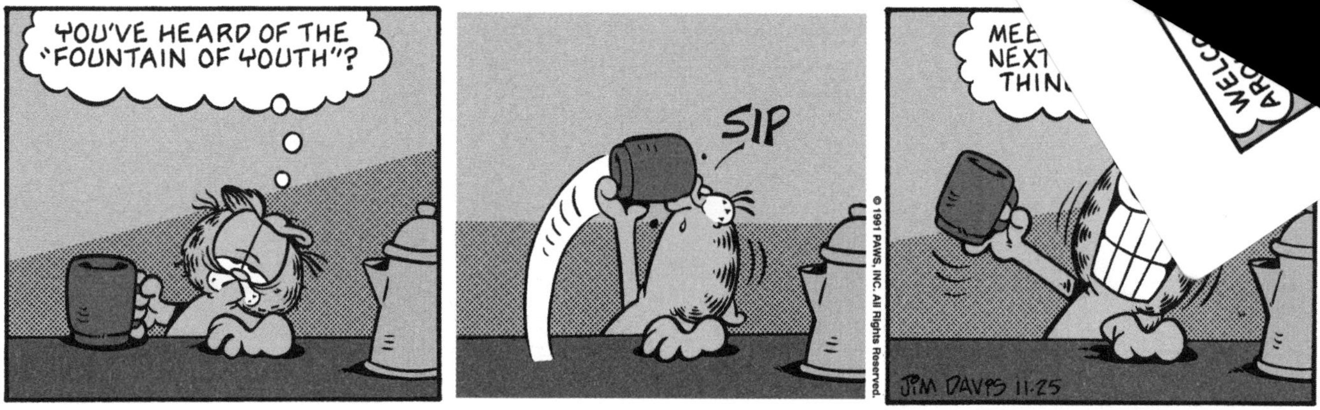
YOU'VE HEARD OF THE "FOUNTAIN OF YOUTH"?
SIP
© 1991 PAWS, INC. All Rights Reserved.
JIM DAVIS 11-25

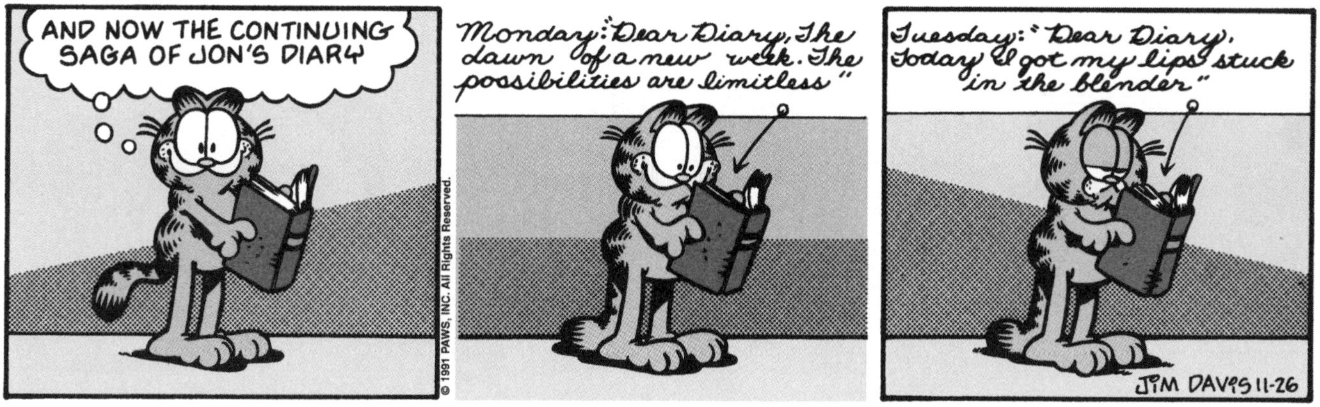
AND NOW THE CONTINUING SAGA OF JON'S DIARY
© 1991 PAWS, INC. All Rights Reserved.
Monday: "Dear Diary, The dawn of a new week. The possibilities are limitless"
Tuesday: "Dear Diary, Today I got my lips stuck in the blender"
JIM DAVIS 11-26

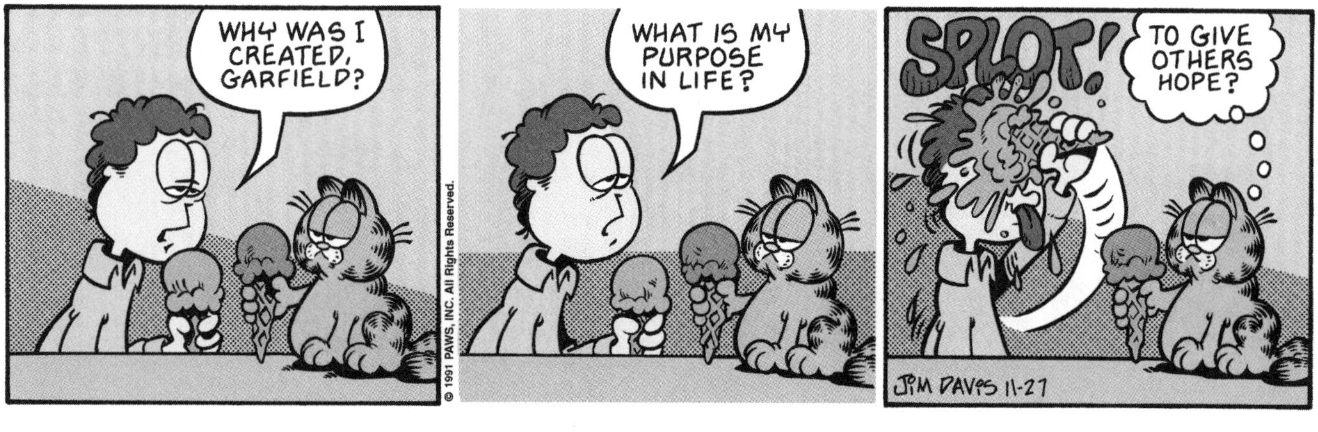
WHY WAS I CREATED, GARFIELD?
© 1991 PAWS, INC. All Rights Reserved.
WHAT IS MY PURPOSE IN LIFE?
SPLOT!
TO GIVE OTHERS HOPE?
JIM DAVIS 11-27

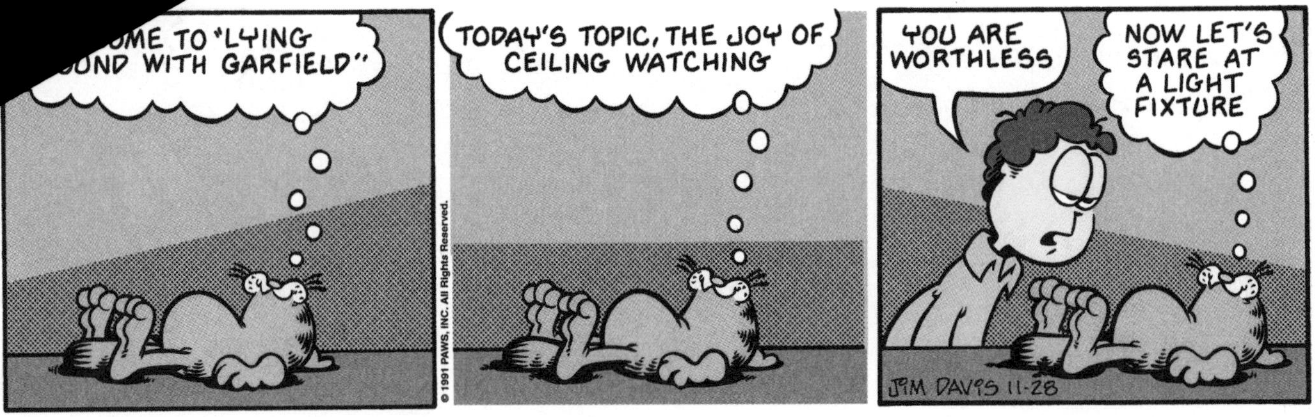

OME TO "LYING
OUND WITH GARFIELD"
© 1991 PAWS, INC. All Rights Reserved.
TODAY'S TOPIC, THE JOY OF CEILING WATCHING
YOU ARE WORTHLESS
NOW LET'S STARE AT A LIGHT FIXTURE
JIM DAVIS 11-28

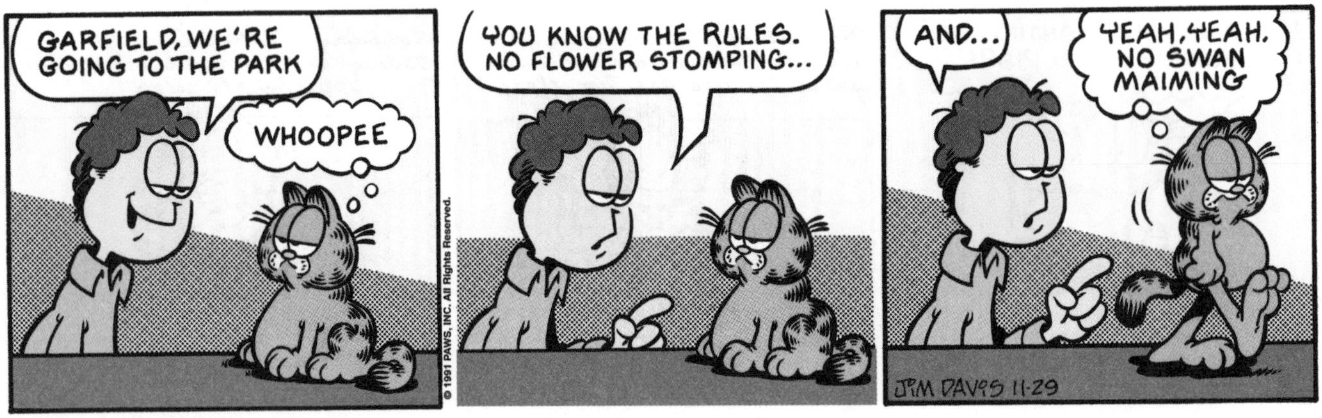

GARFIELD, WE'RE GOING TO THE PARK
WHOOPEE
© 1991 PAWS, INC. All Rights Reserved.
YOU KNOW THE RULES. NO FLOWER STOMPING...
AND...
YEAH, YEAH. NO SWAN MAIMING
JIM DAVIS 11-29

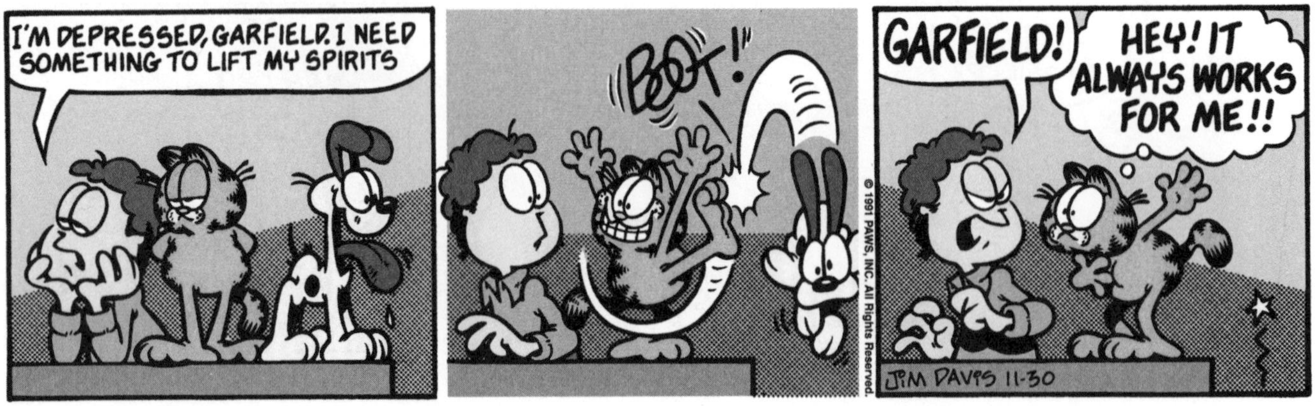

I'M DEPRESSED, GARFIELD. I NEED SOMETHING TO LIFT MY SPIRITS
BOOT!
© 1991 PAWS, INC. All Rights Reserved.
GARFIELD!
HEY! IT ALWAYS WORKS FOR ME!!
JIM DAVIS 11-30

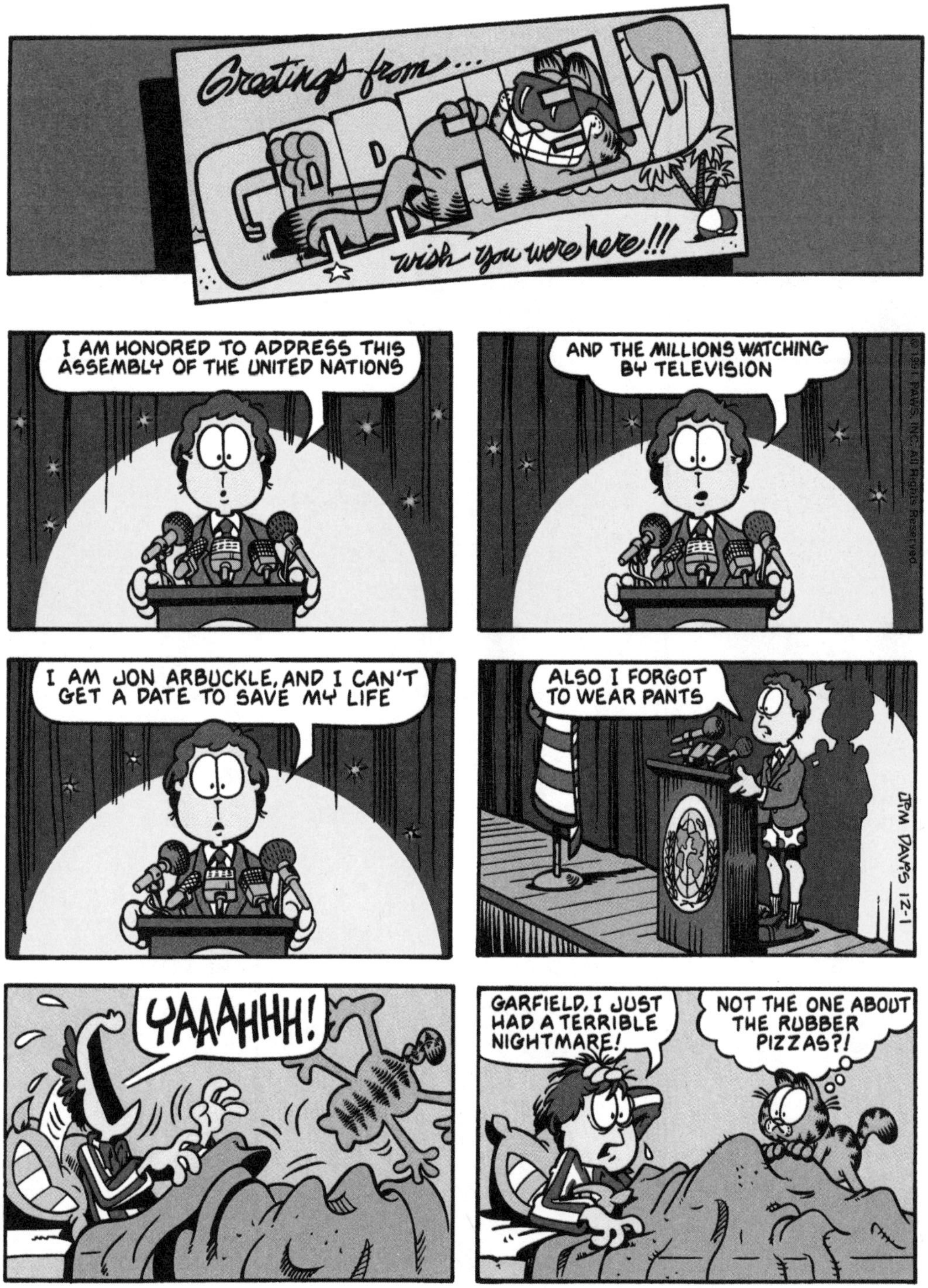
Greetings from...
GARFIELD
wish you were here!!!
I AM HONORED TO ADDRESS THIS ASSEMBLY OF THE UNITED NATIONS
AND THE MILLIONS WATCHING BY TELEVISION
© 1981 PAWS, INC. All Rights Reserved.
I AM JON ARBUCKLE, AND I CAN'T GET A DATE TO SAVE MY LIFE
ALSO I FORGOT TO WEAR PANTS
JIM DAVIS 12-1
YAAAHHH!
GARFIELD, I JUST HAD A TERRIBLE NIGHTMARE!
NOT THE ONE ABOUT THE RUBBER PIZZAS?!

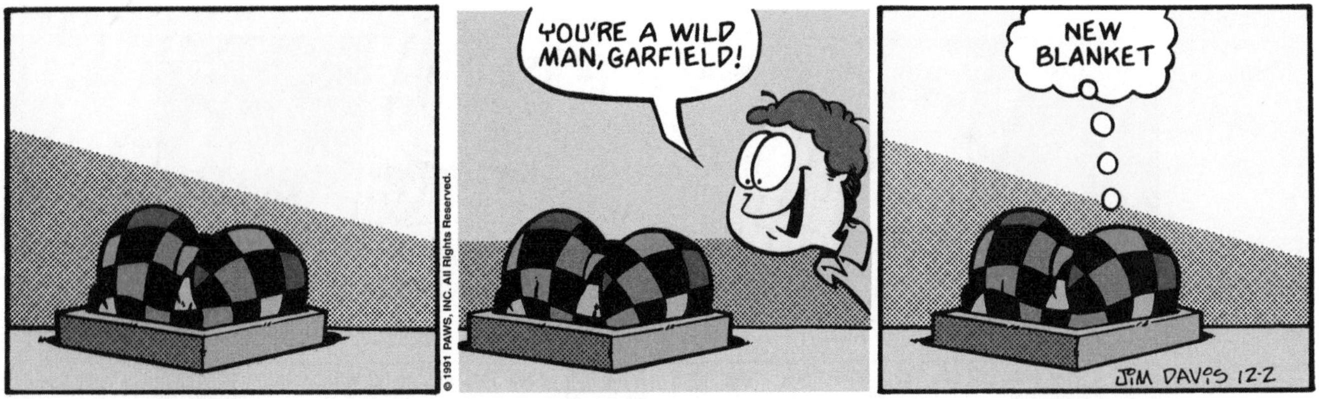
© 1991 PAWS, INC. All Rights Reserved.
YOU'RE A WILD MAN, GARFIELD!
NEW BLANKET
JIM DAVIS 12-2

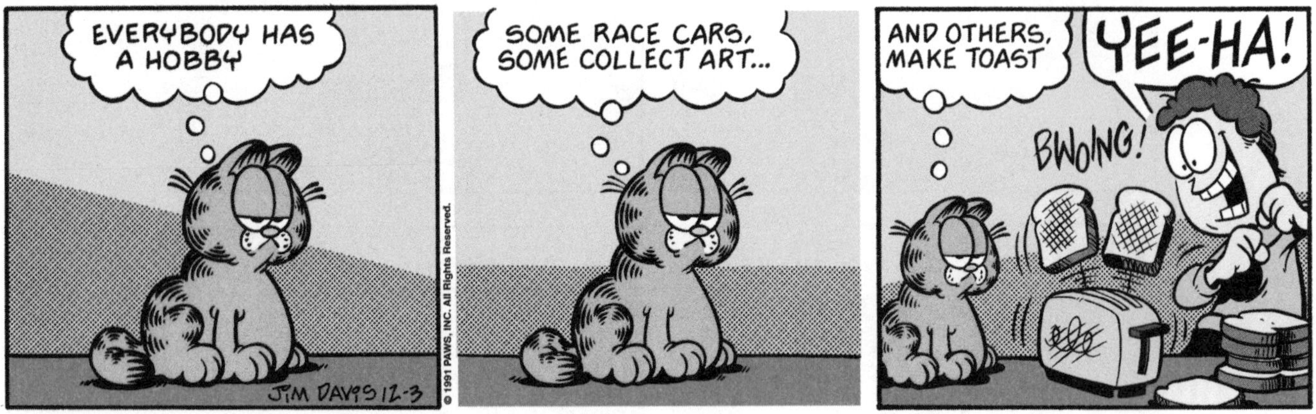
EVERYBODY HAS A HOBBY
JIM DAVIS 12-3
© 1991 PAWS, INC. All Rights Reserved.
SOME RACE CARS, SOME COLLECT ART...
AND OTHERS, MAKE TOAST
YEE-HA!
BWOING!

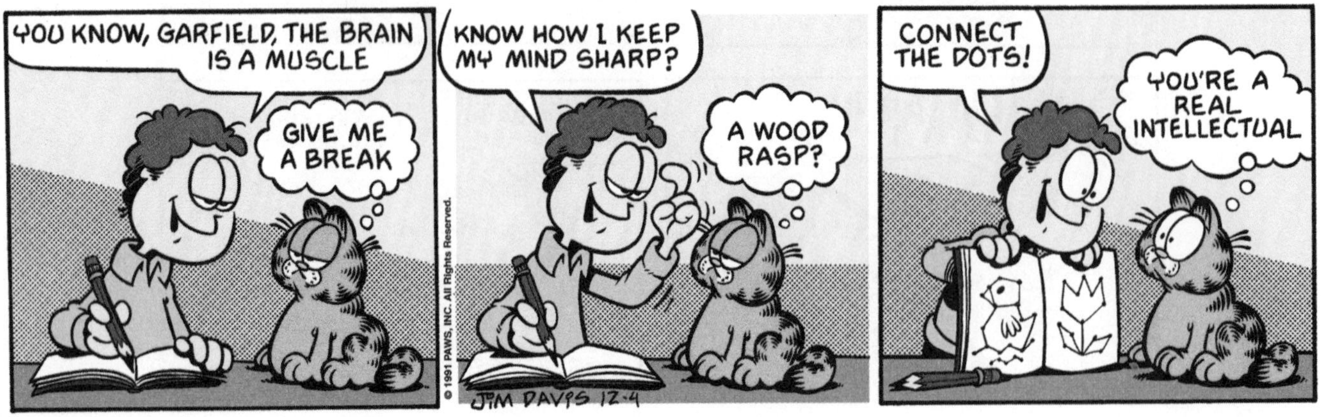
YOU KNOW, GARFIELD, THE BRAIN IS A MUSCLE
GIVE ME A BREAK
© 1991 PAWS, INC. All Rights Reserved.
KNOW HOW I KEEP MY MIND SHARP?
A WOOD RASP?
JIM DAVIS 12-4
CONNECT THE DOTS!
YOU'RE A REAL INTELLECTUAL

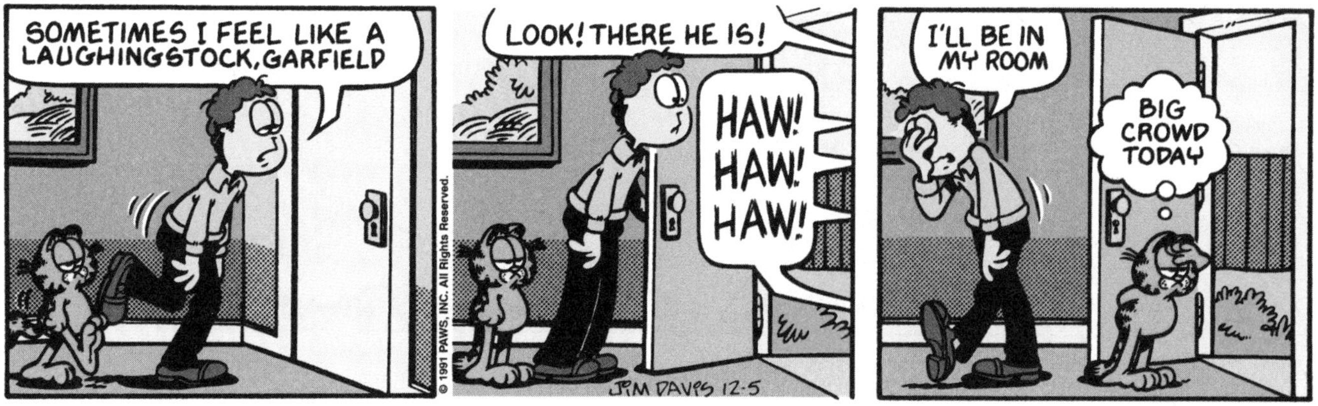
SOMETIMES I FEEL LIKE A LAUGHINGSTOCK, GARFIELD
LOOK! THERE HE IS!
HAW! HAW! HAW!
I'LL BE IN MY ROOM
BIG CROWD TODAY
© 1991 PAWS, INC. All Rights Reserved.
JIM DAVIS 12-5

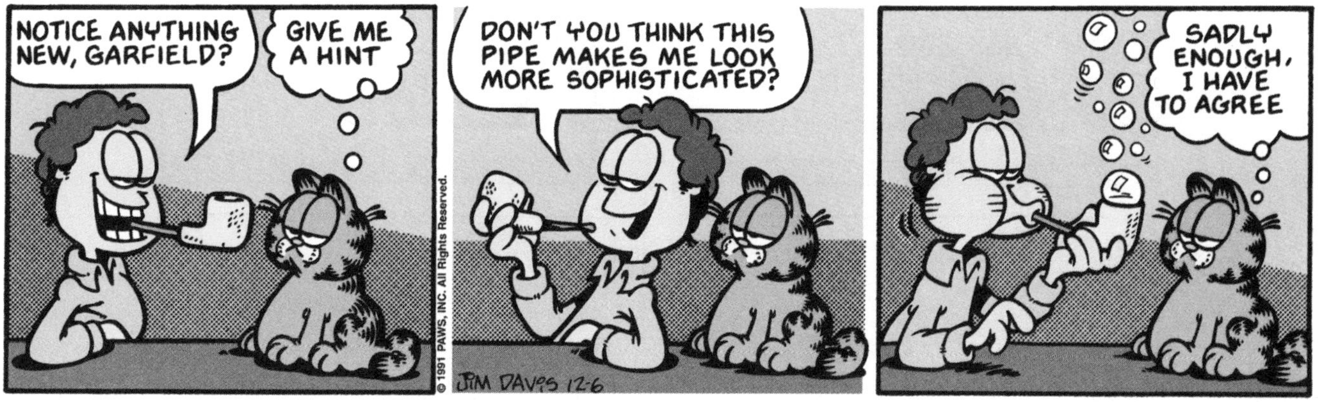
NOTICE ANYTHING NEW, GARFIELD?
GIVE ME A HINT
DON'T YOU THINK THIS PIPE MAKES ME LOOK MORE SOPHISTICATED?
SADLY ENOUGH, I HAVE TO AGREE
© 1991 PAWS, INC. All Rights Reserved.
JIM DAVIS 12-6

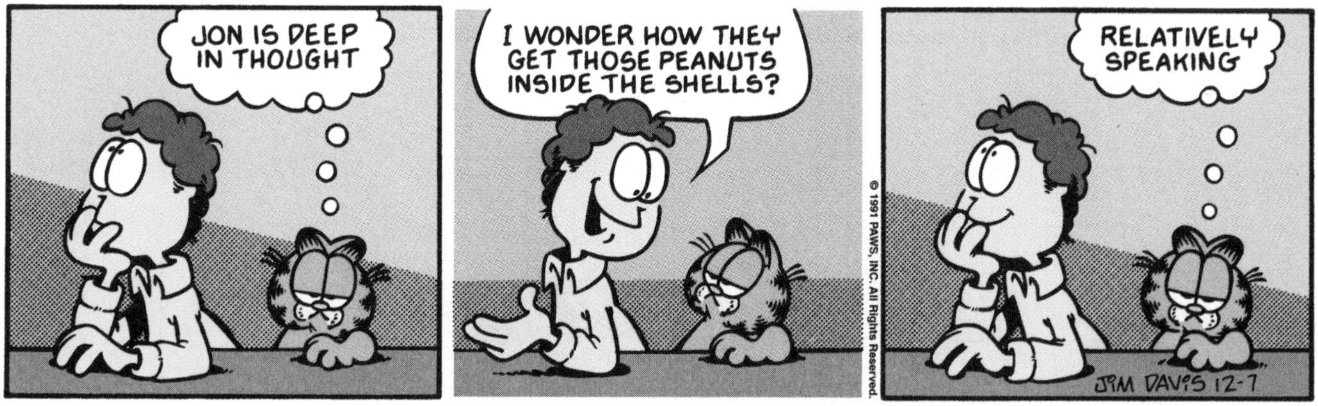
JON IS DEEP IN THOUGHT
I WONDER HOW THEY GET THOSE PEANUTS INSIDE THE SHELLS?
RELATIVELY SPEAKING
© 1991 PAWS, INC. All Rights Reserved.
JIM DAVIS 12-7

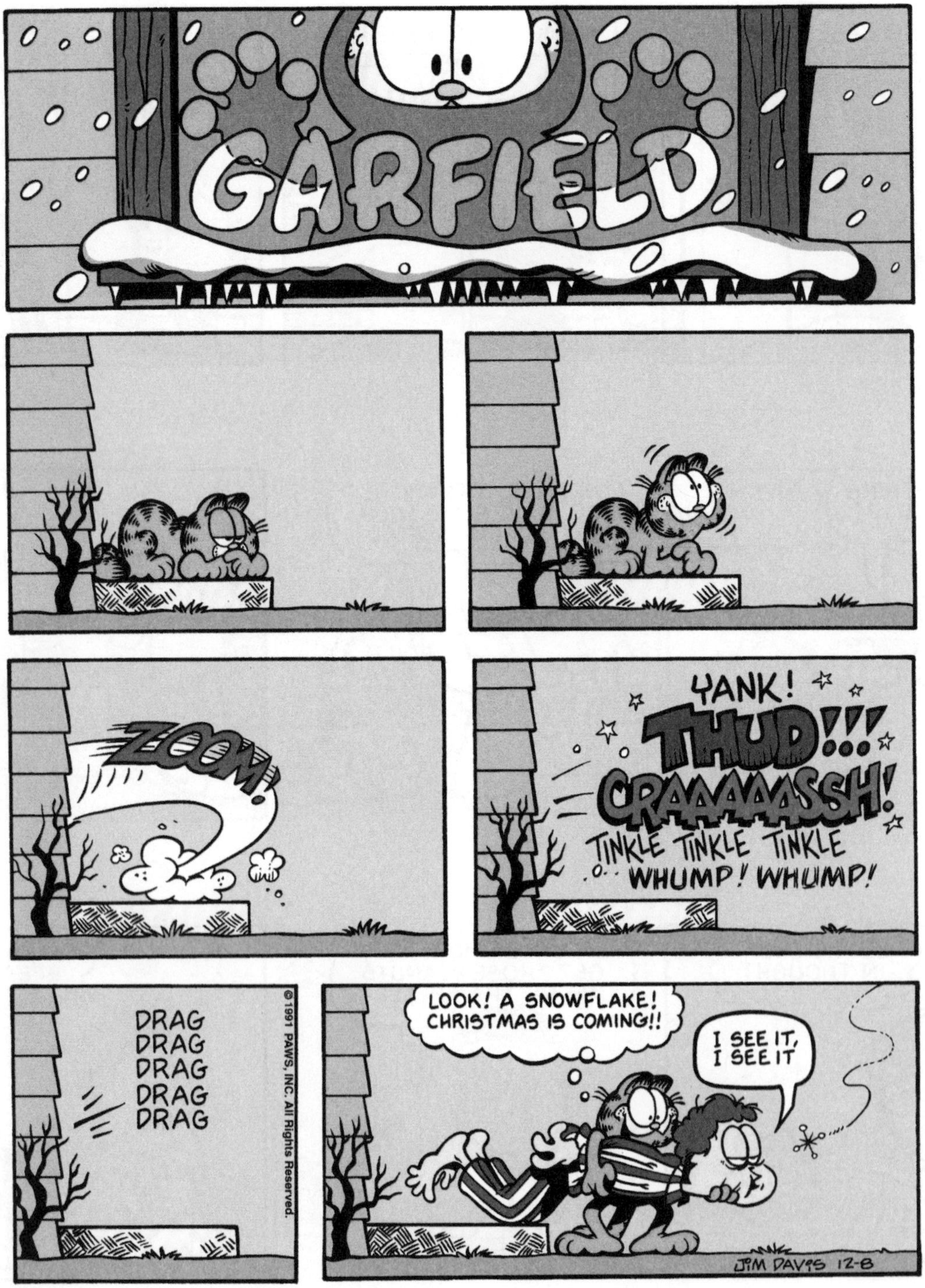
GARFIELD
ZOOM!
YANK!
THUD!!!
CRAAAAASSH!
TINKLE TINKLE TINKLE
WHUMP! WHUMP!
DRAG
DRAG
DRAG
DRAG
DRAG
© 1991 PAWS, INC. All Rights Reserved.
LOOK! A SNOWFLAKE! CHRISTMAS IS COMING!!
I SEE IT, I SEE IT
JIM DAVIS 12-8

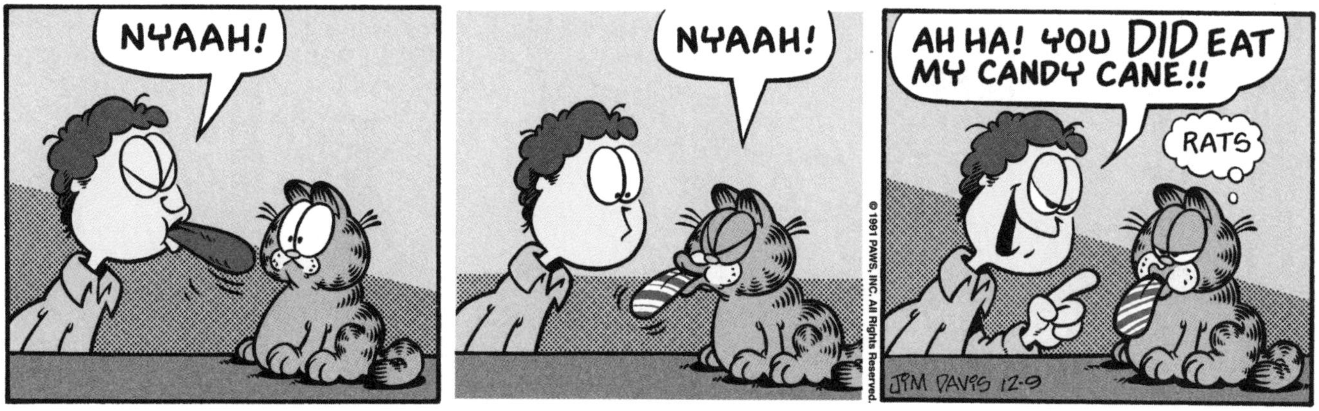
NYAAH!
NYAAH!
AH HA! YOU DID EAT MY CANDY CANE!!
RATS
JIM DAVIS 12-9
© 1991 PAWS, INC. All Rights Reserved.

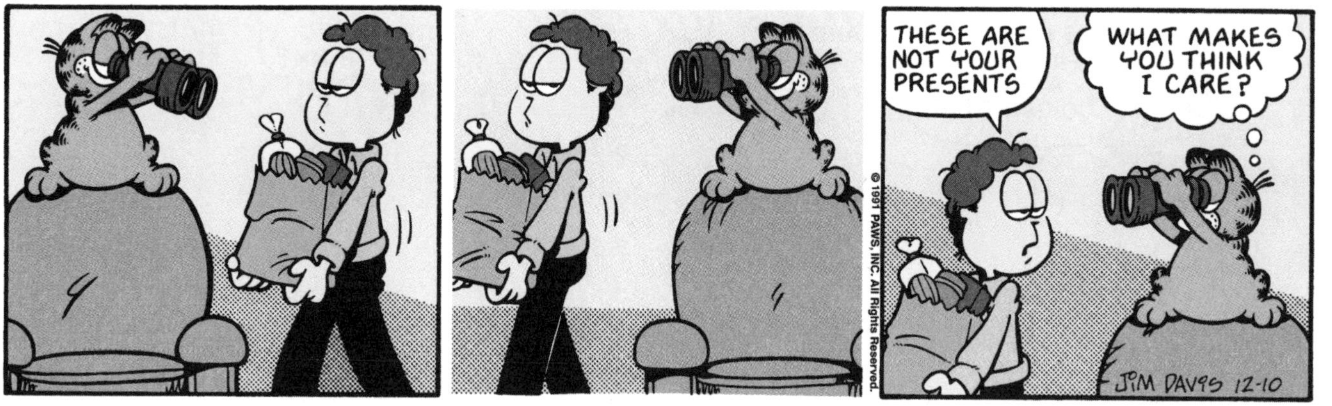
THESE ARE NOT YOUR PRESENTS
WHAT MAKES YOU THINK I CARE?
JIM DAVIS 12-10
© 1991 PAWS, INC. All Rights Reserved.

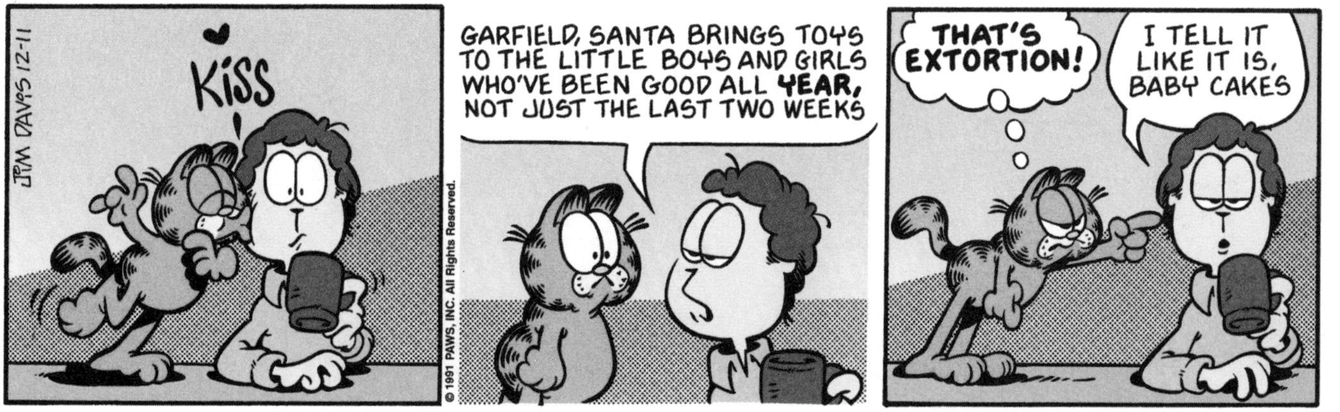
JIM DAVIS 12-11
KISS
GARFIELD, SANTA BRINGS TOYS TO THE LITTLE BOYS AND GIRLS WHO'VE BEEN GOOD ALL YEAR, NOT JUST THE LAST TWO WEEKS
THAT'S EXTORTION!
I TELL IT LIKE IT IS, BABY CAKES
© 1991 PAWS, INC. All Rights Reserved.

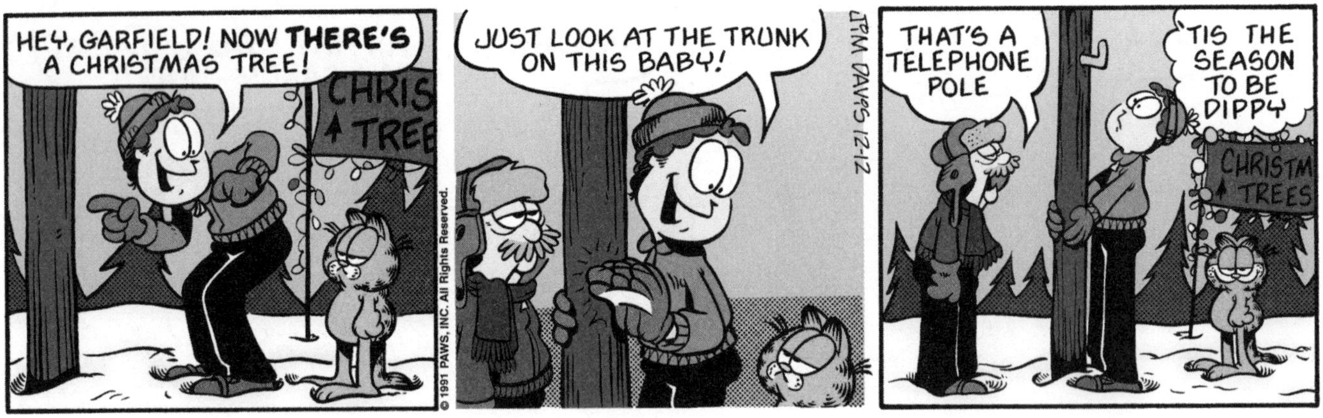
HEY, GARFIELD! NOW **THERE'S** A CHRISTMAS TREE!
CHRIS TREE
© 1991 PAWS, INC. All Rights Reserved.
JUST LOOK AT THE TRUNK ON THIS BABY!
JIM DAVIS 12-12
THAT'S A TELEPHONE POLE
'TIS THE SEASON TO BE DIPPY
CHRISTM TREES

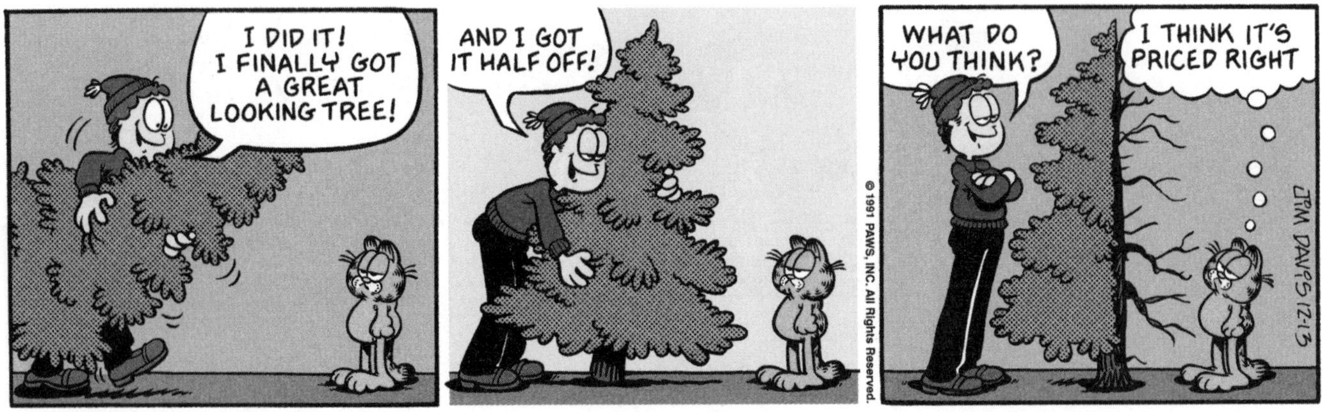
I DID IT! I FINALLY GOT A GREAT LOOKING TREE!
AND I GOT IT HALF OFF!
© 1991 PAWS, INC. All Rights Reserved.
WHAT DO YOU THINK?
I THINK IT'S PRICED RIGHT
JIM DAVIS 12-13

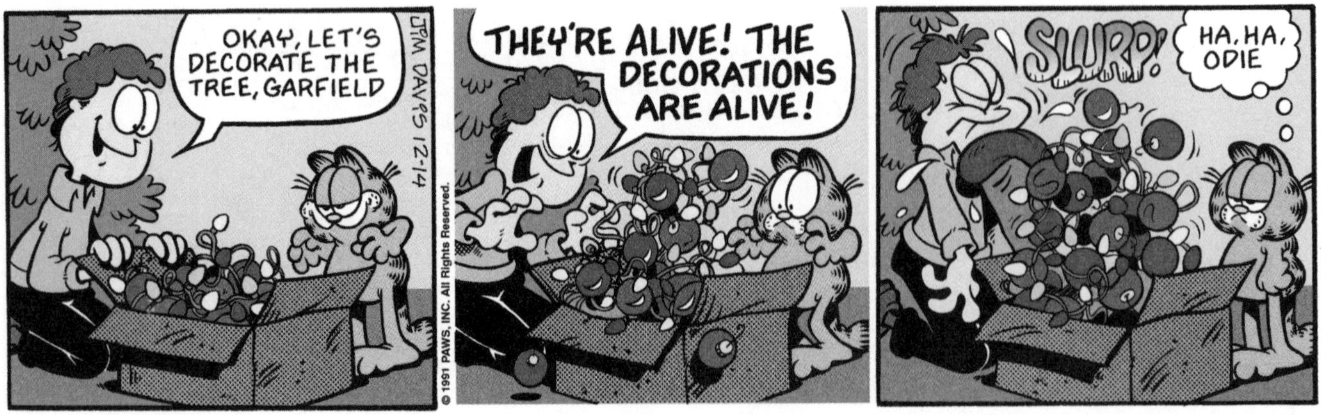
OKAY, LET'S DECORATE THE TREE, GARFIELD
JIM DAVIS 12-14
© 1991 PAWS, INC. All Rights Reserved.
THEY'RE ALIVE! THE DECORATIONS ARE ALIVE!
SLURP!
HA, HA, ODIE

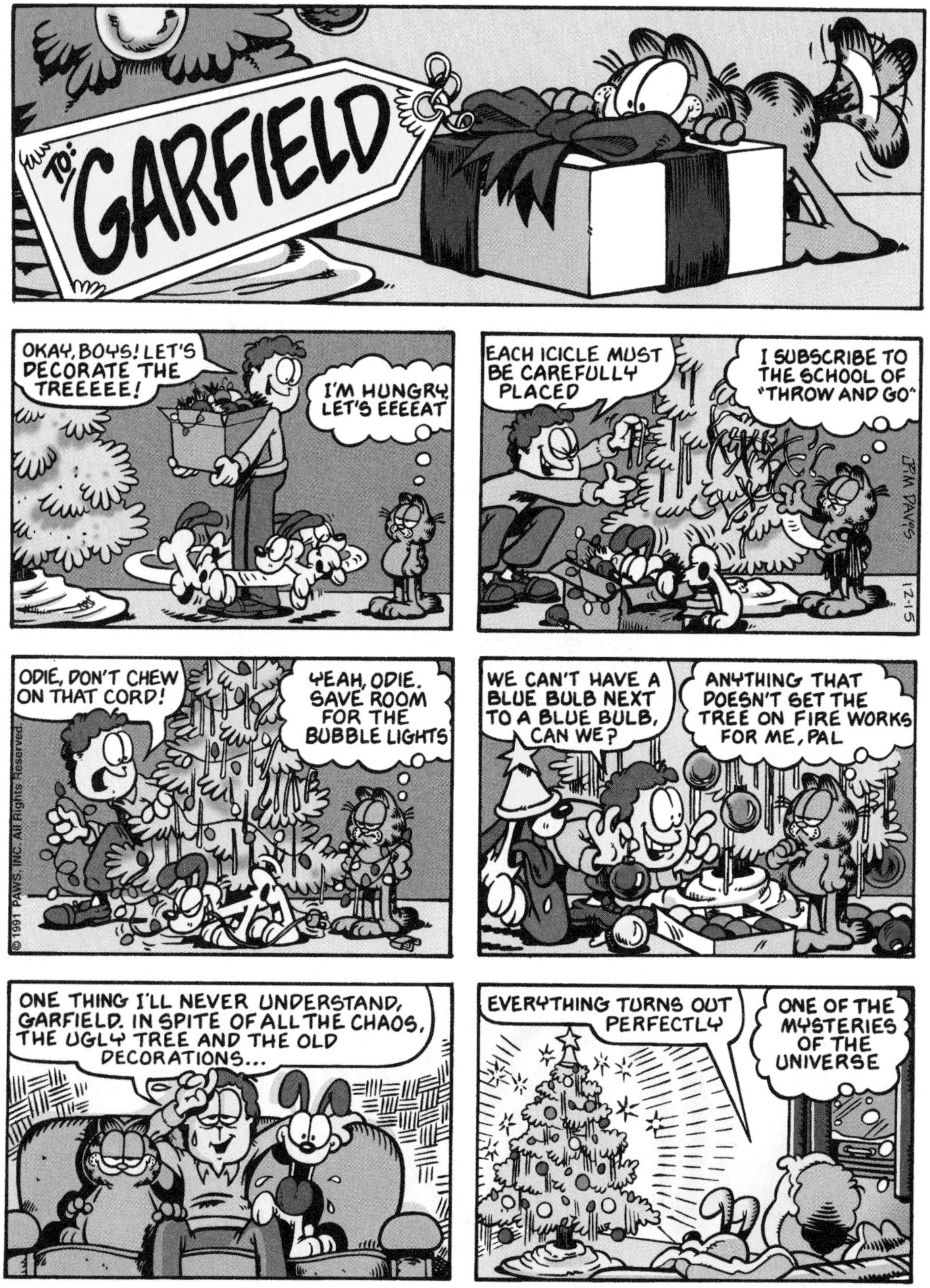

TO: GARFIELD
OKAY, BOYS! LET'S DECORATE THE TREEEEE!
I'M HUNGRY. LET'S EEEEAT
EACH ICICLE MUST BE CAREFULLY PLACED
I SUBSCRIBE TO THE SCHOOL OF "THROW AND GO"
JIM DAVIS
12-15
ODIE, DON'T CHEW ON THAT CORD!
YEAH, ODIE. SAVE ROOM FOR THE BUBBLE LIGHTS
WE CAN'T HAVE A BLUE BULB NEXT TO A BLUE BULB, CAN WE?
ANYTHING THAT DOESN'T SET THE TREE ON FIRE WORKS FOR ME, PAL
ONE THING I'LL NEVER UNDERSTAND, GARFIELD. IN SPITE OF ALL THE CHAOS, THE UGLY TREE AND THE OLD DECORATIONS...
EVERYTHING TURNS OUT PERFECTLY
ONE OF THE MYSTERIES OF THE UNIVERSE

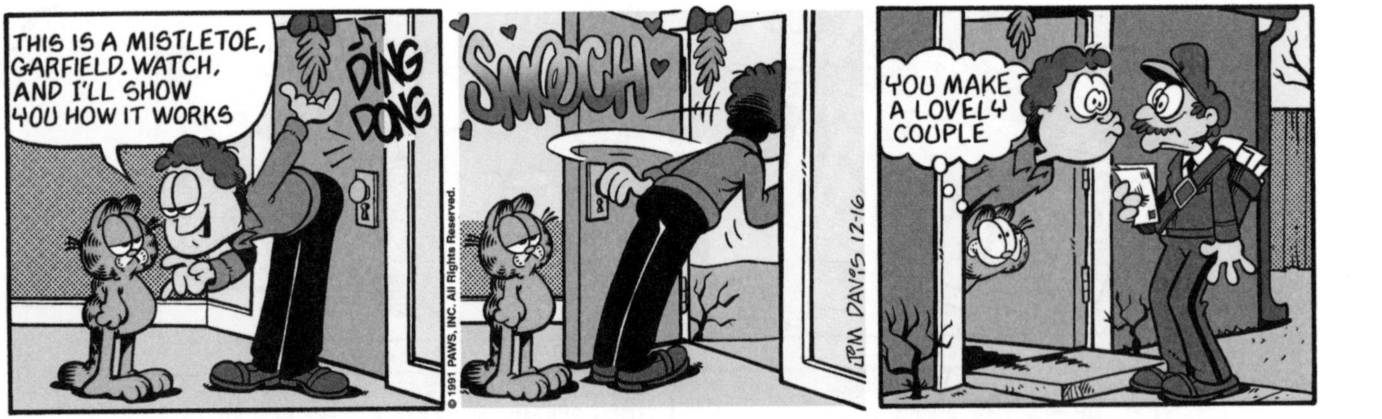
THIS IS A MISTLETOE, GARFIELD. WATCH, AND I'LL SHOW YOU HOW IT WORKS
DING DONG
© 1991 PAWS, INC. All Rights Reserved.
SMOOCH
JIM DAVIS 12-16
YOU MAKE A LOVELY COUPLE

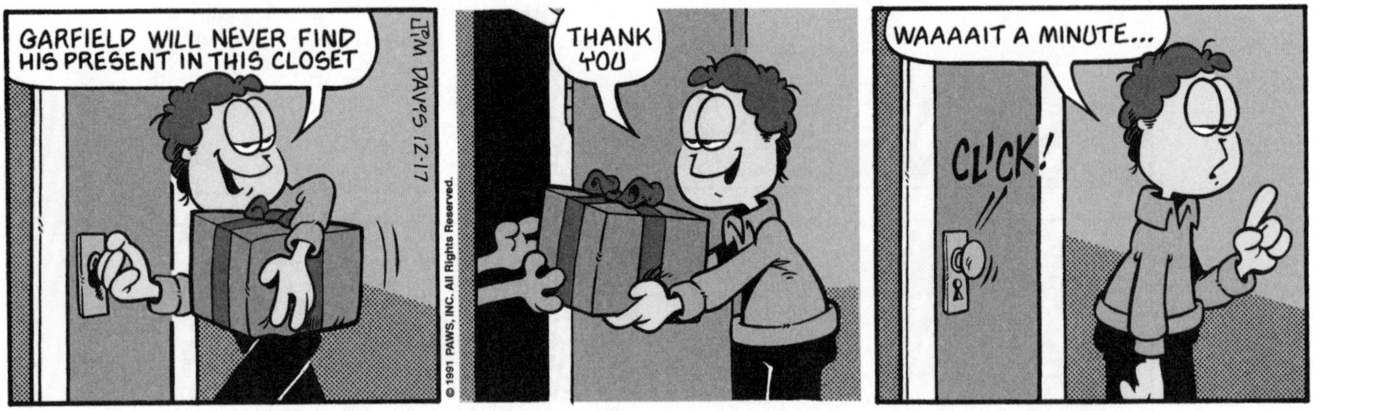
GARFIELD WILL NEVER FIND HIS PRESENT IN THIS CLOSET
JIM DAVIS 12-17
© 1991 PAWS, INC. All Rights Reserved.
THANK YOU
WAAAAIT A MINUTE...
CLICK!

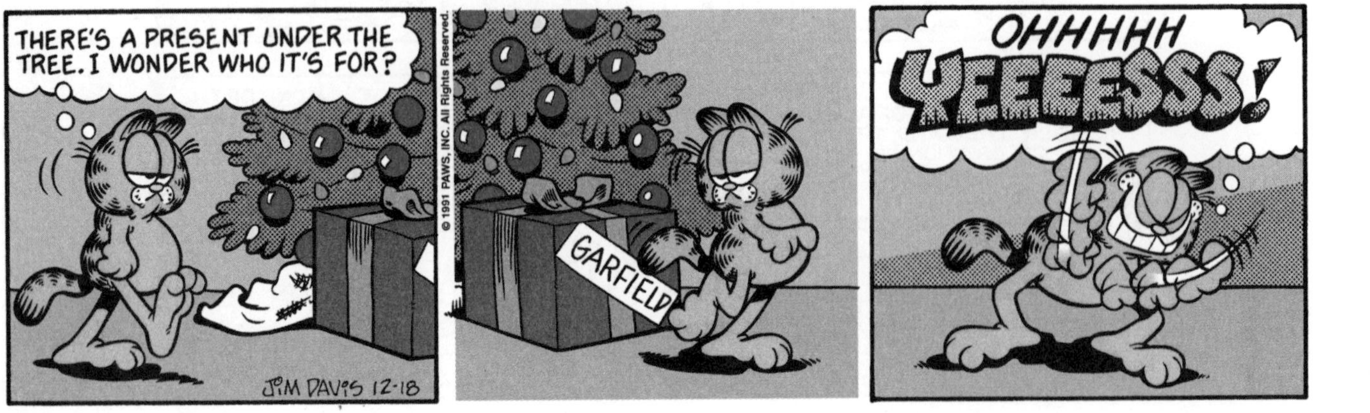
THERE'S A PRESENT UNDER THE TREE. I WONDER WHO IT'S FOR?
JIM DAVIS 12-18
© 1991 PAWS, INC. All Rights Reserved.
GARFIELD
OHHHHH YEEEESSS!

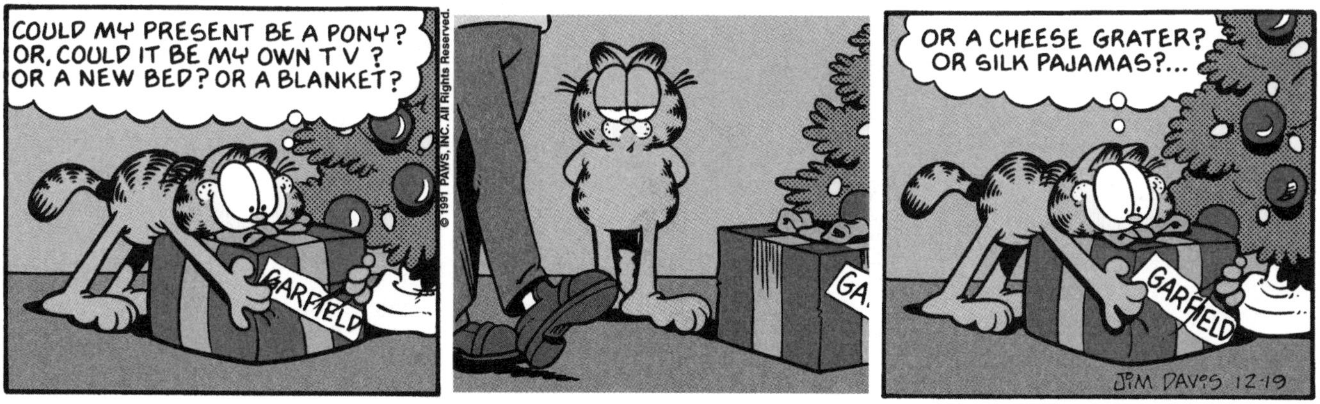
COULD MY PRESENT BE A PONY? OR, COULD IT BE MY OWN T V ? OR A NEW BED? OR A BLANKET?
GARFIELD
© 1991 PAWS, INC. All Rights Reserved.
OR A CHEESE GRATER? OR SILK PAJAMAS?...
GARFIELD
JIM DAVIS 12-19

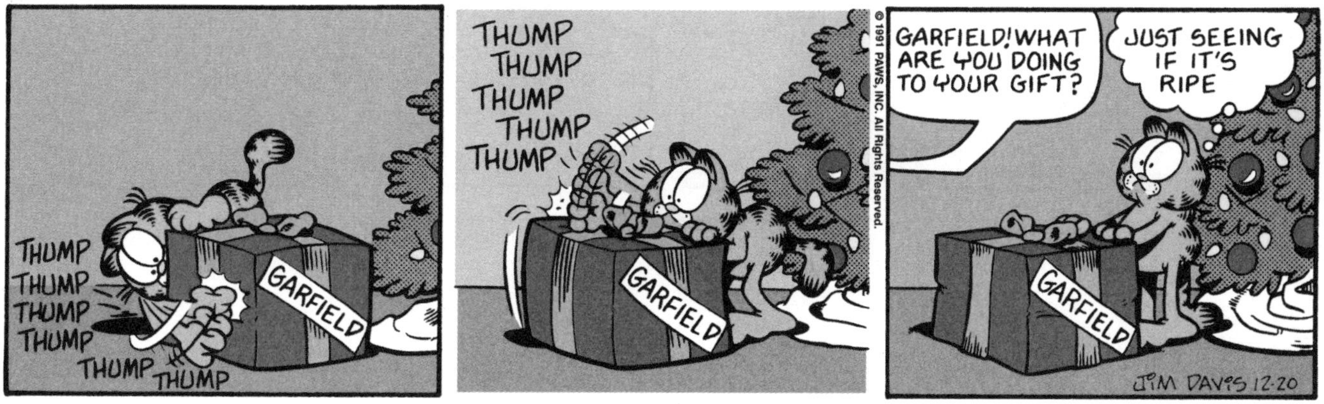
THUMP THUMP THUMP THUMP THUMP THUMP
GARFIELD
THUMP THUMP THUMP THUMP THUMP
GARFIELD
© 1991 PAWS, INC. All Rights Reserved.
GARFIELD! WHAT ARE YOU DOING TO YOUR GIFT?
JUST SEEING IF IT'S RIPE
GARFIELD
JIM DAVIS 12-20

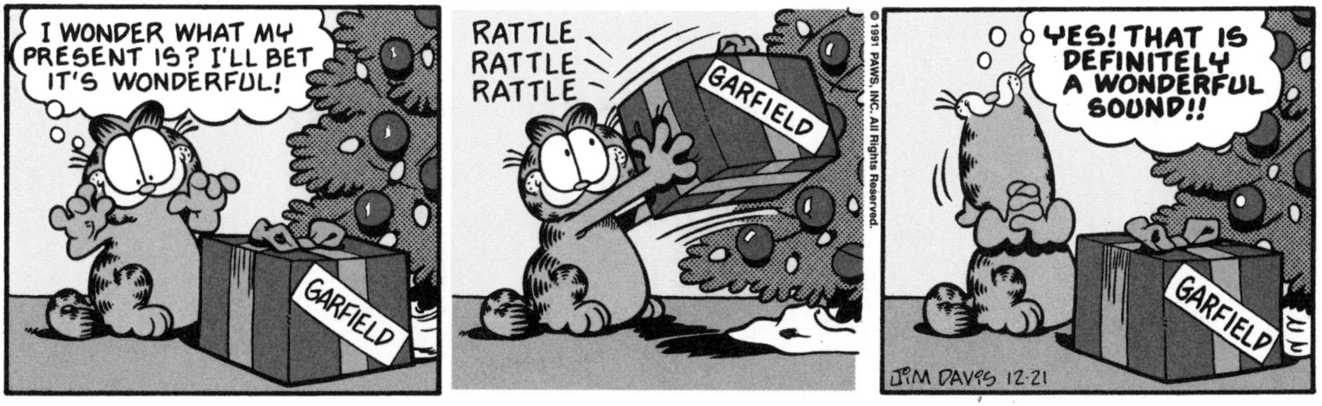
I WONDER WHAT MY PRESENT IS? I'LL BET IT'S WONDERFUL!
GARFIELD
RATTLE RATTLE RATTLE
GARFIELD
© 1991 PAWS, INC. All Rights Reserved.
YES! THAT IS DEFINITELY A WONDERFUL SOUND!!
GARFIELD
JIM DAVIS 12-21

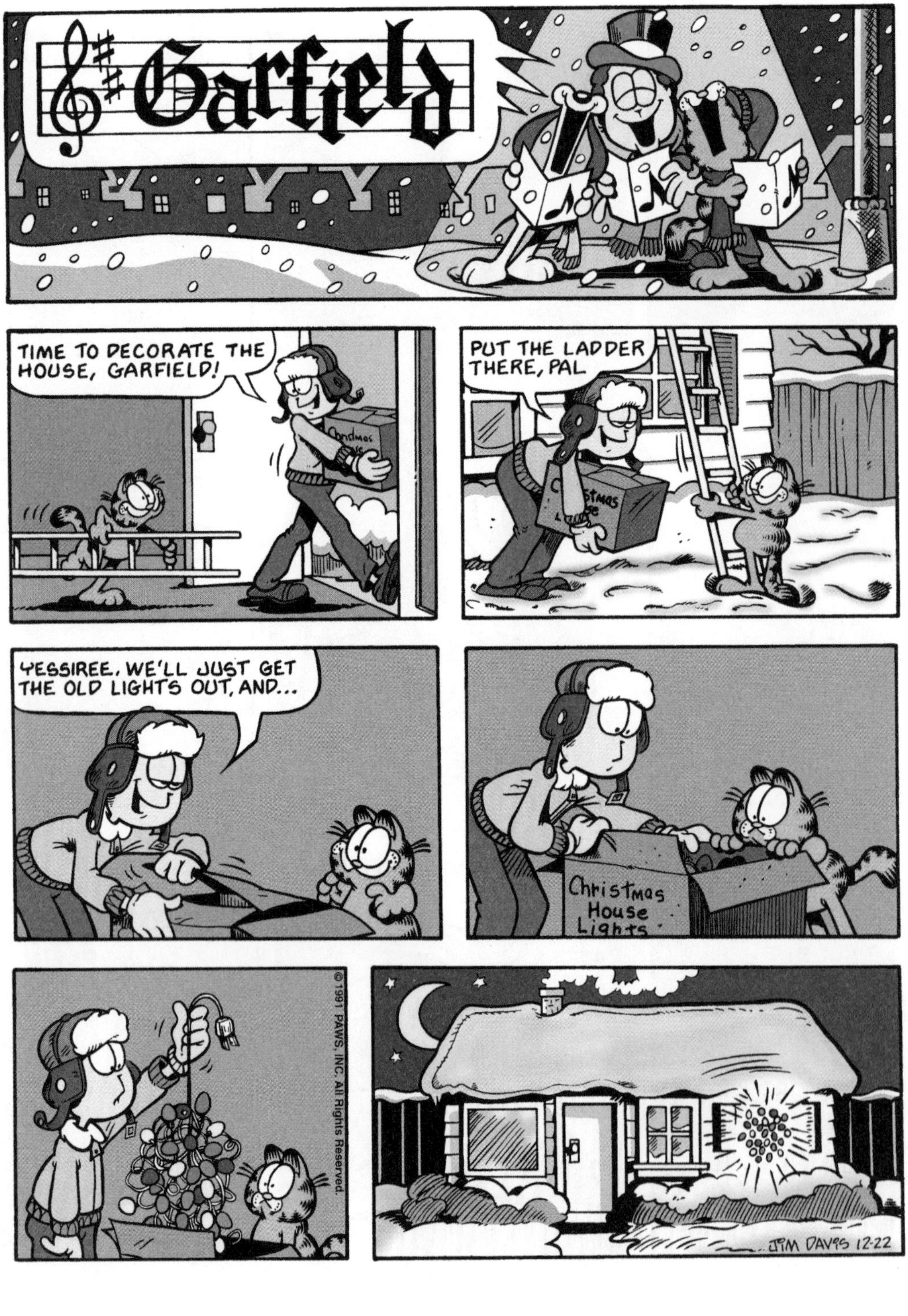
Garfield
TIME TO DECORATE THE HOUSE, GARFIELD!
Christmas
PUT THE LADDER THERE, PAL
YESSIREE. WE'LL JUST GET THE OLD LIGHTS OUT, AND...
Christmas House Lights
© 1991 PAWS, INC. All Rights Reserved.
JIM DAVIS 12-22

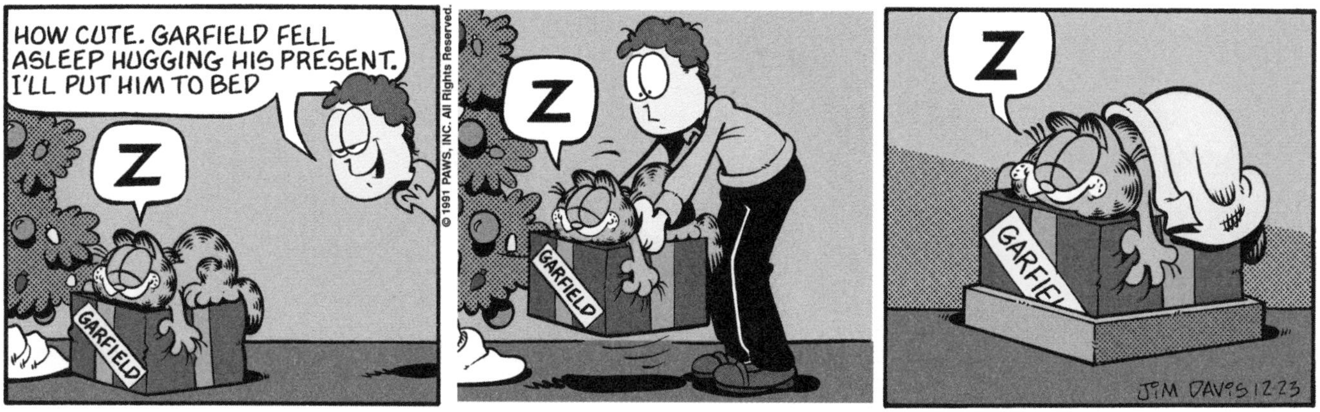
HOW CUTE. GARFIELD FELL ASLEEP HUGGING HIS PRESENT. I'LL PUT HIM TO BED
Z
GARFIELD
© 1991 PAWS, INC. All Rights Reserved.
Z
GARFIELD
Z
GARFIELD
JIM DAVIS 12-23

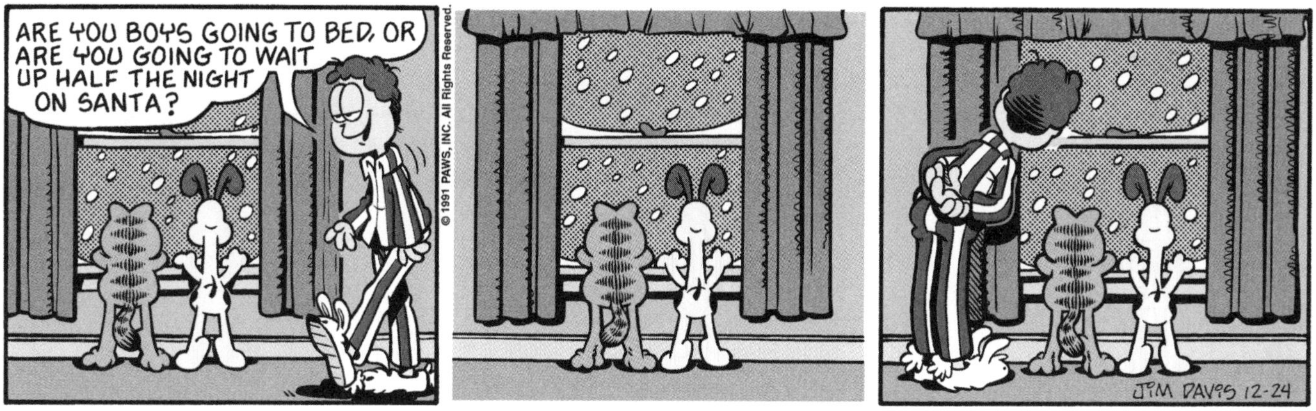
ARE YOU BOYS GOING TO BED, OR ARE YOU GOING TO WAIT UP HALF THE NIGHT ON SANTA?
© 1991 PAWS, INC. All Rights Reserved.
JIM DAVIS 12-24

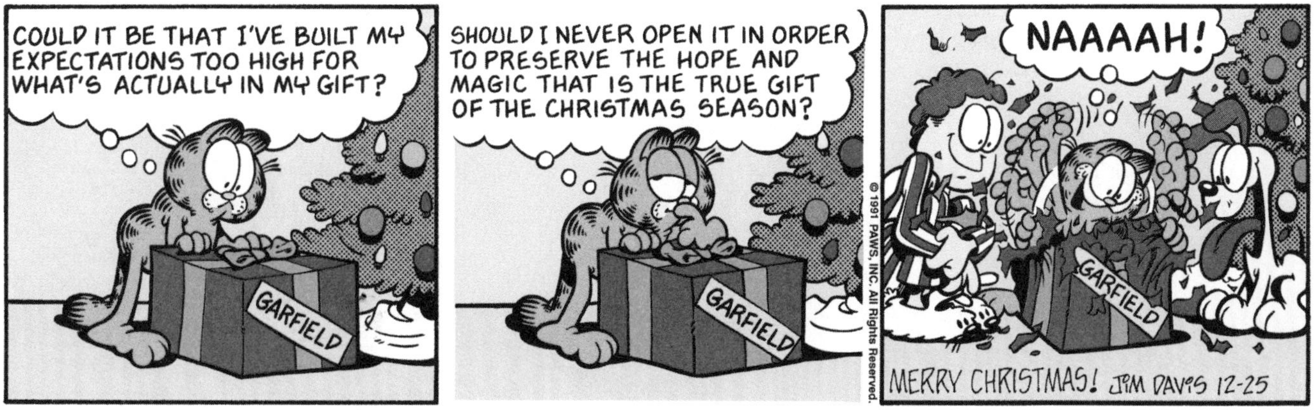
COULD IT BE THAT I'VE BUILT MY EXPECTATIONS TOO HIGH FOR WHAT'S ACTUALLY IN MY GIFT?
GARFIELD
SHOULD I NEVER OPEN IT IN ORDER TO PRESERVE THE HOPE AND MAGIC THAT IS THE TRUE GIFT OF THE CHRISTMAS SEASON?
GARFIELD
© 1991 PAWS, INC. All Rights Reserved.
NAAAAH!
GARFIELD
MERRY CHRISTMAS! JIM DAVIS 12-25

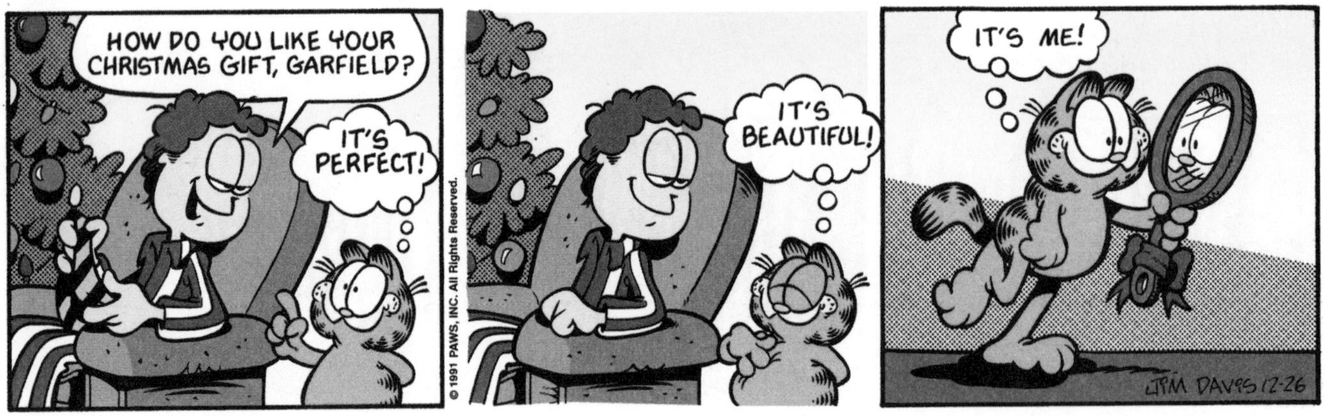
HOW DO YOU LIKE YOUR CHRISTMAS GIFT, GARFIELD?
IT'S PERFECT!
© 1991 PAWS, INC. All Rights Reserved.
IT'S BEAUTIFUL!
IT'S ME!
JIM DAVIS 12-26

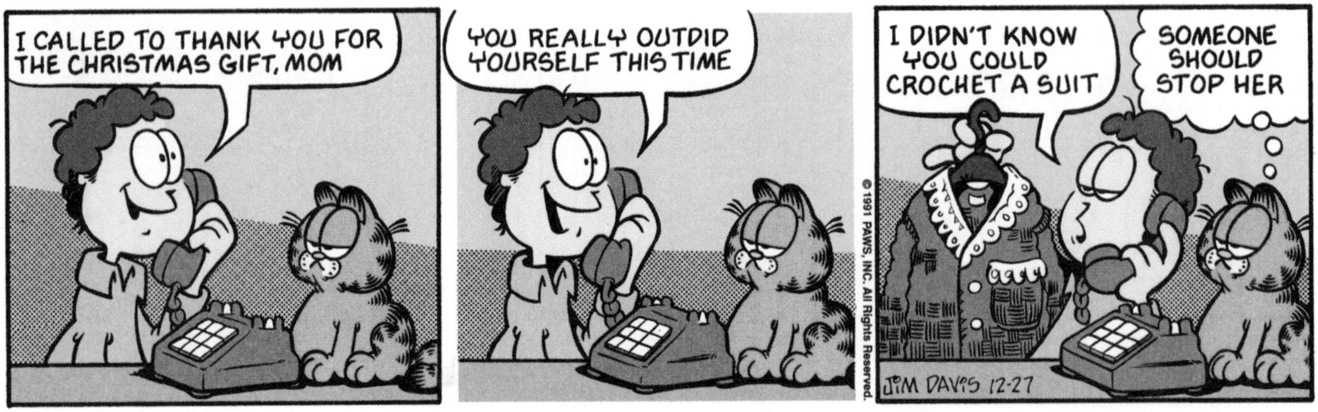
I CALLED TO THANK YOU FOR THE CHRISTMAS GIFT, MOM
YOU REALLY OUTDID YOURSELF THIS TIME
© 1991 PAWS, INC. All Rights Reserved.
I DIDN'T KNOW YOU COULD CROCHET A SUIT
SOMEONE SHOULD STOP HER
JIM DAVIS 12-27

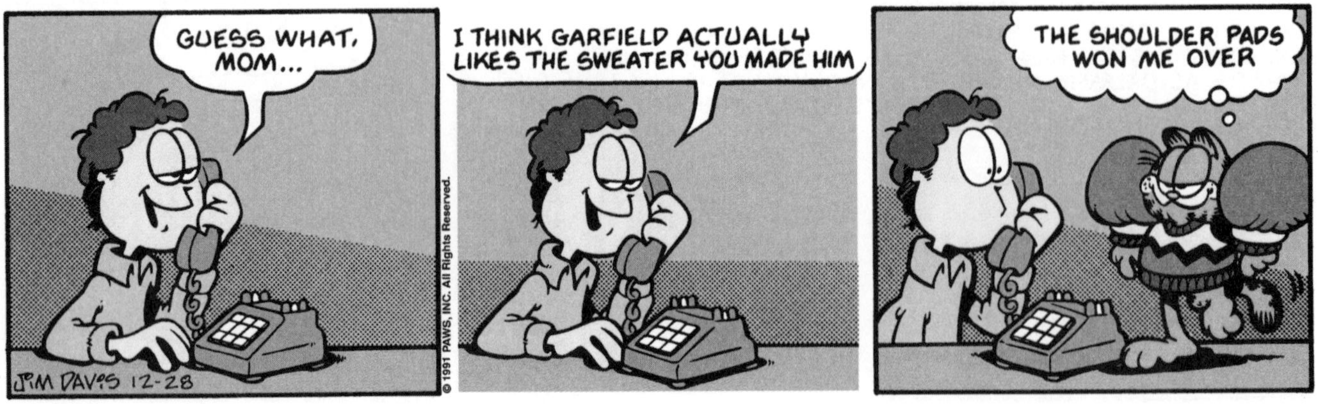
GUESS WHAT, MOM...
JIM DAVIS 12-28
© 1991 PAWS, INC. All Rights Reserved.
I THINK GARFIELD ACTUALLY LIKES THE SWEATER YOU MADE HIM
THE SHOULDER PADS WON ME OVER

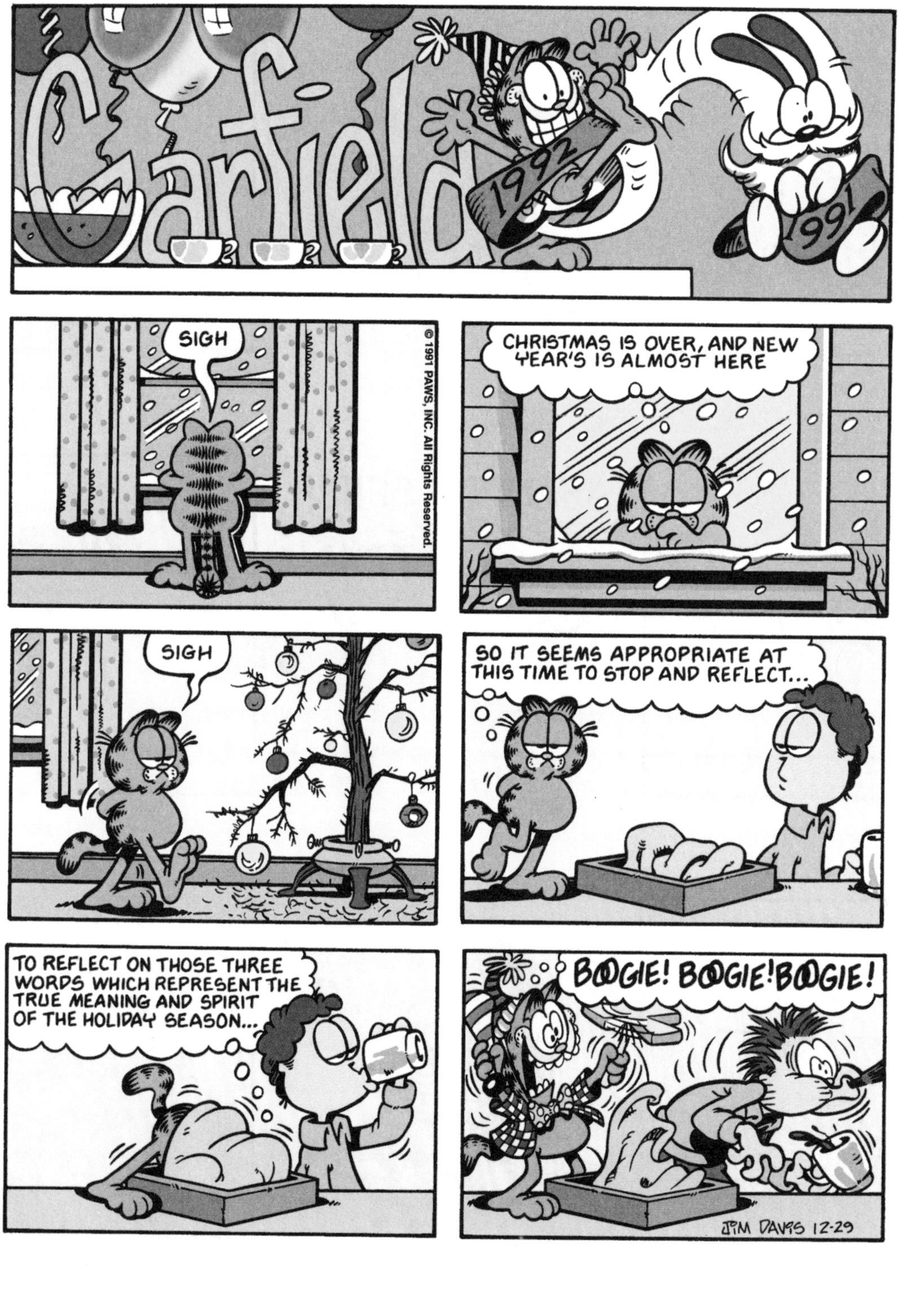
Garfield
1992
1991
SIGH
© 1991 PAWS, INC. All Rights Reserved.
CHRISTMAS IS OVER, AND NEW YEAR'S IS ALMOST HERE
SIGH
SO IT SEEMS APPROPRIATE AT THIS TIME TO STOP AND REFLECT...
TO REFLECT ON THOSE THREE WORDS WHICH REPRESENT THE TRUE MEANING AND SPIRIT OF THE HOLIDAY SEASON...
BOOGIE! BOOGIE! BOOGIE!
JIM DAVIS 12-29

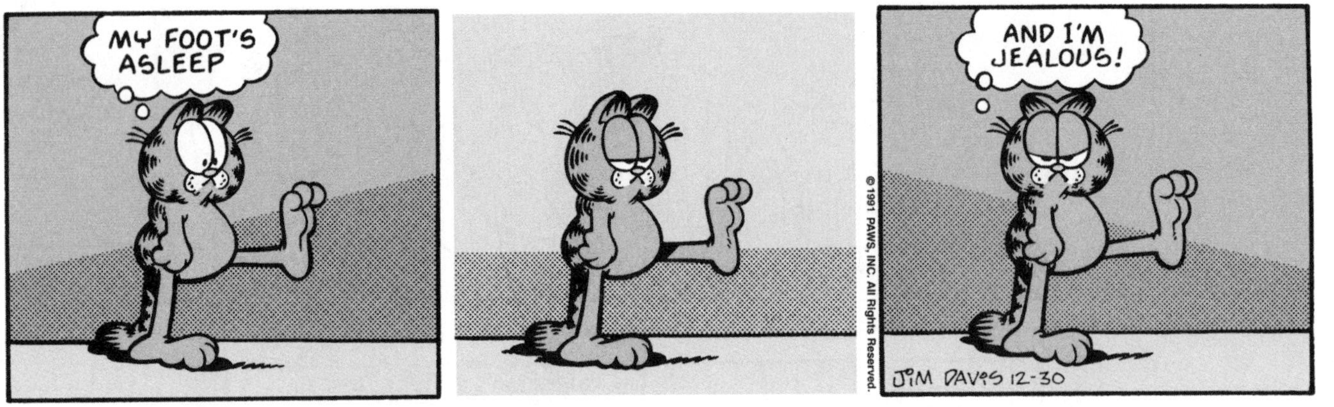
MY FOOT'S ASLEEP
AND I'M JEALOUS!
© 1991 PAWS, INC. All Rights Reserved.
JIM DAVIS 12-30

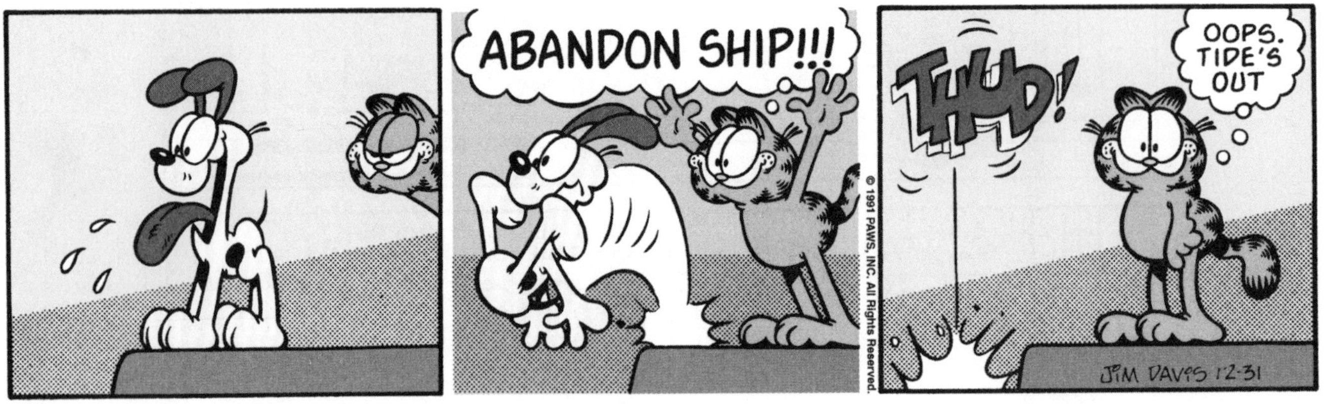
ABANDON SHIP!!!
THUD!
OOPS. TIDE'S OUT
© 1991 PAWS, INC. All Rights Reserved.
JIM DAVIS 12-31

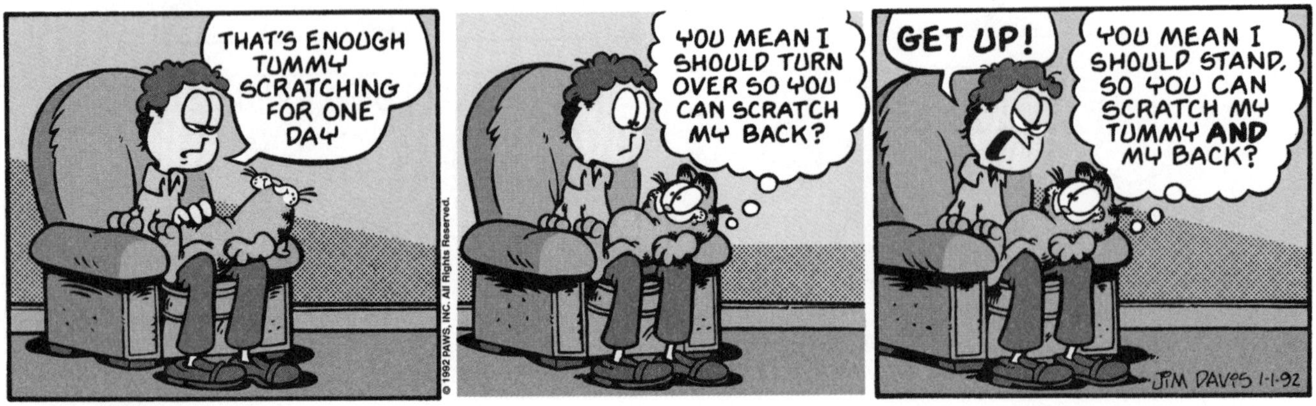
THAT'S ENOUGH TUMMY SCRATCHING FOR ONE DAY
YOU MEAN I SHOULD TURN OVER SO YOU CAN SCRATCH MY BACK?
GET UP!
YOU MEAN I SHOULD STAND, SO YOU CAN SCRATCH MY TUMMY AND MY BACK?
© 1992 PAWS, INC. All Rights Reserved.
JIM DAVIS 1-1-92

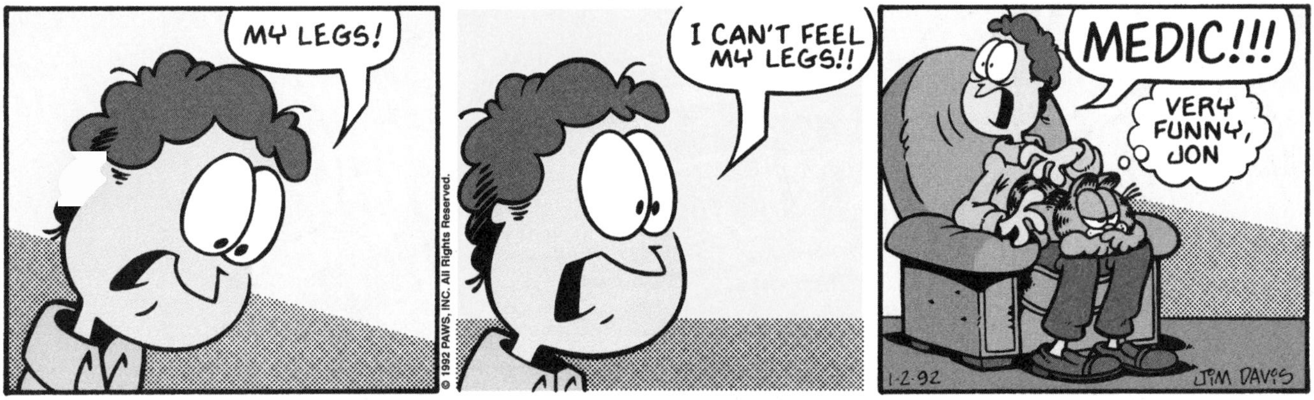
MY LEGS!
© 1992 PAWS, INC. All Rights Reserved.
I CAN'T FEEL MY LEGS!!
MEDIC!!!
VERY FUNNY, JON
1-2-92
JIM DAVIS

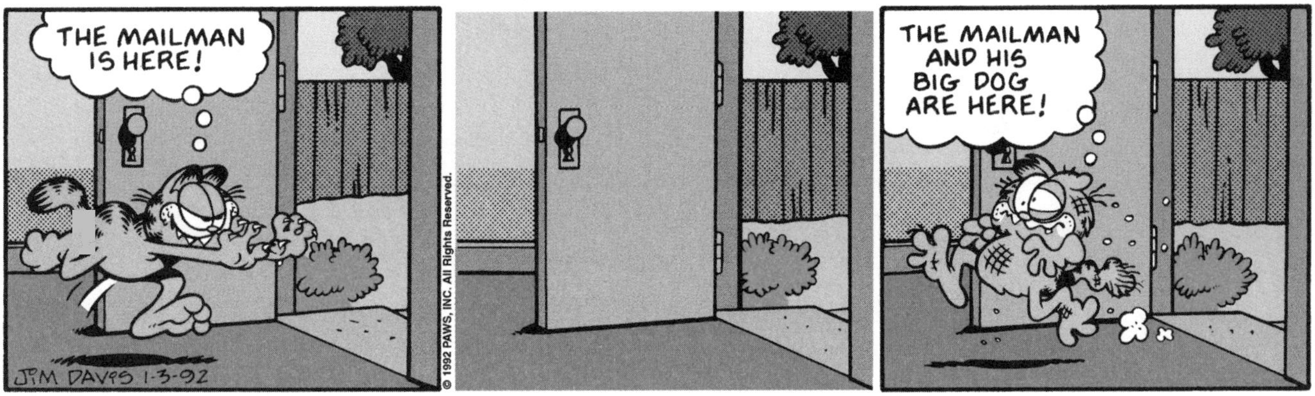
THE MAILMAN IS HERE!
JIM DAVIS 1-3-92
© 1992 PAWS, INC. All Rights Reserved.
THE MAILMAN AND HIS BIG DOG ARE HERE!

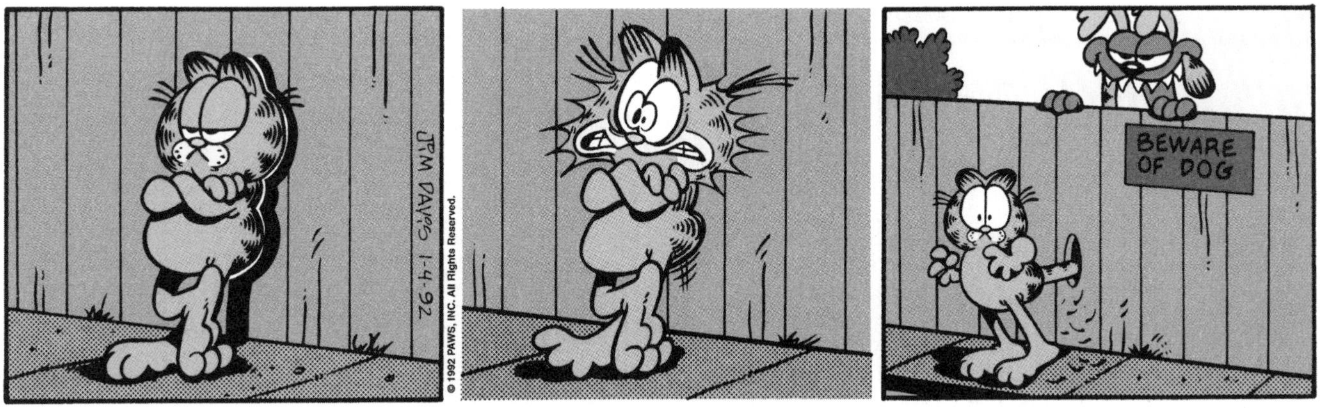
JIM DAVIS 1-4-92
© 1992 PAWS, INC. All Rights Reserved.
BEWARE OF DOG

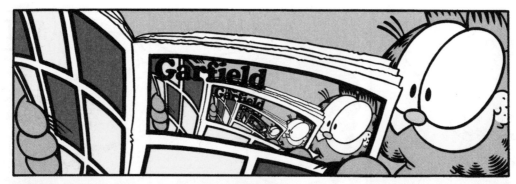

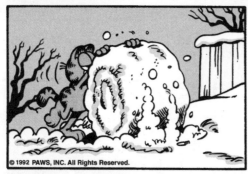

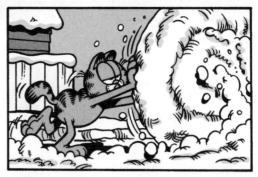

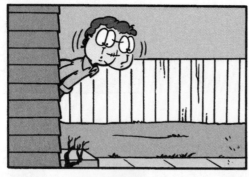

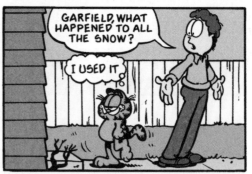

Garfield
Garfield
© 1992 PAWS, INC. All Rights Reserved.
GARFIELD, WHAT HAPPENED TO ALL THE SNOW?
I USED IT
JIM DAVIS 1-5-92

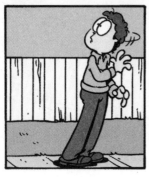

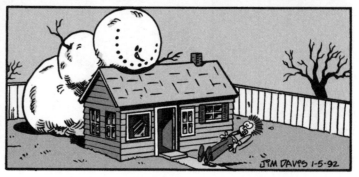

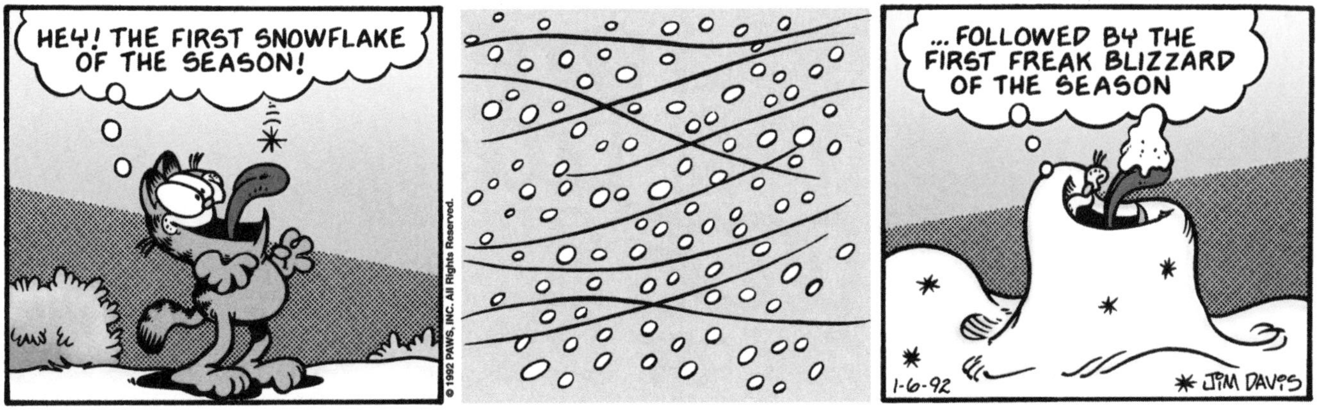
HEY! THE FIRST SNOWFLAKE OF THE SEASON!
... FOLLOWED BY THE FIRST FREAK BLIZZARD OF THE SEASON
© 1992 PAWS, INC. All Rights Reserved.
1-6-92
JIM DAVIS

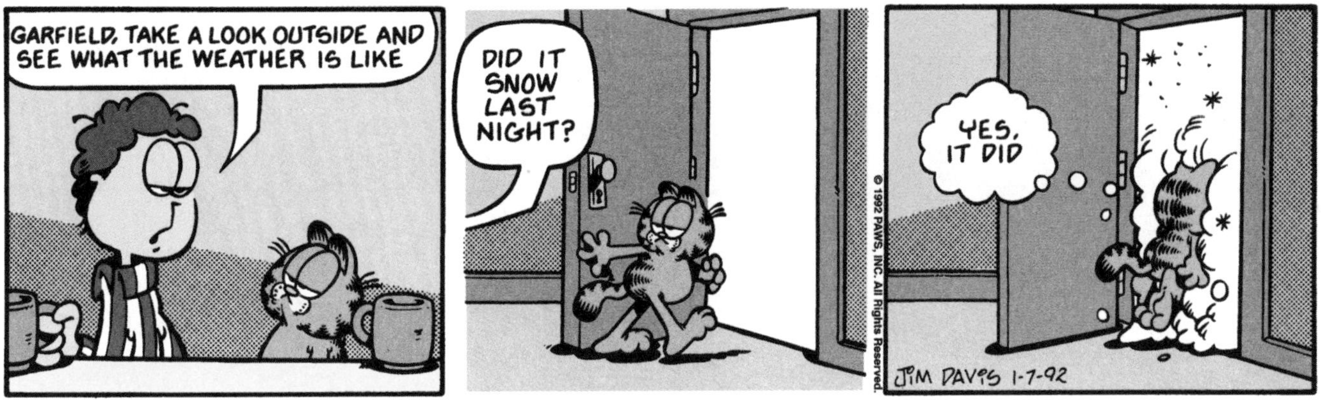
GARFIELD, TAKE A LOOK OUTSIDE AND SEE WHAT THE WEATHER IS LIKE
DID IT SNOW LAST NIGHT?
YES, IT DID
© 1992 PAWS, INC. All Rights Reserved.
JIM DAVIS 1-7-92

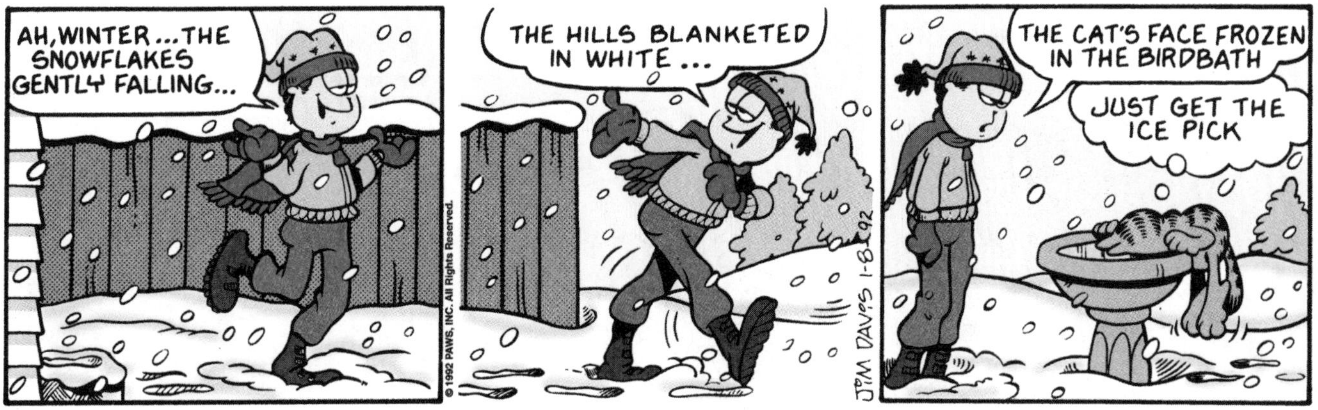
AH, WINTER ... THE SNOWFLAKES GENTLY FALLING...
THE HILLS BLANKETED IN WHITE ...
THE CAT'S FACE FROZEN IN THE BIRDBATH
JUST GET THE ICE PICK
© 1992 PAWS, INC. All Rights Reserved.
JIM DAVIS 1-8-92

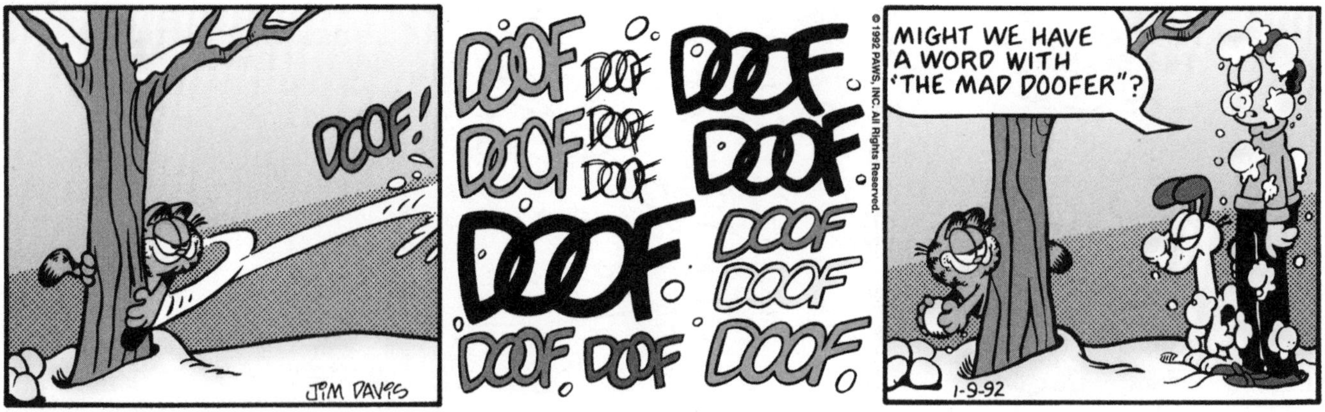
DOOF!
DOOF DOOF DOOF
DOOF DOOF DOOF DOOF
DOOF DOOF
DOOF
DOOF DOOF DOOF
JIM DAVIS
© 1992 PAWS, INC. All Rights Reserved.
MIGHT WE HAVE A WORD WITH "THE MAD DOOFER"?
1-9-92

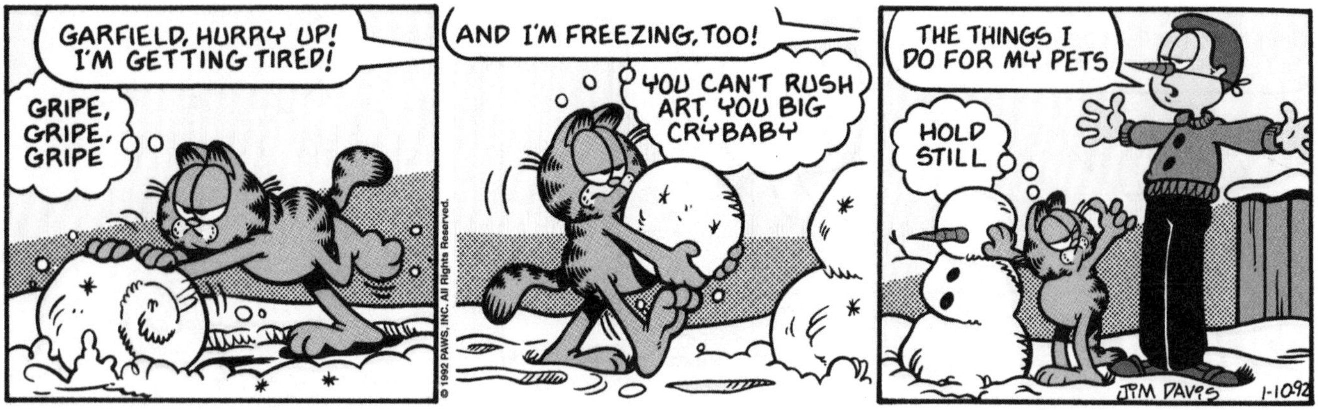
GARFIELD, HURRY UP! I'M GETTING TIRED!
GRIPE, GRIPE, GRIPE
© 1992 PAWS, INC. All Rights Reserved.
AND I'M FREEZING, TOO!
YOU CAN'T RUSH ART, YOU BIG CRYBABY
THE THINGS I DO FOR MY PETS
HOLD STILL
JIM DAVIS
1-10-92

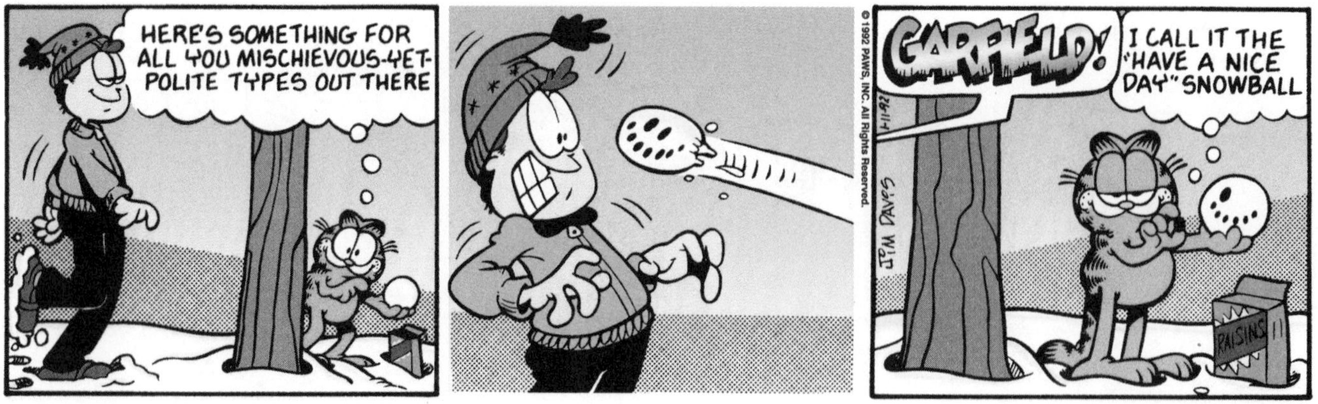
HERE'S SOMETHING FOR ALL YOU MISCHIEVOUS-YET-POLITE TYPES OUT THERE
© 1992 PAWS, INC. All Rights Reserved.
1-11-92
JIM DAVIS
GARFIELD!
I CALL IT THE "HAVE A NICE DAY" SNOWBALL
RAISINS

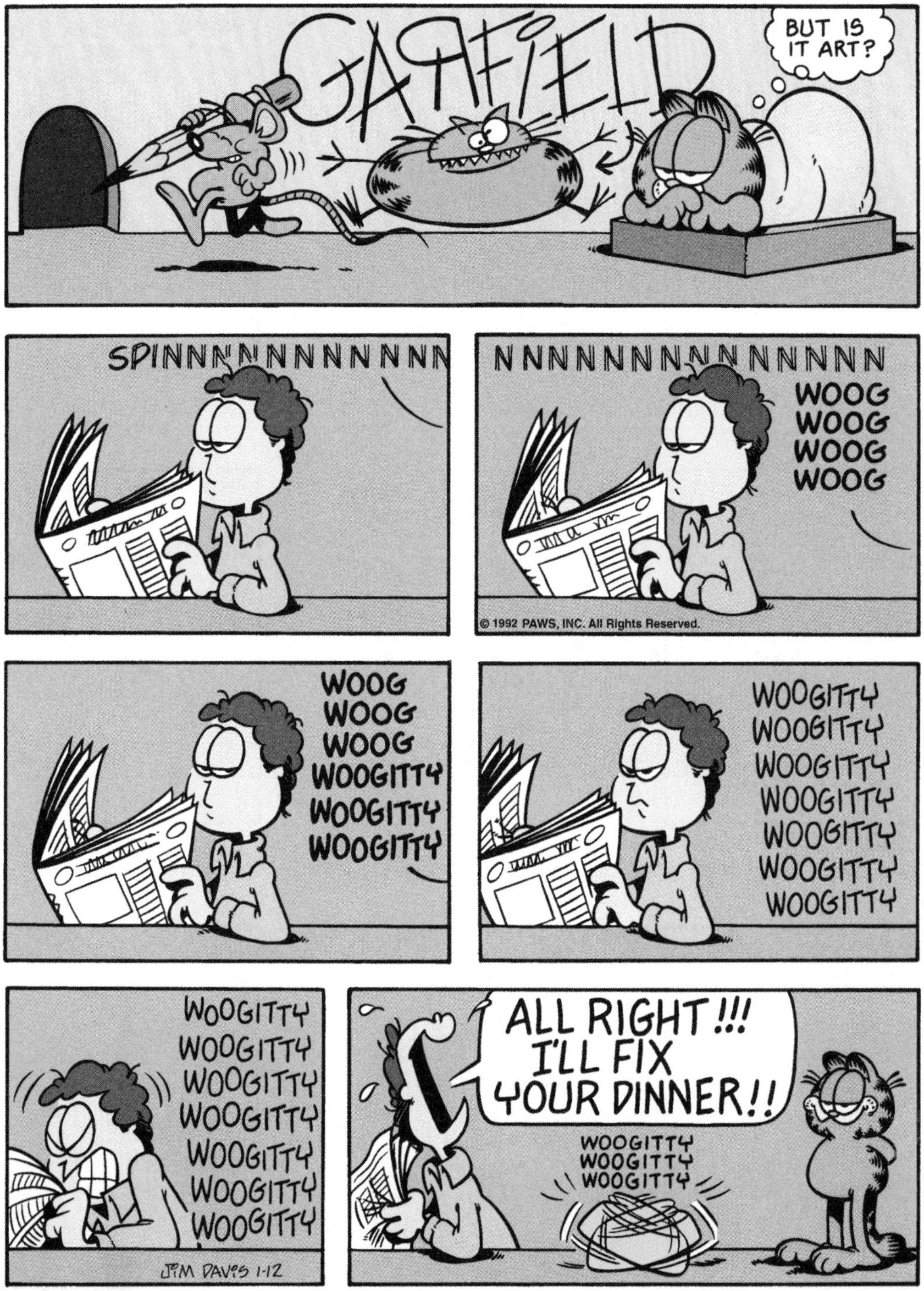
GARFIELD
BUT IS IT ART?
SPINNNNNNNNNNNNN
NNNNNNNNNNNNNNN
WOOG WOOG WOOG WOOG
© 1992 PAWS, INC. All Rights Reserved.
WOOG WOOG WOOG WOOGITTY WOOGITTY WOOGITTY
WOOGITTY WOOGITTY WOOGITTY WOOGITTY WOOGITTY WOOGITTY WOOGITTY
WOOGITTY WOOGITTY WOOGITTY WOOGITTY WOOGITTY WOOGITTY WOOGITTY
JIM DAVIS 1-12
ALL RIGHT!!! I'LL FIX YOUR DINNER!!
WOOGITTY WOOGITTY WOOGITTY

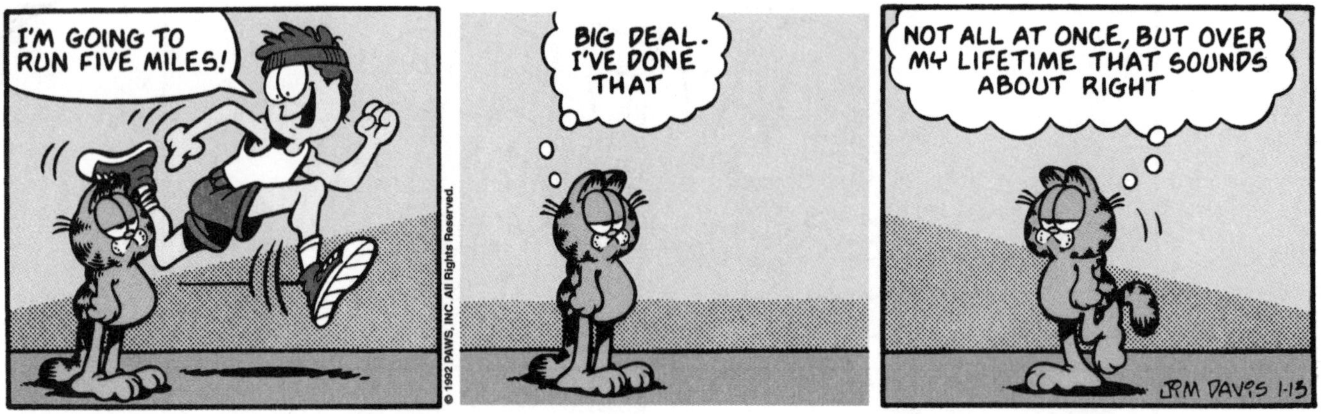
I'M GOING TO RUN FIVE MILES!
BIG DEAL. I'VE DONE THAT
NOT ALL AT ONCE, BUT OVER MY LIFETIME THAT SOUNDS ABOUT RIGHT
JIM DAVIS 1-13

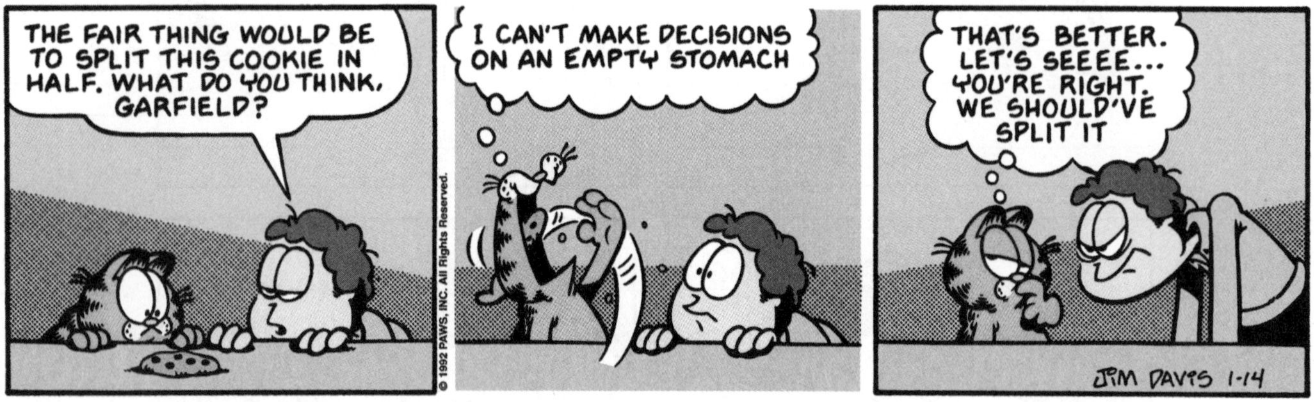
THE FAIR THING WOULD BE TO SPLIT THIS COOKIE IN HALF. WHAT DO YOU THINK, GARFIELD?
I CAN'T MAKE DECISIONS ON AN EMPTY STOMACH
THAT'S BETTER. LET'S SEEEE... YOU'RE RIGHT. WE SHOULD'VE SPLIT IT
JIM DAVIS 1-14

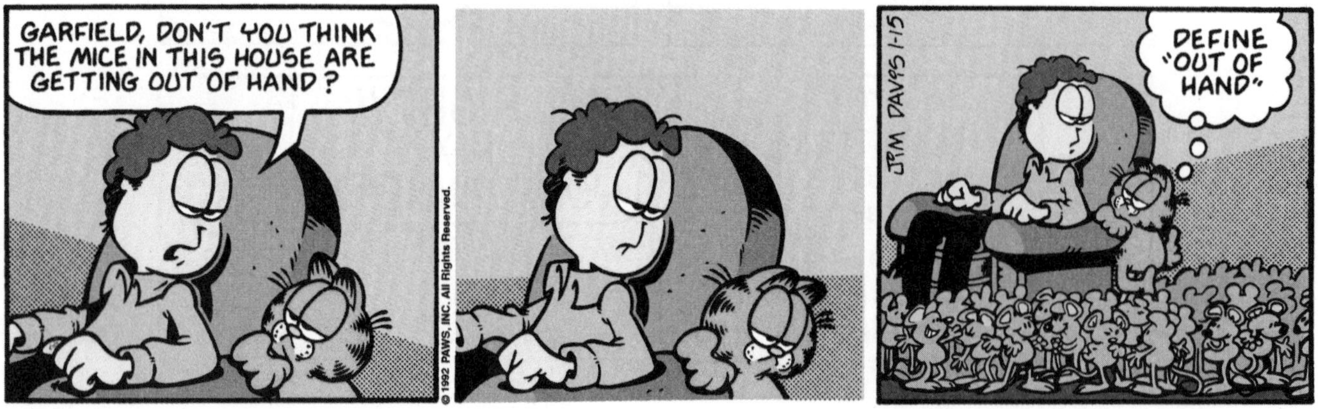
GARFIELD, DON'T YOU THINK THE MICE IN THIS HOUSE ARE GETTING OUT OF HAND?
JIM DAVIS 1-15
DEFINE "OUT OF HAND"

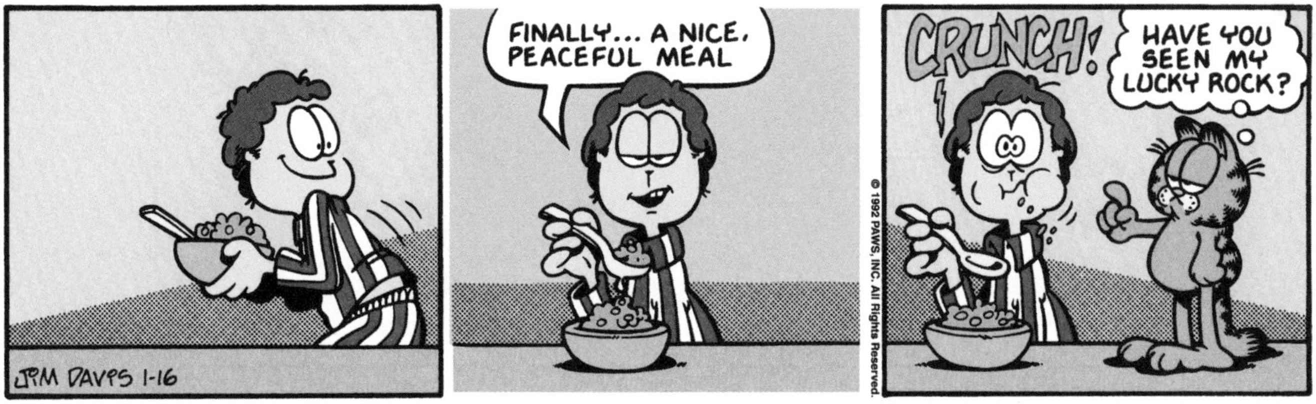
JIM DAVIS 1-16
FINALLY... A NICE, PEACEFUL MEAL
CRUNCH!
HAVE YOU SEEN MY LUCKY ROCK?
© 1992 PAWS, INC. All Rights Reserved.

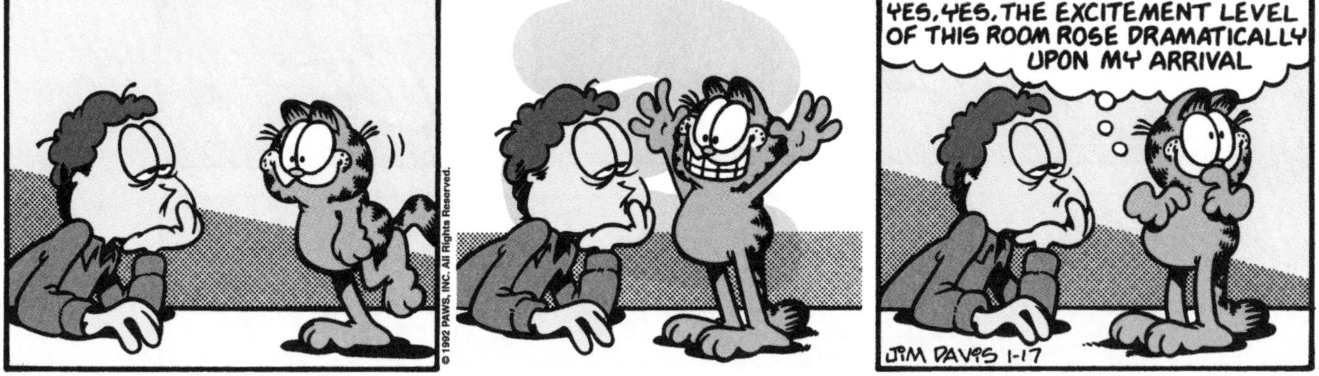
© 1992 PAWS, INC. All Rights Reserved.
YES, YES, THE EXCITEMENT LEVEL OF THIS ROOM ROSE DRAMATICALLY UPON MY ARRIVAL
JIM DAVIS 1-17

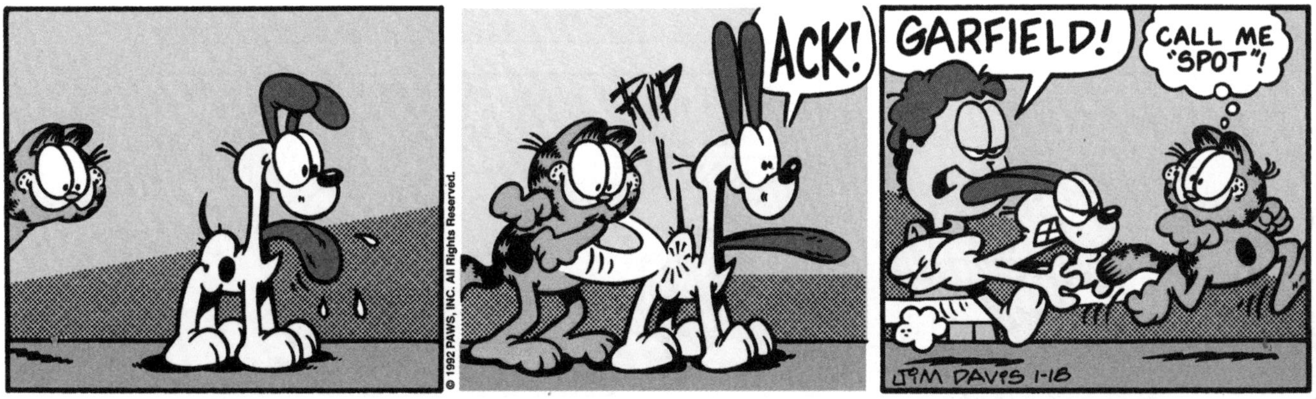
© 1992 PAWS, INC. All Rights Reserved.
RIP
ACK!
GARFIELD!
CALL ME "SPOT"!
JIM DAVIS 1-18

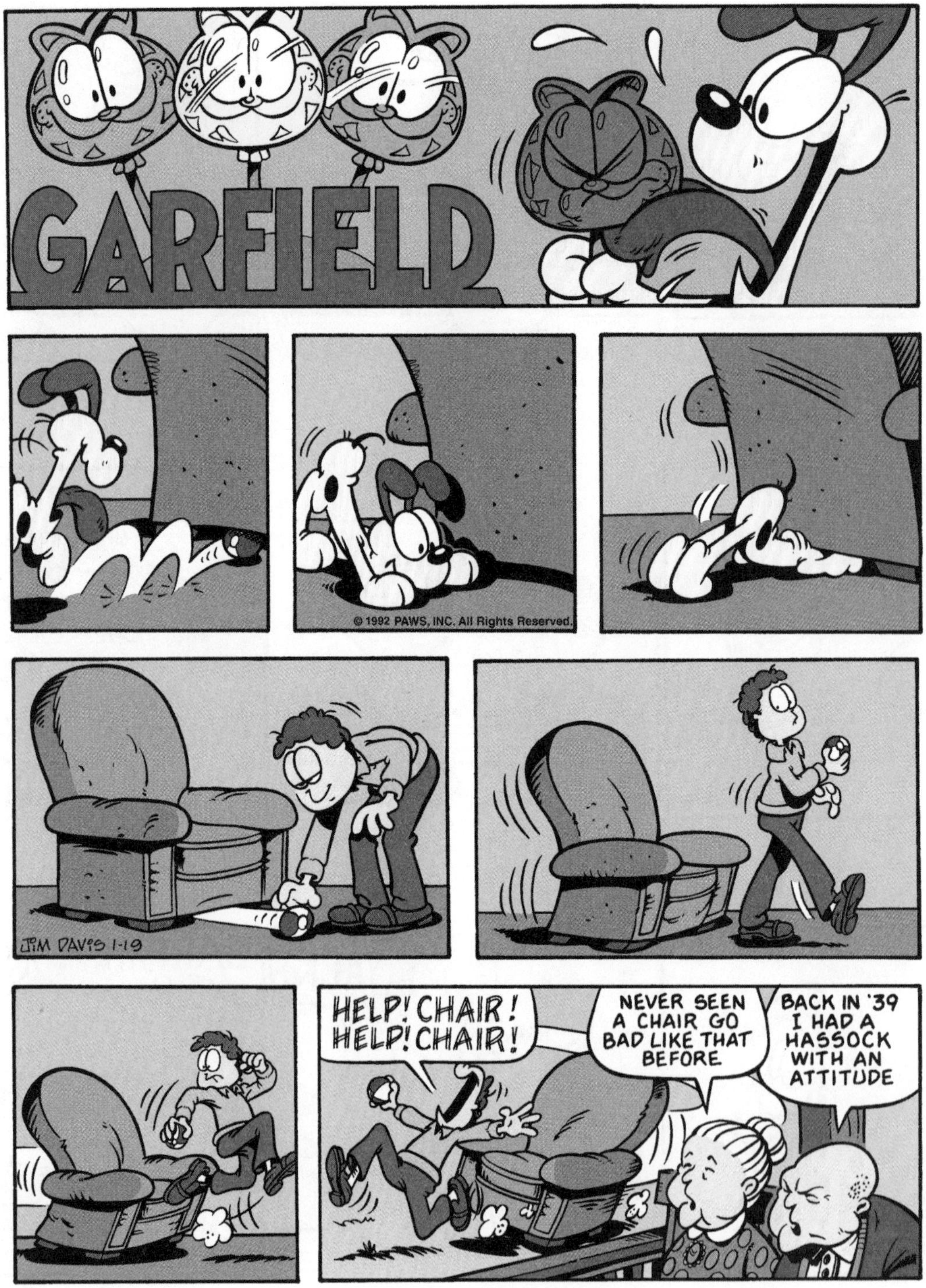
GARFIELD
© 1992 PAWS, INC. All Rights Reserved.
JIM DAVIS 1-19
HELP! CHAIR! HELP! CHAIR!
NEVER SEEN A CHAIR GO BAD LIKE THAT BEFORE
BACK IN '39 I HAD A HASSOCK WITH AN ATTITUDE

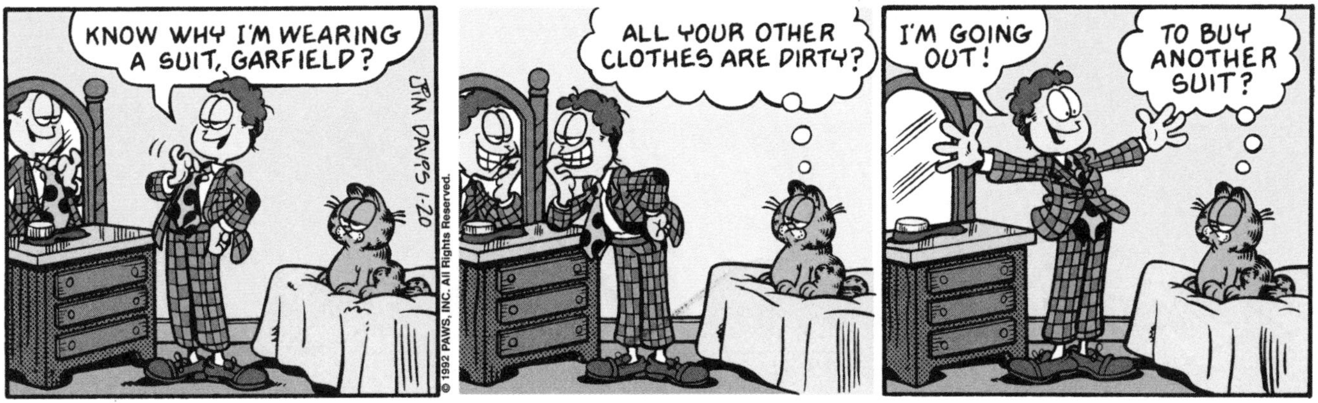
KNOW WHY I'M WEARING A SUIT, GARFIELD?
JIM DAVIS 1-20
© 1992 PAWS, INC. All Rights Reserved.
ALL YOUR OTHER CLOTHES ARE DIRTY?
I'M GOING OUT!
TO BUY ANOTHER SUIT?

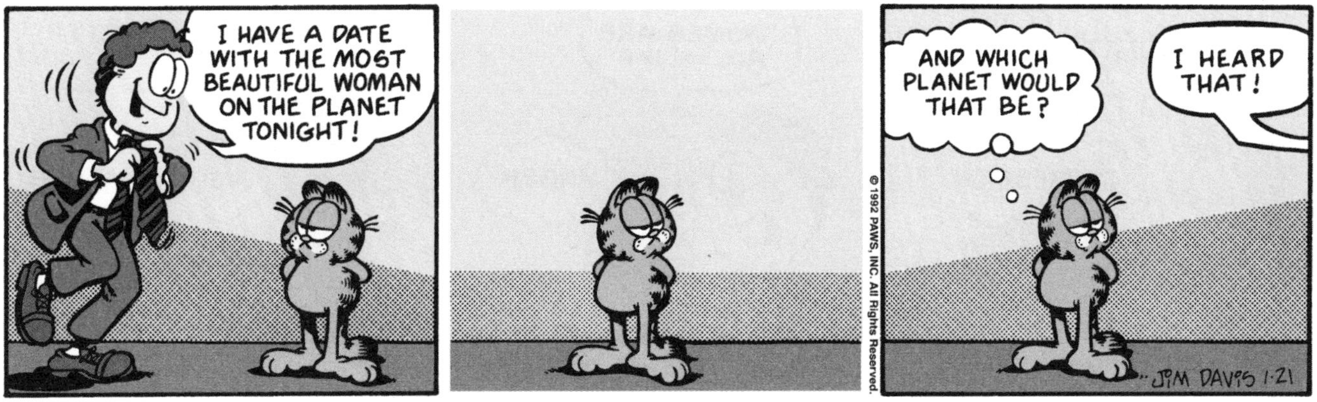
I HAVE A DATE WITH THE MOST BEAUTIFUL WOMAN ON THE PLANET TONIGHT!
© 1992 PAWS, INC. All Rights Reserved.
AND WHICH PLANET WOULD THAT BE?
I HEARD THAT!
JIM DAVIS 1-21

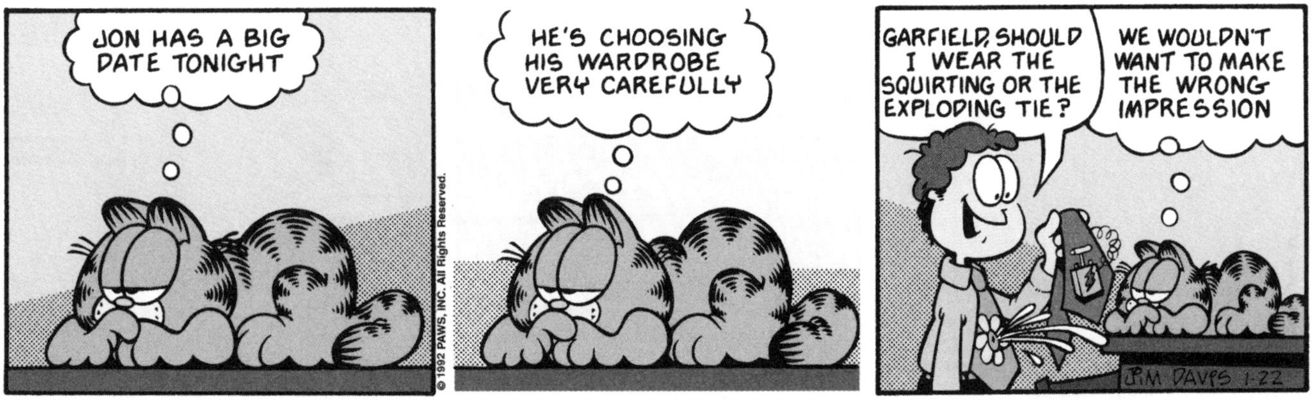
JON HAS A BIG DATE TONIGHT
© 1992 PAWS, INC. All Rights Reserved.
HE'S CHOOSING HIS WARDROBE VERY CAREFULLY
GARFIELD, SHOULD I WEAR THE SQUIRTING OR THE EXPLODING TIE?
WE WOULDN'T WANT TO MAKE THE WRONG IMPRESSION
JIM DAVIS 1-22

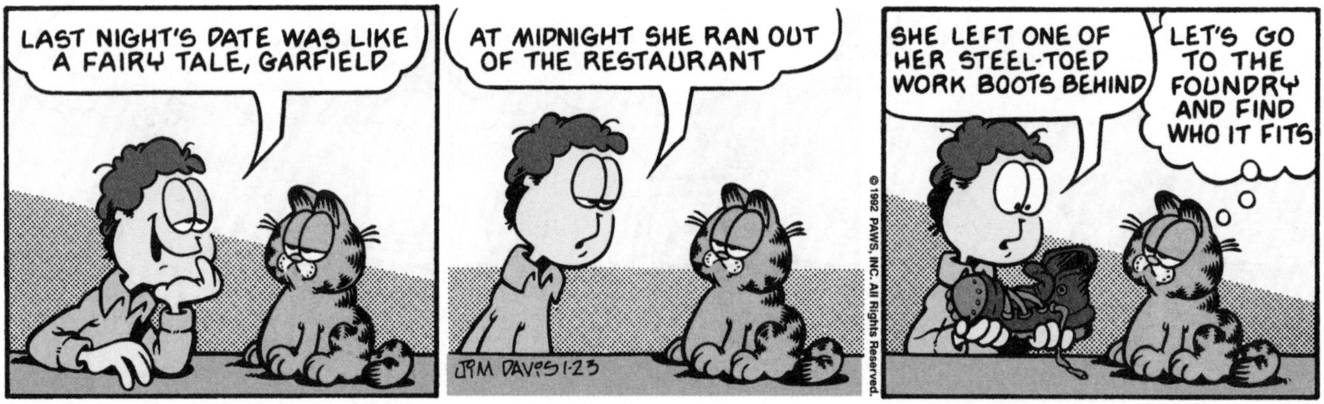
LAST NIGHT'S DATE WAS LIKE A FAIRY TALE, GARFIELD
AT MIDNIGHT SHE RAN OUT OF THE RESTAURANT
JIM DAVIS 1-23
© 1992 PAWS, INC. All Rights Reserved.
SHE LEFT ONE OF HER STEEL-TOED WORK BOOTS BEHIND
LET'S GO TO THE FOUNDRY AND FIND WHO IT FITS

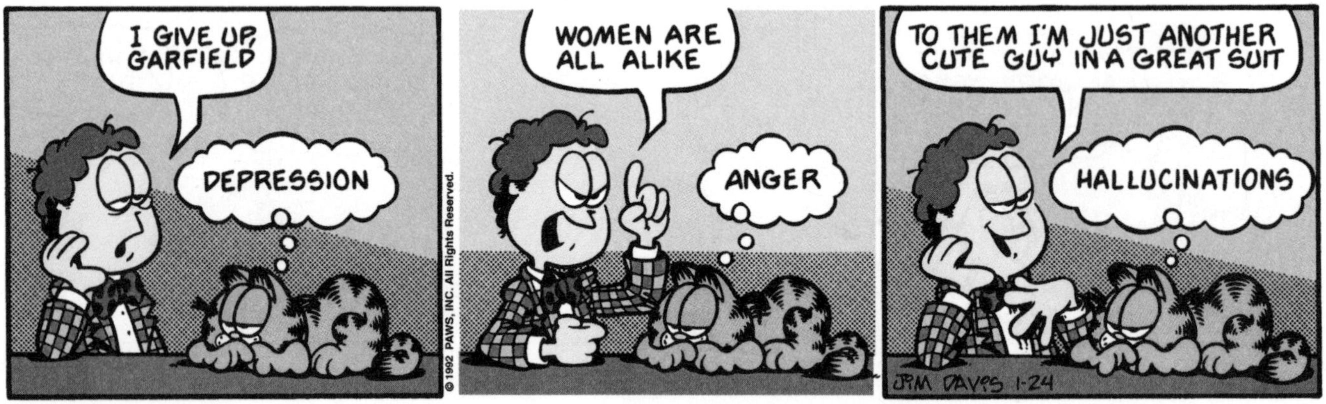
I GIVE UP, GARFIELD
DEPRESSION
© 1992 PAWS, INC. All Rights Reserved.
WOMEN ARE ALL ALIKE
ANGER
TO THEM I'M JUST ANOTHER CUTE GUY IN A GREAT SUIT
HALLUCINATIONS
JIM DAVIS 1-24

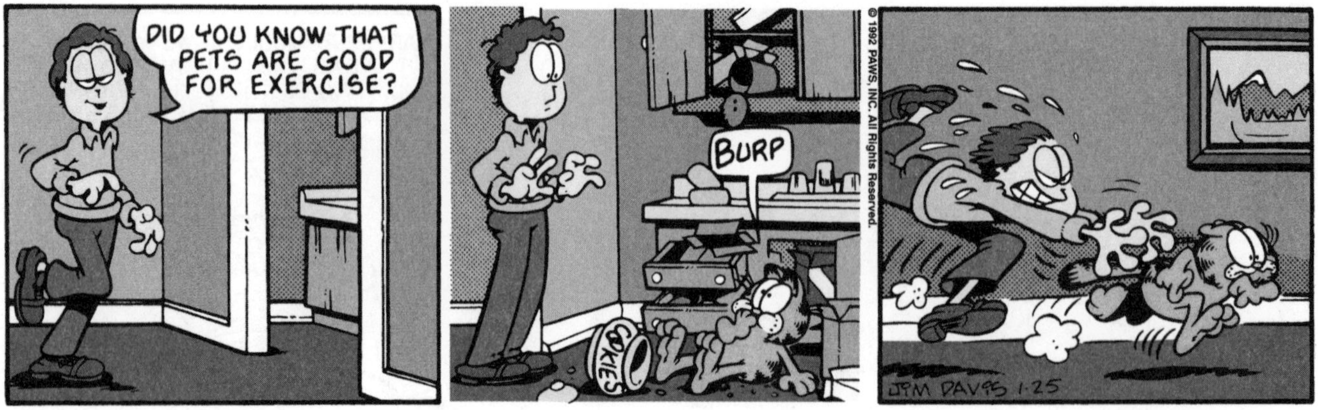
DID YOU KNOW THAT PETS ARE GOOD FOR EXERCISE?
BURP
COOKIES
© 1992 PAWS, INC. All Rights Reserved.
JIM DAVIS 1-25

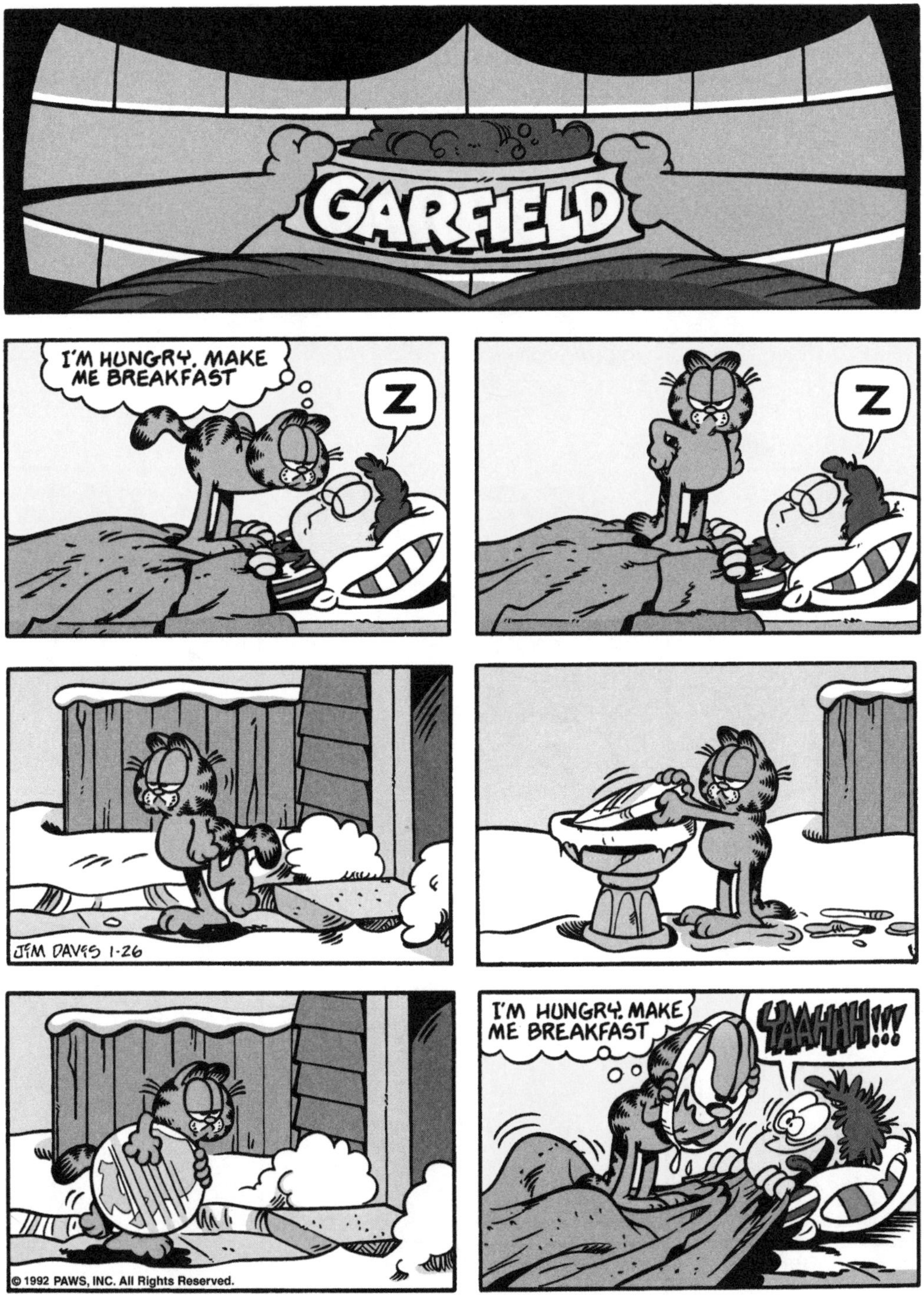
GARFIELD
I'M HUNGRY. MAKE ME BREAKFAST
Z
Z
JIM DAVIS 1-26
© 1992 PAWS, INC. All Rights Reserved.
I'M HUNGRY. MAKE ME BREAKFAST
YAAHHH!!!

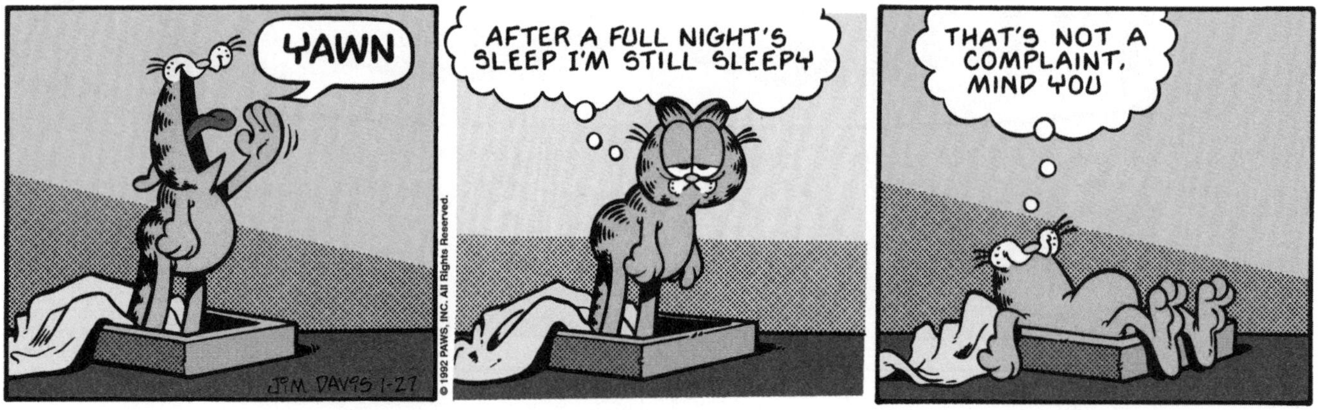
YAWN
JIM DAVIS 1-27
© 1992 PAWS, INC. All Rights Reserved.
AFTER A FULL NIGHT'S SLEEP I'M STILL SLEEPY
THAT'S NOT A COMPLAINT, MIND YOU

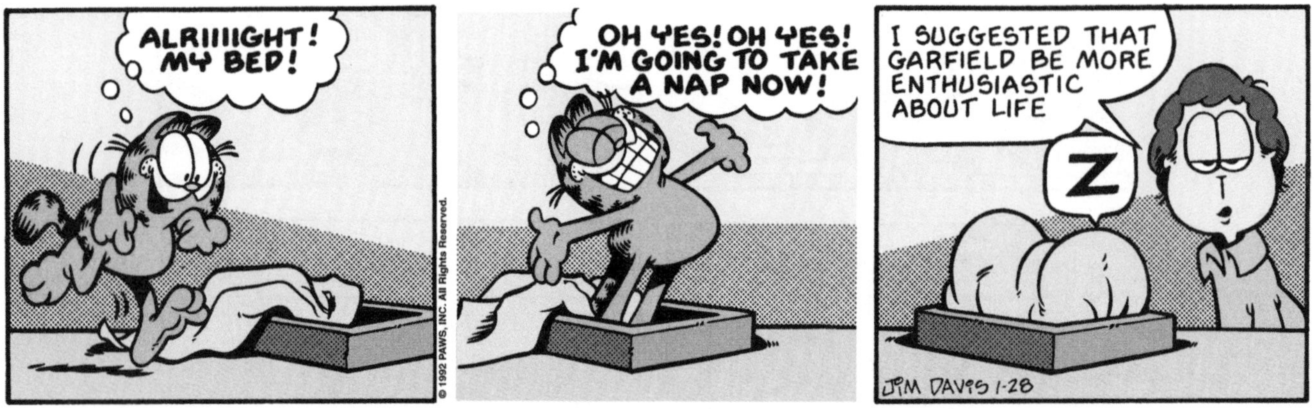
ALRIIIIGHT! MY BED!
© 1992 PAWS, INC. All Rights Reserved.
OH YES! OH YES! I'M GOING TO TAKE A NAP NOW!
I SUGGESTED THAT GARFIELD BE MORE ENTHUSIASTIC ABOUT LIFE
Z
JIM DAVIS 1-28

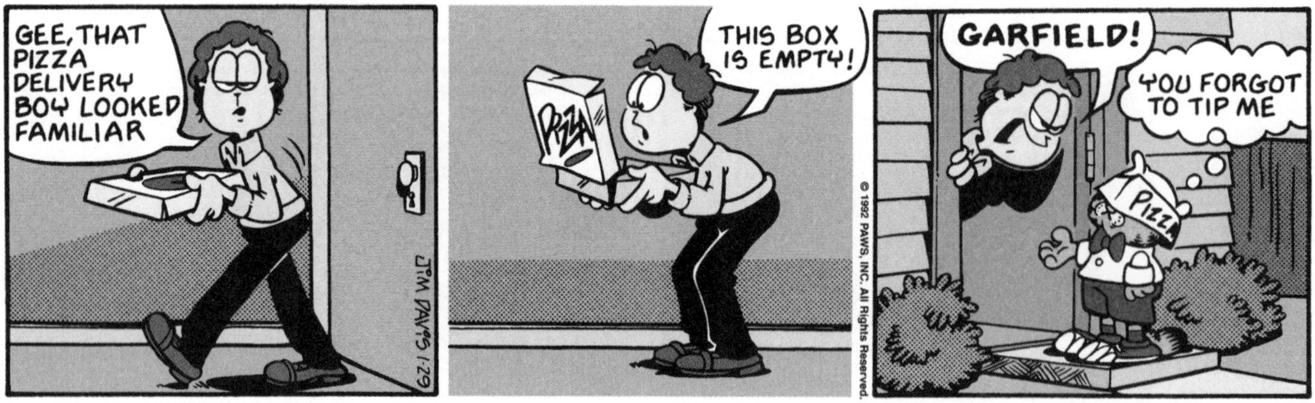
GEE, THAT PIZZA DELIVERY BOY LOOKED FAMILIAR
JIM DAVIS 1-29
THIS BOX IS EMPTY!
PIZZA
© 1992 PAWS, INC. All Rights Reserved.
GARFIELD!
YOU FORGOT TO TIP ME
PIZZA

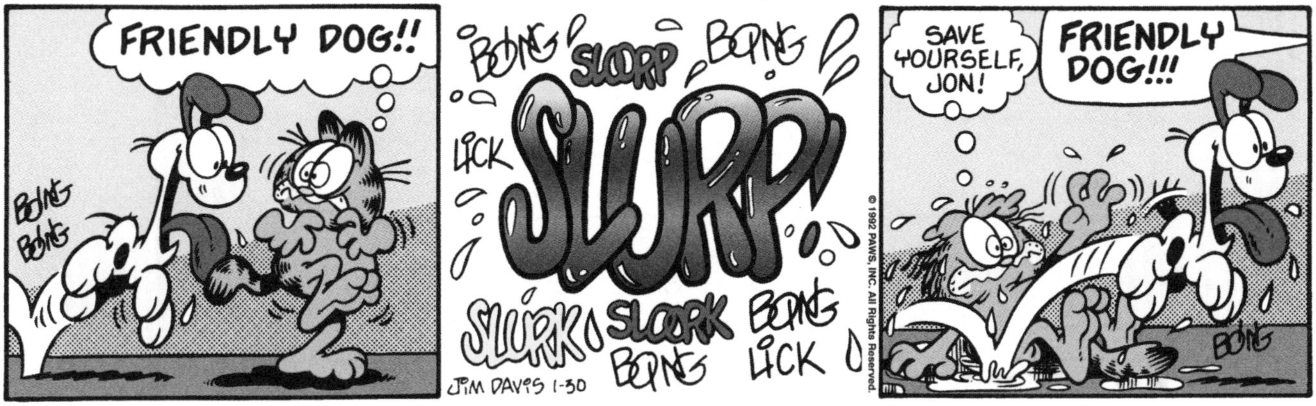
FRIENDLY DOG!!
BOING
BOING
BOING SLOORP BOING
LICK
SLURP
SLURK SLOORK BOING
BOING LICK
JIM DAVIS 1-30
© 1992 PAWS, INC. All Rights Reserved.
SAVE YOURSELF, JON!
FRIENDLY DOG!!!
BOING

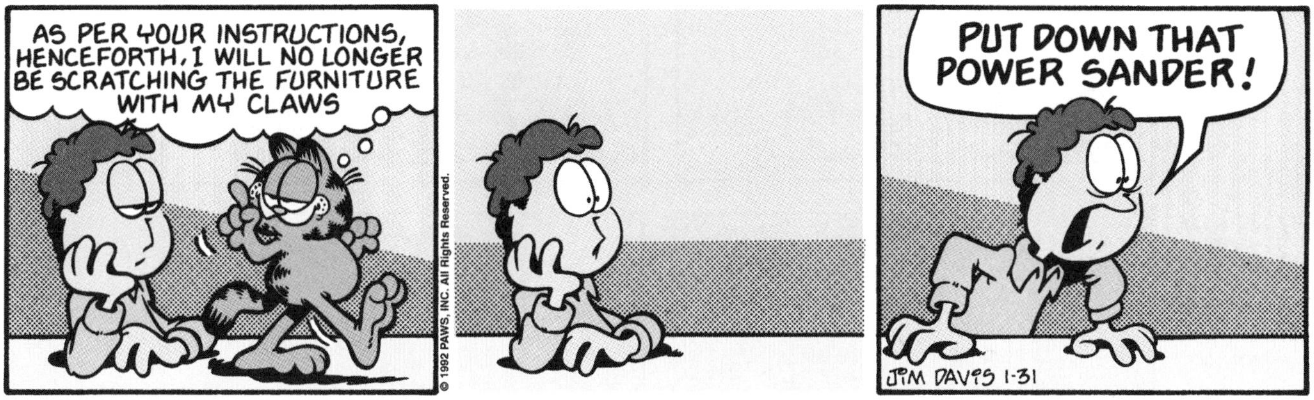
AS PER YOUR INSTRUCTIONS, HENCEFORTH, I WILL NO LONGER BE SCRATCHING THE FURNITURE WITH MY CLAWS
© 1992 PAWS, INC. All Rights Reserved.
PUT DOWN THAT POWER SANDER!
JIM DAVIS 1-31

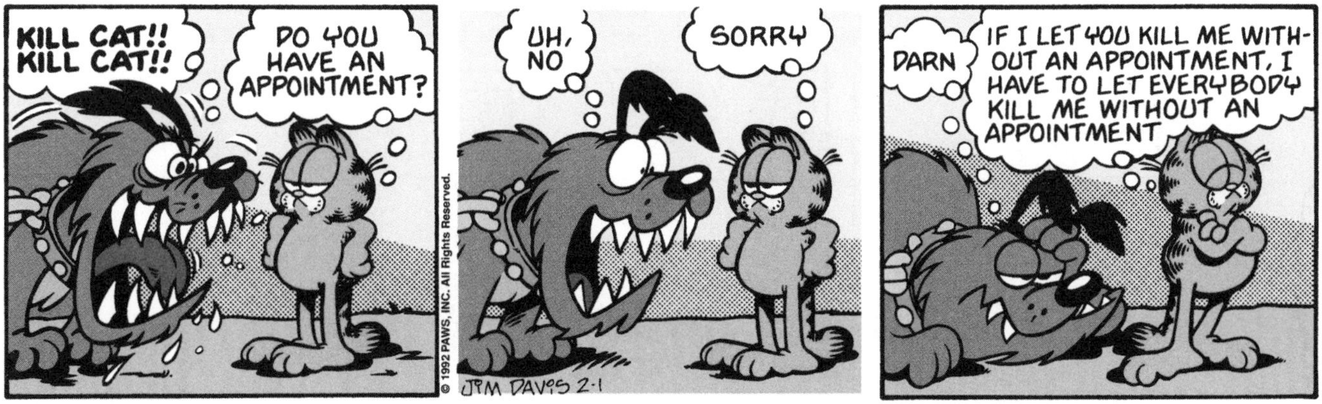
KILL CAT!! KILL CAT!!
DO YOU HAVE AN APPOINTMENT?
© 1992 PAWS, INC. All Rights Reserved.
UH, NO
SORRY
JIM DAVIS 2-1
DARN
IF I LET YOU KILL ME WITHOUT AN APPOINTMENT, I HAVE TO LET EVERYBODY KILL ME WITHOUT AN APPOINTMENT

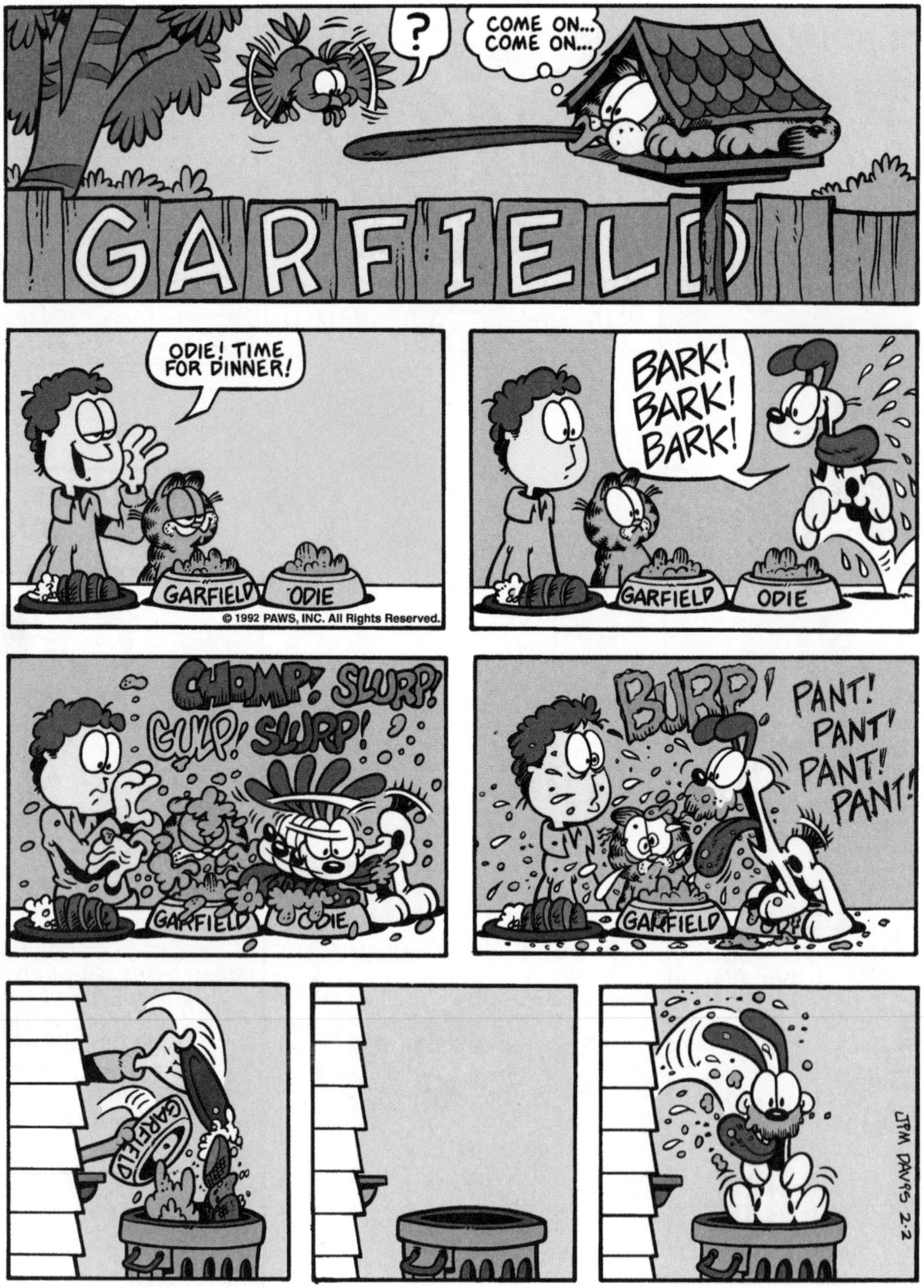
?
COME ON... COME ON...
GARFIELD
ODIE! TIME FOR DINNER!
GARFIELD
ODIE
© 1992 PAWS, INC. All Rights Reserved.
BARK! BARK! BARK!
GARFIELD
ODIE
CHOMP! SLURP!
GULP! SLURP!
GARFIELD
ODIE
BURP!
PANT! PANT! PANT! PANT!
GARFIELD
GARFIELD
JIM DAVIS 2-2

THIS IS THE ALL PET NETWORK
AND NOW IT'S TIME FOR EVERY CAT'S FAVORITE SHOW...
"HARASS THE DOG!"
FINALLY... QUALITY TELEVISION
JIM DAVIS
2-3
© 1992 PAWS, INC. All Rights Reserved.

DON'T CHANGE THE CHANNEL
WE KNOW WHERE YOU LIVE...
THE RATINGS WARS ESCALATE
JIM DAVIS 2-4
© 1992 PAWS, INC. All Rights Reserved.

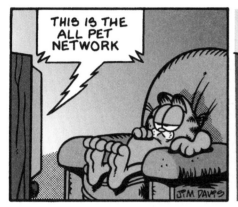

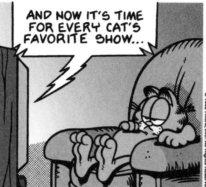

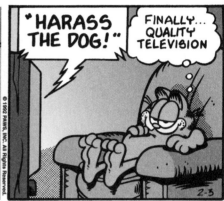

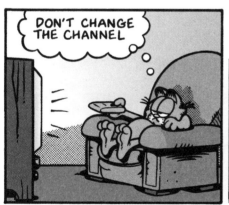

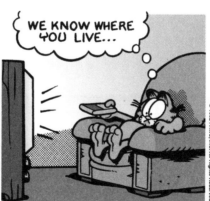

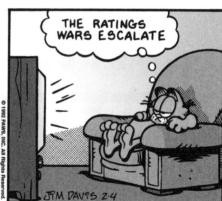

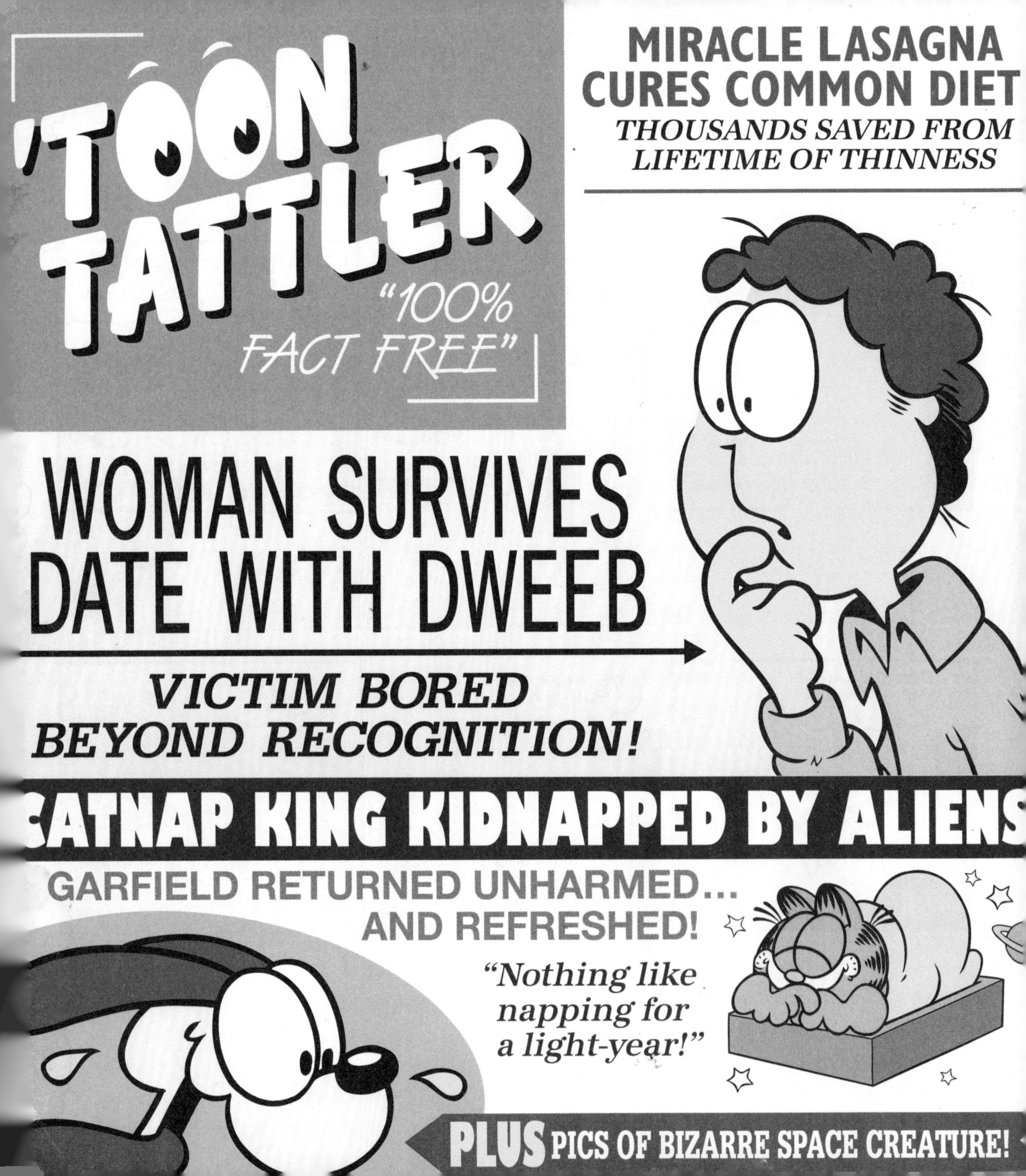
'TOON TATTLER
"100% FACT FREE"
MIRACLE LASAGNA CURES COMMON DIET
THOUSANDS SAVED FROM LIFETIME OF THINNESS
WOMAN SURVIVES DATE WITH DWEEB
VICTIM BORED BEYOND RECOGNITION!
CATNAP KING KIDNAPPED BY ALIENS
GARFIELD RETURNED UNHARMED... AND REFRESHED!
"Nothing like napping for a light-year!"
PLUS PICS OF BIZARRE SPACE CREATURE!